BOARDROOM GAMES
You're Fired!

Peter A. Crossgrove

Book Cover Design: Marla Thompson
Typeset: Greg Salisbury
Author Photographer: Matthew Plexman Photography

DISCLAIMER: This is a work of non-fiction based on Peter Crossgrove's recollections. The information is of a general nature to help you on the subject of business. Readers of this publication agree that neither Peter Crossgrove, nor his publisher will be held responsible or liable for damages that may be alleged or resulting directly or indirectly from their use of this publication. All external links are provided as a resource only and are not guaranteed to remain active for any length of time. Neither the publisher nor the author can be held accountable for the information provided by, or actions resulting from accessing these resources.

This book is dedicated
to the most wonderful parents in the world.

Testimonials

Boardroom Games is required reading for everyone from the first year MBA student to the seasoned CEO to the government leader. Corporate boards have experienced so much change that Peter Crossgrove's behind-the-scenes look is a template for corporate governance for many board members today. Peter's biography is that of a true renaissance man and a miner's miner. Bravo, Peter!
John R Ing, Chairman, CEO Maison Placements Canada Inc.

I trust others will enjoy this book as much as I have. Peter has travelled through so many different worlds and eras. From mining in Sudbury to marketing at Seagram's at age twenty-eight, having the legendary Sam Bronfman's ear, and to starting, building, and fixing companies, all with a complete rolodex of fantastic and influential friends—affecting so many companies and not-for-profit organizations. Peter has lived up to what he learned—leaving everything better than he found it.
Michael Cooper, CEO of Dundee REIT

I read your book and thoroughly enjoyed the journey. To me it is a very Canadian story of your working life. As a young person living in the Sault and having had an opportunity to visit mines, it was fun to reflect with you on your experiences. It was also interesting to see the threads that lead you from one experience to another along your very active and productive professional life. And what wonderful experiences you have had! There are names of those you encountered I knew, but many more were only known to me through you and the media. As you moved in and out of Judy's and my life, we always found you on to another adventure. We loved the stories. Thank you for the read.
Ken Burgess, Former co-owner of Harlequin Enterprises

If you want to know anything or anybody connected to leadership in mining, real estate, health care, or either corporate or not-for-profit governance in Canada, Peter A. Crossgrove is the person to ask. Peter's experience in these and other fields is vast. An indefatigable hard-nosed former football player, he is an example of that rare combination of a tough executive and a deeply caring, ethical human being who holds himself and others to a high standard of integrity. Reading Boardroom Games is a trip through the highways (and back alleys) of Canada's corporate world guided by a man who has been intimate with successive Premiers of Ontario, with business tycoons and CEOs in North America and elsewhere, but also with miners, fishermen, pilots, and farmers from Copper Cliff to Sudbury to Manitoulin Island. Mr. Crossgrove has as well made a career of philanthropy and leadership in the health care field. He richly deserved his induction into the Order of Canada that finally came his way. His memoir deserves to be read.

Frederick H. Lowy, OC, MD, LLD (HON), FRCPC.

Acknowledgements

The person I need to thank the most is the lovely lady in Victoria, British Columbia—Miriam Sanua—who pulled my scattered thoughts together to produce what I hope is an interesting, educational, and an enjoyable read. In addition, I must thank my talented assistant Rocio Zavala, who constantly helped me in getting the material to Miriam.

My thanks go to Michael Cooper for contributing his thoughts to the foreword regarding the co-operative work and experiences we have both participated in on corporate boards. He highlights the importance of building friendships and cordial working and personal relationships that can and need to be built around the boardroom table, as well as with company management. Around all the need for brevity, focus, and seriousness of business, sincerity and a sense of humour is just as important. I have made mention of Michael and his wonderful capabilities and dedication to his work, which has afforded him the success he deserves.

I also wish to say thank you to Dr. Alan Hudson for writing the foreword from the perspective of the health care system, and the hospital boards of the Toronto hospitals of which I have been a part. In addressing the relationship between himself as CEO and myself as board chairman, he talks of the existence of an "inter-co-independence" in the work we participated in and enjoyed together. He has succinctly honed with clarity and candour—he speaks frankly and with open honesty, expressing the depths and heights in the management of health care systems, hospitals and hospital boards, and leadership in the boards as it finds itself today. I am grateful for his valuable insights as well as helpful suggestions.

My sincere thanks also go to Dr. Frederick Lowy for reading the manuscript and writing for the foreword. His comments greatly summarize what I have attempted to share with you the reader through all my varied experiences both in the field and around the boardroom table. Fred's position as confidant to physicians and surgeons, senior management and staff, as well as sitting on both hospital boards, meant he straddled the fence of opinion, reality, and raw emotion, and is a testament to his leadership abilities based on personal integrity, openness, and honesty. His support through the hospital mergers was definitely appreciated.

Thank you to the following people who took the time to read the manuscript as it developed, and suggested meaningful clarifications: Ned Goodman, Conrad Black, Tim Ryan, Alan McFarland, Fraser Fell, and Gerald Panneton. Thank you to John Ing for his testimonial and pertinent and relevant conversations around the title of the book. To Ken Burgess—thank you for your testimonial, which adds a light-hearted frame of reference recalling the weaving of people, places, and experiences throughout the manuscript. To Tony Griffiths, Corporate Catalyst: A Chronicle of the (Mis)Management of Canadian Business from a Veteran Insider, and Eric Sprott, The Sprott School of Business—thank you! Both your favourable comments and pointers add a valuable dimension to the flow of the book.

Thank you Joanne Kearney of Smithcom for your offer to enquire of and take the time to acquire additional photographs other than the originals from the family collection from Vale Canada, for which I am greatly appreciative, and also for offering support with the marketing of the book. I thank Emily Robb for her invaluable assistance, and acknowledge the Vale Archive for their kind permission to publish the photographs and images from their archives, which so aptly portray the historical significance of the period in time and location in Sudbury and outlying areas of northern Ontario that I reminisce about.

Kristen Bertrand and Curators Jim Fortin and Samantha Morel of the City of Greater Sudbury Heritage Museum very kindly facilitated the process of forwarding the photographs from the Museum, which I am sure will be of great interest to you. Thank you Kristen, Jim, and Samantha for your prompt and courteous response to my request and granting permission for the use of the photographs for the book.

Megan Fostka, Krystal Koo, and Jessica Venter of Dundee Realty have supported me in obtaining photographs for the book as well. Thank you for your time and interest.

My thanks also go to Kevin O'Brien of Osler, Hoskin and Harcourt LLP for his invaluable review of the book. To Julie and Greg Salisbury and team at Influence Publishing—thank you for so wholeheartedly embracing the message of Boardroom Games, and your diligence and attention to see the manuscript through to print and publication.

While writing this book, I have been building a cottage on Manitoulin

Island and a house on Ramsey Lake in Sudbury; and since I did not have the time, my son Keith took on the construction co-ordination of both properties. I have to say Keith has done a great job. And I am most thankful to him for the time and dedication he has put into these projects.

I am pleased too that my son Alex got to read the manuscript while still in the editing stage and that he added some additional insights on the historical growth of Sudbury through the mining and lumbering industries. He also helped in recalling some realities and the practicalities on health insurance coverage and processes—as you will read in the book. Thank you Alex, I am glad too that I did write the book.

> *Coming together is a beginning; keeping together is progress; working together is success.*
> **Henry Ford**

CONTENTS

Chapter 4:

Chapter 5:

PART TWO

Chapter 6:

Chapter 7:

PART THREE

Chapter 8:

Chapter 11:

Photos:

Chapter 12:

PART FIVE

Chapter 13:

Chapter 14:

PART SIX

Chapter 15:

Foreword

Peter Crossgrove: Board Experiences, Relationships and Mentoring

Shortly after the Initial Public Offering (IPO) of Dundee Industrial REIT in October of 2012, we held our inaugural board dinner at the restaurant Mistura's private dining room. It was a chance for management and the board to get to know each other. Many of us had been involved in Dundee REIT, so most were very familiar with each other, and some others were not as familiar.

We spent time providing the board with the feedback we got from investors, and discussed what projects we had ahead, as well as our strategy for the coming months. After we finished the business part of the dinner, everyone began by introducing themselves to each other and relating something personal to the group there. After a while, when we were all feeling pretty comfortable, Peter started telling stories. Peter spoke about growing up in Sudbury, and referred to all of his friends by their nicknames. His stories were so funny we couldn't stop laughing. As Peter got on a role, he couldn't stop himself from laughing. So there we all were, listening to Peter's stories and watching a seventy-five-year-old man fill the room with his joyful life.

I first met Peter fittingly in a boardroom. We were in the middle of the Camreal acquisition, and Peter played an influential role in the completion of the transaction. We had agreed to add directors from Camreal to our board. And that is how I got to know Peter. After the transaction was completed, we provided Peter with an office near where I sat. We were office neighbours for most of the years we have known each other, until he became the acting CEO of Excellon a couple of years ago. For many years, Peter and I would share a coffee, and he would listen to me and provide advice. He was always available to me. He later got me involved in Cancer Care, and to a lesser extent (making a donation), to the University Health Network.

I was running a company for the very first time and every time we grew, I was running the biggest company I had ever run. There is so much more to a business than the math or strategy. How to deal with the people inside and outside of the company is very hard. Peter would help me whenever I asked. Since I met him fifteen years ago, I have watched Peter travel all over the world to help CARE, Cancer Care, Princess Margaret, and the University Hospital. He has always stepped in to help companies in trouble, but if there was one thing I saw him do the most, it was to take calls from people who had just found out a loved one had been diagnosed with cancer. You could see his posture change after one of those phone calls. He always helped because he knew how difficult a time it would be. He would speak to the doctors to find out what could be done. And he continued to monitor what was going on, and provide any help or comfort he could. There are countless people who have relied on Peter when they were at their most vulnerable—and Peter never disappointed.

In the boardroom, Peter does not enjoy extra words. He knows what matters and what doesn't, and wants to spend time on the important stuff. He has all the time for new ideas or conversations that lead to meaningful discussions. However, he isn't very interested in listening to self-serving comments from board members or management. Over the years, we must have been in at least ninety meetings together. And as he says, he has only missed a few meetings in person—and when he did, he usually called in from some place I had never heard of on work for CARE. He is not shy in asking and probing with difficult questions—yet he is not confrontational. I have never seen anyone run an audit committee meeting better than Peter. He has also singlehandedly reduced our audit fees by beating up the auditors from time to time.

One of my favourite board meetings was when we went to Saskatoon to see our properties as well as have our meeting. We stayed at a hotel we owned that was in the wrong part of town, and made almost all of its money from the gambling video games in the bar and our off-site beer sales. Detlef Bierbaum, another great contributor to our company from Camreal, is a German aristocrat in nature, and was somewhat less than enthused about staying at our hotel. Peter told Detlef that he learned from mining that you can sleep anywhere provided you drink enough first. Good enough for me, but Detlef would ask every quarter and every year thereafter if we had sold the hotel, and we would all laugh thinking about Peter's advice.

What was so special about watching Peter laughing so hard at our inaugural board dinner for Dundee Industrial was that Peter rarely talks about himself. He was sharing stories from his life that we had never heard before.

When I read Peter's book, I learned so many things that I never knew of Peter and his life. There are so many names of famous people, politicians, and successful business people, but Peter never drops any names. I also have no experience growing up in a small town, a mining town, or northern Ontario. Peter shows me that world, and it helps me understand how he became the way he is: always up for a practical joke, taking his various roles seriously, as well as enjoying the people around him.

Peter has never asked anything for himself in all the years I have known him. He has been generous of his time. He has encouraged me when I needed it, and from time to time he has suggested that I could do better. He does it gently, but you hear him loudly. The only times he ever asked me for anything was to remind me that I had been doing pretty well, and others haven't—and they could use my help. I always said yes.

I trust others will enjoy this book as much as I have. Peter has travelled through so many different worlds and eras. From mining in Sudbury to marketing at Seagrams at age twenty-eight; having the legendary Sam Bronfman's ear; to starting, building, and fixing companies; all with a complete rolodex of fantastic and influential friends—affecting so many companies and not-for-profit organizations. Peter has lived up to what he learned—leaving everything better than he found it.

Michael Cooper, CEO of Dundee REIT

The Board Chairman & CEO Relationship: The Health and Hospital Perspective

Peter Crossgrove's view of the optimal function of board members and CEOs is central to many of the stories related in this book. The affinity between the board chairman and CEO is not explicitly addressed in these memoirs, although that interaction is a crucial link in any successful company. My experiences with the author were solely on the non-profit side. Peter was successively Chairman of the Toronto Hospital, Princess

Margaret Hospital, three times Chairman of the Canadian Association of Provincial Cancer Agencies, as well as Cancer Care Ontario, and I was successively CEO of those institutions.

The top-down merger of The Toronto General Hospital (tracing its roots to the aftermath of the War of 1812), and The Toronto Western Hospital (100 years old), created "The Toronto Hospital." Vic Stoughton (TGH) was appointed CEO of that new entity. Chairman of Toronto General Hospital, Alf Powis, graciously stepped away so that Chairman Peter Crossgrove of Toronto Western Hospital could assume the chairmanship of the new entity.

Spectators of the macabre sport of hospital mergers will know that there is an over-reaching anatomical rule governing these war games—the heart is master of the brain! This is understandable as the contestants may have been born in one of the institutions, have had their own or a loved one's life saved at a particular hospital or endured the sadness of a relative's passing in a particular ward. Many have donated funds or volunteer hours to one of the hospitals. Thus, highly emotional and tendentious arguments, frequently not germane to the discussion, coloured sane judgment.

Peter rode out the post merger maelstrom in masterly fashion and was about to retire from the volunteer chairman's role when he unexpectedly had to stay on an extra year to see in my arrival as the new CEO. One day I was in the operating room, and the next I was CEO of Canada's largest teaching hospital. The most charitable view expressed was that I knew next to nothing about the business of leading an extraordinarily complicated institution.

Peter coached sports in his youth. The essence of coaching is that you tell the players what to do but you don't play the game yourself. Mentoring incorporates a different skill set and Peter had had great experience in tutoring CEOs through his many business adventures. On several occasions Peter had stepped off a board to assume a temporary CEO role while a search was underway so he understood the relationship from both vantage points.

I called Peter several times a week. My first question, "Where are you?" came as he would be gallivanting anywhere from Claridge's in London, to an office in Sydney, to a mine in New Guinea. Peter regarded the hospital chair's role as a serious avocation and always stopped what he was doing to take my call. I cannot recall Mr. Crossgrove ever telling me what to do.

The response for my request for advice was, "Have you thought of this approach?" or, "Why not give Fraser Elliott a call," or, "Watch out for this issue or it'll bite you next week." Thus Peter mentored me by allowing me to look into his vast business experience. He never undercut my authority and allowed me to grow in confidence as we jointly enjoyed some early wins. Peter gave a stock answer to anyone who attempted an end-run around the CEO: "Go and chat to Alan about that." The end runs soon ceased.

The chairman of the board is just that. It is an adage that he or she is not the board. Peter had an uncanny sense of when he could make a governance decision on behalf of the board, and when an issue had to be taken through board committees for ultimate debate at the full board. Getting immediate governance decisions allowed the institution to maintain momentum in many crucial negotiations, and the board always backed Peter when it subsequently received the compendium—a sign of the confidence they had in his judgment.

In the early 1990s, the quality of hospital boards in Ontario varied greatly. Some board chairs regarded the role as a social sinecure while others worked diligently but heavily under the influence of the physicians. A few arrivistes attempted to use their positions for personal gain in the community. Medical jargon frequently flummoxed well-meaning board members. Most hospital boards understood their accountability for financial prudence, although some purposely ran deficits in the sure and certain hope that the government would bail them out. Many boards however did not appreciate their absolute responsibility for the quality of care in their institutions. The very term quality was frequently not understood in this context, and it was not until the elements being measured (death rates, infection rates, medication error rates, wait-times, customer satisfaction, etc.), were reported, that the term was fully comprehended.

The Ontario Nurses' Association represented the interests of the nurses and the Ontario Medical Association the interests of physicians. Just who was responsible for the interests of the patients? The patients were shareholders by virtue of paying taxes and were consumers of the services provided at the hospital. Peter Crossgrove insisted that Quality of Care receive a major time allocation at any board agenda. Thus he laid the foundation on which subsequent computer program advances could build out detailed and sophisticated "quality management and customer satisfaction" programs. The main function of the board was to represent the interests of the patients on behalf of all the taxpayers and the government of Ontario. Peter firmly believed that volunteer board members would disengage if key decisions were being made by a select few so he seldom called executive committees.

The Toronto Hospital subsequently absorbed Doctor's Hospital and merged with Princess Margaret Hospital. Subsequently, PMH became a major component of Cancer Care Ontario. (Previously PMH, one of the world's largest medical radiation centres, had not been a member of CCO—a ludicrous situation.) A new entity, University Health Network, was created. A single board governed this over-arching entity. Members of the Board of UHN were extraordinarily accomplished and dedicated to their governance roles. All were teachers of mine and many remain close friends. Peter maintained a collegial and friendly atmosphere amongst these strong individuals. Careful preparation of board agendas allowed good debate and only rarely altercations.

The healthcare industry is appropriately and heavily regulated, and Peter distinguished actions that were mandatory from those entrepreneurial adventures that might be undertaken. The Trustees were courteous and supportive of my role, but never shy. Following one of my more spectacular PR fumblings, Matt Barrett remarked across the board table that he thought I had "the diplomatic skills of Idi Amin." I would nip down to the bank and catch Matt between his meetings. In response to the problem I posed, Matt would regale me with two or three hysterically funny stories and then make an erudite proposal to solve my problem. No CEO has ever been the recipient of so much experience and wisdom encompassed in the lives of various board members.

In Ontario hospitals, the relationship of the board chair and board members to the CEO varied. One Toronto institution was notorious because various board committees attempted to manage the institution. We never understood how the CEO could do his job. In several instances, the boards were so weak that the physicians ran key elements of the hospital, frequently to their personal advantage, in a fee-for-service environment.

In some smaller towns, doctors and board members chatted to each other across neighbourhood fences, effectively undercutting the role of the CEO. In several towns, mayors and minor politicians expressed their personal ambitions through hospital board activity. The provincial wide "Ontario Wait Times" project exposed these variations in governance excellence. The Ontario Hospital Association led a determined effort to obtain a more uniform standard of governance, and there has been a steady transformation away from paternalistic and provider-centred care to patient-centred care. (Many were surprised at the emphasis on the latter concept because they had mistakenly thought that this had been the predominant principle all along.)

All UHN and Cancer Care Ontario board members fully understood that theirs was governance and not a management role, and I was left to run the hospitals and systems, understanding that I was 100 percent accountable to the board. I took on that responsibility with pleasure. There were some moments of consternation and grinding disappointment, but overall I felt that I had the best job in the world. "Authority, responsibility, and accountability," were at one locus and the board could not have been more supportive. Peter and I laughed a lot and encouraged each other in darker moments.

The foundations laid at the genesis of The Toronto Hospital have been built on by the devoted actions of Peter Crossgrove's successors. Fraser Fell, Fred Eaton, Tony Fell, and Phillip Orsino maintained this high level of voluntary public service. Tom Closson succeeded me as CEO and brought his system engineering talents to the management role.

UHN is a teaching hospital and trains more professionals than any hospital in Canada. A better distinguishing description is that of "a research-intensive hospital," and Peter fostered that domain from the start. Currently UHN's annual expenditures are $1.8 billion: $310 million for research, $950 million from government, and about an additional $300 million pass-through payment to physicians. Very few Toronto companies have this level of annual expenditure. UHN recently received a 98 percent score at its national accreditation and the current duo of Chairman John Mulvihill and CEO Dr. Bob Bell are rated the best in Canada.

With the plethora of government issues relating to patient care, teaching and research, and with the constant demand of maintaining a balanced budget, Peter had to be on top of a very wide range of issues and their political implications. Tempered by his personal political experience, Peter understood realpolitik. The direction of healthcare in Ontario is not strictly a party political affair. Patient demographics and provincial finances are issues that face all provincial parties, regardless of their political stripe. The enormous expenditure in healthcare in Ontario, however, creates very significant political sensitivities for the government of the day.

Peter regarded most reporters as pariahs and he had a healthy distrust of their craft. He firmly believed that the CEO, not the chairman, should be the voice of the organization. Nevertheless, Peter was very sensitive to reputational risk and maintained good relations with the government of the day behind the scenes. His plain speech, never unctuous or oleaginous, clearly stated his view, and he delighted in pointing out to the Minister of the day that he had been in this branch of public service for decades longer than she or he had.

The government contributes the lion's share of the UHN budget, but expenditures exceed income. Philanthropists contribute a significant part of the shortfall. Hospital Foundations are governed by their own boards, and their magnificent work has to be coordinated with the function of the hospital as a whole. UHN is, by design, the largest research hospital in Canada and donated dollars provide a critical foundation for world-leading research programs. The Ontario government understandably only funds major capital equipment of proven diagnostic or therapeutic value. The leading clinical programs, however, are constantly inventing or evaluating new equipment of as yet unproven value. These new machines carry a high price tag and are not funded by the government. The taxpayer and philanthropic donors usually fund purpose-built hospital wings jointly.

Thus the hospital has to raise funds constantly to support these non-tax payer funded initiatives. Peter has led single-purpose fundraising campaigns very successfully. Chairing a fundraising campaign is a time-consuming occupation. The citizens of Ontario are extraordinarily generous, but donors are besieged by requests from a variety of worthy causes and, appropriately, require detailed explanations of hospital projects.

Peter would frequently call me to tip me off that a potential donor was about to be a patient at one of the hospitals. I had a very strict rule in my own practice: "In their pajamas, all patients are to be managed in identical fashion." If you are doing your best for your patient, how can you do more than your best for the supposed VIP in the next bed? Changing the crucial roles played by nurses, junior interns, and senior residents in-patient care, because the patient is a VIP, invariably results in the VIP receiving inferior care. I responded to Peter's "heads up" by reinforcing family communication. Before going home at night I would visit the patient and then report progress to the family. This little extra attention usually helped when Peter met the patient at a social event six months later and suggested they make a donation to the hospital. In turn, Peter became a target of all those whom he had approached when those hospital donors would invariably call on him to support their own causes.

Much has been written of the roles of board chairman, lead director, and CEO in the private sector. The power of these roles varies. If the chairman holds the majority of the voting shares, the CEO finds absolutely fascinating what the board chairman finds mildly interesting. In the public sector the chairman and CEO roles are always separate. The voluntary chairman holds the same equity as every other taxpayer in Ontario.

I respected Peter Crossgrove's business acumen, and he my medical accomplishments. Hopefully, this synergy served our customers well and provided a stimulating and exciting environment in which healthcare providers worked. Peter and I worked very hard, laughed a lot, and endured a little pain. Above all else we shared the emotion that we were incredibly fortunate to be given successive and combined but different leadership roles in the service of our fellow Canadians—be they patients, payers, or providers.

If I had to pick one characteristic of Peter's performance I would remark that seldom has so much time, effort, and care been given unselfishly behind the scenes. Few truly appreciated his great contribution to the success of TTH, UHN, Princess Margaret Hospital, and Cancer Care

Ontario. Until he was honoured by The Order of Canada, Peter received little kudos for his enormous public service. His lack of egotism never demanded personal recognition and he lived the values he had been taught growing up in de Nort.

Alan R. Hudson, OC, MB ChB, FRCSEd, FRCSC, DD(Hon), FCS SA(Hon), LLD (Hon)

A Life of Success and Sharing

If you want to know anything or anybody connected to leadership in mining, real estate, health care, or either corporate or not-for-profit governance in Canada, Peter A. Crossgrove is the person to ask. Peter's experience in these and other fields is vast. An indefatigable hard-nosed former football player, he is an example of that rare combination of a tough executive and a deeply caring, ethical human being who holds himself and others to a high standard of integrity. Reading Boardroom Games is a trip through the highways (and back alleys) of Canada's corporate world guided by a man who has been intimate with successive Premiers of Ontario, with business tycoons and CEOs in North America and elsewhere, but also with miners, fishermen, pilots, and farmers from Copper Cliff to Sudbury to Manitoulin Island. Mr. Crossgrove has as well made a career of philanthropy and leadership in the healthcare field.

I first met Peter in the mid-1980s when he was vice-chair, then Chair of the Board of Trustees of the Toronto Western Hospital. I was then Dean of the University of Toronto's faculty of Medicine. Since all staff physicians, residents, and medical students were also members of the Faculty of Medicine, I represented the University on the Boards of most of the University affiliated teaching hospitals, including the Toronto Western and the Toronto General. As is described in Chapter 14 of this memoir, the difficult and contentious work that resulted in the merger of these two hospitals involved the Boards, the senior management, the staff of both institutions, and myself. As Peter notes, I was the only person who at the time was a member of both Boards of Trustees. As Dean, I was also the confidant of the senior physicians and surgeons of both hospitals as well as a member of the Department of Psychiatry of both hospital staffs. I therefore was able, as a participant observer, to see Peter Crossgrove in action.

Peter is entirely goal-directed. He is able to apply his corporate experience, his contacts, his persuasive powers and especially his determination to overcome obstacles to reach an objective that he feels is worthwhile. The merger of the two hospitals from what was then called the Toronto Hospital led, in due course to the present University Health Network that now includes also the Ontario Cancer Institute, Princess Margaret Hospital (whose Board Peter later came to chair) and the Toronto Rehabilitation Institute. This has created a downtown Toronto academic and clinical powerhouse. Peter Crossgrove is one of its original architects. He richly deserved his induction into the Order of Canada that finally came his way. His memoir deserves to be read.

Frederick H. Lowy, OC, MD, LLD (HON), FRCPC

Introduction

Men are developed the same way gold is mined. Several tons of dirt must be moved to get an ounce of gold. But you don't go into the mine looking for dirt. You go in looking for gold.
Dale Carnegie

Why am I bothering to write this book? There is no one reason. There are several. First of all, people I know and worked with suggested that I write a book, having found my experiences both interesting and funny as I relate them. Of course, my children, who have no idea what I do or have done, may be enlightened by this book. When I am with my children and grandchildren I would rather talk about them. And besides, a lot of what I was or am doing is confidential, because I am often an insider. My CV is included in the Afterword. It outlines the forty-six or so corporate boards and twenty-three not-for-profit boards that I have served on.

I chose the title Boardroom Games to illustrate the interplay between the business of life and the life of business—it's a game! You have a desire to do something great with your life—you create an intention, assume a position, take strategic actions towards your vision, and finally get to look back and view the outcome. Standing by my principles has led me to fire up or piss off Corporate Canada and, in some instances, get fired. The outcomes are what they are. I have no regrets. I feel good about it all.

This book is sectioned off into six parts. In Part One: I begin my life story from the time I was completing studies at Concordia and embarking on an MBA program at Western University, which was a great experience. This time in my life was essentially one of those nexus points, a crossroads, where we make decisions in the early days of our lives based on an idea of what we are going to do, who we think we are going to become in our lives, and what type of work we are going to pursue. And we take the action steps to facilitate the vision we hold in our minds and passion we hold in our hearts. I go on to talk about my life post-university days. I had a young family and focused my attention on building myself out into the business world. The doors opened and I was given an opportunity to meet Charles Bronfman. Our initial interview was to open up a new world for me in terms of the possibilities I could and would seek out even at my young age. Starting with Seagram, I gained valuable experience in the corporate world. Going on from there, life took me in various directions as I built my portfolio of experience. Being a natural networker and connector, I continue to be amazed at the unfolding of situations connecting those that need connecting. Through my acceptance into the Toronto YPO chapter, northern Ontario got opened up. I was briefly involved in politics, further cementing political relationships, where I was able to make a number of suggestions and contributions for the continued development of the region up north.

Moving to Toronto through Part Two highlights the blossoming, if you will, of greater opportunities and new relationships that came my way. While working in various capacities to turn companies around, I tapped into my innate business savvy and acumen and found success at those endeavours. I learnt, as well, how to negotiate the intricacies of the boardroom, board members, and board situations. It is my sincere hope that university business students and grads may be able to take away for themselves some useful lessons from these various experiences.

As my journey continues in Part Three: here we move into the mining sector and various mining boards that I have sat on. If you don't know much if anything about the mining industry, I am sure you will be intrigued. I grew up around mining and started at a tender age working in the mines. It consumed my life; it was and always has been part of my life and in my blood. Precious minerals and ore have played a strategic part in the development of Canada and on the global stage. Ethical values and morals will always test one because it is so easy to be "led" by the allure of gold. I have expressed a number of personal opinions regarding the integral running of the mining boards. And I present numerous stories documenting various outcomes and events. As this book goes to print, some situations seem to be making headlines over questionable activities regarding particular boards. It remains to be seen how these play out. Because I am so passionate about good board governance, I repeat a number of times the duties and responsibilities to the shareholders and public at large. Standing my ground has pissed off some and gotten me thrown off boards. Fired!

Moving on to Part Four: Some of what I have done is quite interesting to me, and I hope it is for you too. The philanthropic and not-for-profit world opened up to me when I volunteered to work on the hospital boards. I learned much from the health industry and not-for-profits from the perspective of the hospitals. For instance, on the not-for-profit side came about the creation of The University Health Centre in downtown Toronto—recognized as the greatest acute care facility in the world. Other activities have included chairing the Generation Campaign and the Munk Cardiac Centre Campaign, as well as devoting several months of the year for twelve years as a volunteer for CARE Canada and CARE International. Of course working with CARE has been most pleasurable.

The public at large really has no idea about the intricacies and complexities of running hospitals, and in coping with the plethora of health issues and challenges. There are so many very wonderful people who have devoted and dedicated their lives to the well-being of others. Science and medical technology continues to evolve and advance to immeasurable heights where specialists are able to do wonderful things in support of furthering peoples' health and better quality of life. Having had the distinct pleasure of meeting and working with so many of these very talented and dedicated individuals has given me a broader holistic approach and application in melding the business model into that of the philanthropic and not-for-profit.

This work confirmed and reiterates my understanding, again instilled in me by my parents, of how important it is for us each to give of our time and energy to philanthropic endeavours. We are needed, and our support—in whichever way it comes—is always welcomed and appreciated. One feels a great sense of satisfaction and fulfillment working to share of ourselves what we can without any expectation of remuneration: free and gratis. I know that is how I have felt and continue to feel today. That's the best way to do it—I was always taught. We have lost that. And I hope in some small way with some of these stories, that message is conveyed to our youth: to reclaim the valuable moral and ethical sense of working together in a sense of unity and purpose towards the betterment of our communities.

Part Five in summation on the corporate board side: some of the more memorable experiences include being one of the founders of the Masonite company; being thrown off the Eaton board after fifteen years, or being kicked off the board as CEO of Placer Dome after the most successful year in their history, as well the best corporate board I sat on—United Dominion. And through all these business and board experiences, I have travelled much of the world—visiting and spending time in some eighty countries, where I have learned much about different cultures and the adaptation around progress these communities have undergone.

From a historical perspective in my life and the life of this book, we come full circle. We go back in time and I am happy to share with you the reader the first part of my life that now draws you into the world that established my upbringing, environment, the cultural setting for the ideals, passions, sets of values, and motivation that took me out into the business world. Part Six deals with my background growing up in northern Ontario, my family life, schooling, and early start in getting out into the workforce at a tender and very young age. As well to mention the influence the International Nickel Company (Inco, and now Vale) had on Sudbury and Copper Cliff as a mining community that flourished—well supported by the all-encompassing infrastructure of the company.

My desire to learn as much as I could about business was in part a value shared to me by my father. You learned from an early age that in order to make your way in the world you would have to get out into it and work your way up. I feel it's important to document historically the path many of us took in the very early days. You could say I have seen it all. That's the way life was many decades ago. It was not easy. In fact, sometimes it was just downright uncomfortable, as you will come to read. However, I made the best of it.

I would say in highlighting that day-and-age when modern conveniences were starting to see the light of day, we appreciated what we had and were able to accomplish. My parents, in particular, instilled in me the discipline and importance of good values, ethics, and morals no matter what.

Our youth today are so accustomed to the technological wonders, gizmos, and gadgets that have brought the entire globe to the palms of our hands in nanoseconds; you wonder if they have any concept of life in the yester-year. Is there any shred of appreciation for the previous generations and what they went through to create the opportunities for this present fast-instant gratification-world to manifest? The keyword here is appreciation and gratitude. Brian Tracy sums it up with his thoughts on gratitude:

"Develop an attitude of gratitude, and give thanks for everything that happens to you, knowing that every step forward is a step toward achieving something bigger and better than your current situation."
Brian Tracy, Author

This section will be of interest to both the millennials (otherwise known as the generation Y age group—or "echo-boomers" of the early 1980s to 2000s), even generation X age group (born between the 1950s and 1980s), contemplating their present and future careers, working or re-working their way through school—both in the historical context of life, and how numerous successful businessmen and women today made their start from humble, hard-working beginnings. Most did not have silver spoons dished to them.

Stories have a wonderful way of illustrating life lessons: something of which textbooks are devoid. Human nature and the complex interaction of relationships, being what they are, will steer the ship one way or another despite what textbooks define.

Older generations, "Yes, how well I remember those days," I suspect, will recall their own upbringing—the struggles, the successes—and look back appreciatively at the valuable experiences that got them where they are today.

Coming from a small burgeoning community in northern Ontario, I was amongst a generation of many young hopefuls looking to make our way in the world. And the opportunities the small northern communities presented as they have grown and flourished gave rise to many mega-successful people who went humbly on from the early days to having a great impact in shaping not only Canadian society today, but also internationally. This is history in the making; history in progress.

From the point of view of both business and philanthropic or not-for-profit boards, I feel that I have something to say to current board members, future board members, investors, and students. I have had the benefit of a great education at the taxpayer's expense. And I may have an opportunity by relating my experiences to help improve the way things are governed, and the way investors look at companies and their boards of directors.

Most people say the board is there to monitor the activities of the company and report to shareholders. They also think that the board's major job is to pick the CEO and approve corporate strategy. I try to explain why having the right people on the various board committees and that having the proper committee mandate is so important, for example, when I compare mining companies Barrick and Detour Gold.

My experiences of acquiring Interior Door (a small door company based in Mississauga Ontario), doing $5 million in sales with the McConnell family for $2.5 million dollars, hiring and working with Philip Orsino to see it become Masonite the largest door company in the world, and being sold to KKR for $3.2 billion has been personally fulfilling.

My outlines and pointers on good board and corporate governance I trust will instill some insight into the balance bridging what we learn in the textbook of business strategies and the textbook of life: values, morals, and ethics around the reality of human relationships. I walked away from the table after witnessing the audacity of some bright whippersnappers who forgot their humanity, replacing it with heartless and inconsiderate, but what they claimed were strategic, boardroom games. They thought they were being really smart. Here wisdom and experience was pit against the brashness of youth. And I felt the need to stand for what I felt was morally right and correct by not associating myself with their strategies. My instincts proved to be true and right. Another time it was a blessing to be voted off because of one man's thirst for personal control. Well it looks like perhaps that has caught up with him. I go on to list my thoughts and opinions on both values and skillsets required to optimize the functioning of a good board representing the company and shareholders with integrity. Really, it is just about applying old-fashioned work ethics at the end of the day.

The one thing I have learned for sure is that the basic principals of success are quite portable: integrity, hard work, intelligence, strategic thinking, and the respect for those people working with you. If the people around and below you in an organization do not perform, you're a dead duck. Core values, ethics, diligent focus, and action such as those just mentioned, sustain good growth and success in all endeavours. A good leader is good to his or her people, and is well respected by peers, colleagues, and employees.

I have travelled extensively and experienced different cultures. I had the opportunity to make a difference to the lives of companies that have been failing and helped to put them back on track. I call a spade a spade. There is no beating around the bush when I am focused on the task at hand. I expect that out of all of my interactions with people and experiences. In fact, I resigned from the Toronto Club after being persuaded to change my vote to permit an individual—whose integrity I questioned—to join the club. I withdrew my black ball after rescinding my vote. I was committed to upholding my values on integrity and following through on that. No ifs, ands, or buts. I have also learned not to take myself so seriously. I feel it's important to take each situation with a grain of salt—do your best, for all the right reasons, and then let go.

My life has been mostly intriguing, adventuresome not only around the world, but also around boardroom tables. I have worked extremely hard to get to where I am today. I feel good about myself and about what I have brought to the table. I know there is a silver lining in each and every experience—it's the number one reason why we should be doing what we do, and it's also about what we do with these experiences in our hearts and minds that ultimately counts.

In conclusion: I find it quite exciting to be involved at such a high level of business activity at my age. I am happy to share my experiences and stories with you, the reader. There is a lesson to glean from whatever your station in life:

Students in university, business, or mining school: interested in the world of business and boardrooms, values-based ethical business practices, taking risks with integrity, and the power of alliances and connections.

Business and not-for-profit: for those intrigued in what makes a successful businessperson and how to take those skills and their application in the world of philanthropy, not-for-profit and volunteering. I certainly have found them most interestingly instructive. And perhaps new-up-and-coming students can take what they can from my experiences and apply them in radically new ways. Since life and the way we do things is changing at an incredible speed, students will have the background, foundation, and interest to run with what they have been taught and to adapt their skillsets and values to fit with new models of business and not-for-profit for the future.

History buffs: the fascination for evolving communities of early Canadian life and culture, social economic development is nurtured here, and illustrating the intriguing colourful personalities who built the foundations and laid the cornerstones upon which the most successful businesses today have majorly contributed to Canadian society. No doubt a little piece of history.

And also for my children and grandchildren, who might now know what their father and grandfather has been up to all these years. I share with you my personal stories and experiences in the hope that they will resonate as interesting—a good learning perhaps. And with this comes the understanding of life as I have known and experienced it—that it will at least have brought some greater purpose and pleasure to the writing of this book.

"There are three hungers that people are trying to feed throughout their lives. The first is to connect deeply with the creative spirit of life. The second is to know and express your gifts and talents. The third is to know that our lives matter. Fulfillment comes from feeding these three hungers."
Richard Leider, Executive

Three things to govern: temper, tongue and conduct.
Three things to cultivate: courage, affection and gentleness.
Three things to commend: thrift, industry and promptness,
Three things to admire: dignity, intellectual power and gracefulness.
Three things to give: alms to the needy, comfort to the sad, and appreciation to the
worthy – From Priorities.

From the INCO TRIANGLE publication - December 1951
www.SudburyMuseums.ca

PART ONE

CHAPTER 1

The Highs of University Education

The MBA program was a very stimulating environment of high achievers. Choose to set your sights high, believe in your talents and abilities, be open to learning, and success will find you.

I consider myself fortunate to have had a rich schooling and university education. Starting out at McGill in the geology course, my life switched tracks when I made the decision to move over to commerce. Unbeknownst to my father who, at the time, had high hopes when I was done, that I would be joining him and his father in the generational commitment to the mining town company of Inco in Copper Cliff, northern Ontario. (Full details of Inco and Vale, as it is now known today, are talked about at length later in the book.) I realized and wanted to follow the path that felt truthful to my needs, goals, and the pathways I was hoping to open up for my life. University was now very much part, parcel, and platform for my ongoing direction into the business world. I explored the educational options available to me and made calculated decisions based on my vision for my future working life. I moved over to Concordia University at some point and took every available opportunity to study and expand my knowledge of the business world by taking a course in industrial relations at Laurentian in the summers while I worked at the same time just to broaden my skillsets and understanding the commerce model. All these formative years blended an upbringing of substantially different and unique experiences, both educationally and experientially out in the field throughout my young working life.

Western was a wonderful experience: the MBA program was a very stimulating environment of high achievers. In those days an MBA was a rare thing. I enjoyed the challenge of the course. I felt it was a good foundation and preparation for the work I was to pursue later regarding both my own businesses and other businesses I was to be entrusted to turn around.

Our MBA year has two sections of sixty students. We had a woman in our group—the only woman in either section. Nowadays, I believe over half the classes are women, which is wonderful. In those days they wanted you to have a few years of work experience before you were accepted. I think the average class age was about twenty-seven. We were in study groups of four or five people. Each group worked on case preparation business cases that we were given to analyze and recommend the best way forward in dealing with problems the company was facing. We also tended to socialize with the same group and their wives.

In the summer of 1965 I was at Western writing the teaching manual for a well-known textbook written by Dave Leighton and Don Thain, called Canadian Problems in Marketing. In the late afternoons, Tim Ryan, one of my fellow students working at the university, and I would go out and play golf on either of the two great public golf courses they had in London. The student green fees were two dollars. Tim was running and writing computer programs using the Fortran program, whereby punching in information meant it would be programmed on punch cards. These cards were put into this large computer, which sat in an air-conditioned room. It was a long laborious process that might take a couple of hours. We left the machine to its devices and would head out for a round of golf. Tim and I are still friends to this day.

Interviews: Meeting Charles Bronfman of Seagrams

One interesting recollection was in my second year when everyone was going on to take job interviews in various places. A lot of the students were going to Montreal, and of course my wife wanted to go to Montreal. I already knew I had won a Sloan Fellowship in the Doctoral Program at Harvard University competing with people from around the world. I had graduated pretty close to the top of my class. I would have been at the top, but I took one extra course, and instead of having four fours, I think I had four fours and a three. Although I had taken more courses, I still had four fours. They took the average and Morlie Hanford was declared the top student. I've never quite forgiven Western for that. In any event, I had no money; so I had to sign up for some job interviews, and I went to Montreal together with my wife because all the women were going. Back in those days, flying was different. We were a little late getting to the airplane; everybody knew we were coming, so they got the plane to hold up. You couldn't do that on Air Canada today. We were flying from London to Toronto and on to Montreal where the interviews were held. We all wanted to go to Montreal for a good time.

I took about six interviews, and I was offered jobs everywhere. Probably because I was on the Dean's List. One of the interviews was with Seagram Company Limited in the liquor business, and the name of the person in charge of personnel was Gill Mead. Seagram wanted a marketing person. They never had a marketing person who had gone to university. All their marketing people had formerly been whiskey salesmen who had come up through the ranks. They weren't marketing people. They were sales-men. Charles Bronfman said he wanted a marketing person. I finally told Gill Mead I wasn't interested, and he said he'd have to take me down to meet Charles Bronfman. Charles and I started to chat, and he asked Gill to leave. He closed the door and we had a long talk.

I told Charles, "I've got to tell you the truth. I'm embarrassed about it, but this is the way it is. I have no money. So I was taking job interviews in Montreal so my wife and I could have a bit of a holiday."

Bronfman accepted that, and offered that if I ever decided to leave Harvard I could come to Seagram's. So that was the deal. I went to Harvard and was able to skip the first year probably because I'd written exams without taking the courses. I'd been there about a year work-ing away and probably had about another eight months to go, but my wife was getting very itchy because I had bought a house in Lexington, Massachusetts. We really had no money, and I was working so hard trying to cut down the time I was there. I had a son who I never saw, and I never really saw my wife. And even when I had time with her, I was tired. Saturday nights were the only nights off. I worked every night in an office in the stacks at Harvard, and worked when I was at home. It finally came down to if I didn't get out of there my wife was going to leave me. You ask if I had any regrets regarding not completing the Doctorate? Well yes, I do suppose I did. I had worked extremely hard to finish it ahead of schedule. With little more than eight months to complete it, the pressure between family and the work created too much stress in the family. Still I did appreciate what I got out of the work I had completed. And I can accept the skillsets and learning contributed overall to my portfolio of attributes and experience. I resigned myself to letting it go for the sake of my family's well-being. But was well motivated to move forward and make a great life for my family and myself.

I called Charles and asked if he still had the job available, and he said sure. I went to Montreal. I put my house up for sale, which was difficult in Boston at that time. It took a while because there was a newspaper strike and you couldn't sell anything. Everything was done through the newspaper in those days. That house was at 32 Grassland Street, in Lexington. It was a lovely house and lovely area to live in. I did get it sold. In the meantime we rented a fourplex in Ville Saint-Laurent. The company gave me a car, a nice office, an unlimited expense account, and I was on my way. I felt I was fortunate and excited to have the opportunity to work with the Seagram Company more or less straight out the gate.

Going to Work at the Seagram Company Limited

What a learning experience for me. Ever since then I have never hesitated to ask anyone for an opinion.

I started out in marketing with Calvert Distillers, one of the Seagram subs, and in a couple years I worked up to being in charge of marketing for Seagram. Through that period I became very fond of Charles Bronfman. He's a very great guy and smart as hell. I had a hard time because the guys who worked for me were ex-whiskey salesmen, had been around a long time, and were close to Mr. Sam and Charles.

Mr. Sam liked me. I think because I came from Sudbury, and he had a hotel in what is now called Thunder Bay, amalgamated back then from two towns called Fort William and Port Arthur. It was 1,500 miles west of Sudbury but nevertheless in northern Ontario. He used to come into my office and sometimes fall asleep. I'd be on the phone or in a meeting or something; he'd wake up and it was as though he never missed a stroke. I don't know how he did that.

Another time he was sitting there and complaining about being hot, and I said, "Well, Mr. Sam, you're wearing a sweater."

To which he responded, "You know I have a lot of time for the Scots. When they start to wear a sweater in the fall, they don't take it off until the spring. So I will keep wearing the sweater."

He just loved to come in and talk about the business. One time we were having a management meeting in the boardroom and Mr. Sam was able to walk out of his office directly into the boardroom. He came into a meeting in which we were talking about Seagram's sales.

He blurted out, "That no good son of mine who works in New York just bought a movie company in Hollywood so he could get laid."

Jack Clifford, one of the old time vice presidents, said, "Yes, but Mr. Sam, he's your son."

Mr. Sam replied, "Yes and I'll fix him." He continued, "I will call Leo Kolber right now and tell him to sell it." Leo was head of CEMP, and Leo sold it to Kerkorian.

Mr. Sam knew Sam Rothschild very well. Sam was the Seagram salesman for northern Ontario, and I knew Sam Rothschild well too. I ran into him when I had been selling for Edwards Sudbury, and he was also a friend of my parents. Sam was the first Jewish hockey player in the NHL—he played for the Montreal Maroons who played in the NHL between 1924 and 1938, winning the Stanley Cup in 1926 and 1935.

Of Gin and Rum

That brings up another interesting point: Mr. Sam was indeed a high-end marketer. He believed in promoting Chivas Regal, Crown Royal because of the high margins, although he drank VO. Hence the creation of Boodles British Gin is quite interesting. I remember him coming in to see me about that.

He said, "You know, Peter, I was in London and I was driving by this club, the Boodles Club, and I thought that it would be a good name for a gin."

I found that interesting—he went on, "Yes and it will be made by Cock Russell."

"Who are they?" I asked.

"Well, we just bought the company. They make the reins and leather rigging for horses. They've been at it since 1512; it's a pretty small company," was his response.

So we started developing this gin "Boodles," which was a very high-end gin. When ready for marketing, it was launched as a British Gin made by Cock and Russell since 1512. Of course everybody thought it was made in England, but it wasn't. It was made at the Chivas Distillery in Scotland.

Mr. Sam was a great and brilliant marketer, and he knew the numbers. I knew that when he came into my office. Even in those days we had the computer printout on sales from every store in Ontario. Some provinces were not that far advanced. He could ask me about the store numbers in one of the Sudbury stores and I was lucky—always fortunate enough; if I didn't know, I didn't pretend to know. I didn't bluff and I'd always say I'd get back to him, which I did. It was a good lesson to not bullshit and to be straight up.

One time I was working on a new bottle for Captain Morgan Rum. I took the bottle in for Mr. Sam to look at.

He commented that it looked pretty good and he queried, "But what does Mr. Cox think of it?"

Mr. Cox was the commissionaire who came in at 4:30 p.m. everyday and sat inside the entrance until midnight. In my mind I asked myself, Well what would he know about it? I went down to see Mr. Cox who was about thirty years older than I was. He always looked pretty elegant in his commissionaire's uniform. I gave him the bottle.

He looked at it and asked, "Mr. Crossgrove—how tall is the bottle?"

I replied that I didn't know and asked why that would be important.

He told me, "I keep my liquor on a shelf over the fridge and it looks a little too tall."

Well, in those days, many of the average people stored their liquor in the same place. Shelves were a standard size and this bottle was about a half inch too tall. What a learning experience for me. Ever since then I have never hesitated to ask for an opinion from anyone.

Working Life and Family Dynamics

The Seagram Office was right across Peel Street from the Mount Royal Hotel in Montreal. It was a beautiful, distinct, and relatively small building, and was full of original works from the Group of Seven. The blending room was in the basement and if we were in Montreal, we would go down and try products every day. We tried a different type of product every day. If today was gin, we tasted our competitors' and ours. We were supposed to spit it out into big milk cans and then rinse with distilled water. Then we would cross the street to have lunch at the Mount Royal Hotel. My first boss there was Reg Wilson who would have me sign the luncheon bill so it wouldn't be charged to him. What he didn't know was that I always signed his name and put on a big tip. I was only twenty-eight at the time; however, I was not about to be played for a pushover by seniority. I didn't have to say anything though. My actions spoke volumes. I guess that's why he wound up working for me.

An interesting fact was the largest volume of distilled spirit sold in Canada at that time, by a large margin, was basically only sold in the province of Quebec, and was Du Kypers Geneva Gin. In my view, it tasted terrible. They had a great marketing strategy. For every case sold in a parish, the priest and the doctor received twenty-five cents each. In addition, at Christmas and Easter, the company put flowers in the church. So if the priest visited your house and you asked if he would like a drink, he would say, "Yes thanks, Gros Gin," which is what it was referred to as. If you had the flu or another ailment, the doctor would tell you to take a shot of Gros Gin.

When I went to Montreal and started to work for Seagram's, I moved up very quickly. The only job ahead of me was Charles's job I guess. Senior management couldn't get any equity because Mr. Sam was ticked off. The reason was because during the war, some of the senior people had options. They were overseas and partying in London; and I guess the stock was under pressure. They were exercising their options, selling the stock and partying. He declared, "The employees would never get options again." So management would not be able to build up any substantial wealth. Although we had a car provided, and I had the use of the jet, we always had suites entertaining big people when they came to town. It was a pretty interesting job from that point of view. I knew if I didn't give it up soon, I'd never give it up. It was a nice lifestyle but they owned you. Anyway, I did decide to leave later.

Quebec and the Maritimes

While working at Seagram's, it was hard to find French Canadians with academic backgrounds who were interested in business and marketing. We really needed that, particularly for the Maritimes and Quebec. Academics seemed to want to be priests, lawyers, engineers, and doctors. I had a good friend from Sudbury, Bob Gougeon, who had gone to Upper Canada and the University of Western Ontario. He was the wine sales manager for a company in Hamilton. I asked him if he would like to come to Montreal when he called me to tell me he was looking for a job. I was very fond of him and his wife Dorothy. We would send him on French courses to Berlitz, and Bob would be the Assistant Sales Manager for the Province of Quebec. He agreed and moved to Hudson. He did a good job for Seagram's.

When working at Seagram's we lived out in Hudson on the Lake of Two Mountains, which was one of the most wonderful places in the world to live. Bob was out there in Hudson too, and we had a good time. Hudson had a good yacht club. You could go back and forth to Montreal by train if you chose to. It was about a forty-five-minute run on the train, or you could drive downtown if you wanted. I always went to work at about 5:30 a.m. so I never had to worry about traffic, and I generally came home before or after rush hour, managing to skip the traffic.

Seagram's Manager of the Maritime Division was Earle Annette. He grew up in New Carlisle, (on the Gaspé Peninsula, St. Lawrence River in the province of Quebec), with Rene Levesque, who became the Premier of Quebec. Earle's father owned the only hotel in New Carlisle. One Saturday morning when he was still in school, Earle was working early at his dad's hotel front desk during World War II. A man came to the desk using Canadian currency that had been replaced by a newer version. Earle thought that his suit looked foreign too. After he checked in and went to his room, Earle went to see the police chief. He told the chief that he had a German spy in the hotel who must have been dropped off by a German submarine. The police chief told me Earle was crazy, and the discussion went on for a couple of days. Earle then insisted he phone the Quebec Provincial Police. They came and sure enough he was a spy and they arrested him. Several years later on a well-known Canadian TV show, they had the police chief on their program, and gave him all the credit for catching the spy, who was the only one ever caught in Canada I believe. Earle was not too happy about that.

When Earle worked for Seagram's, he lived in Halifax and occasionally I would be invited on a Canadian war ship for lunch in the Officer's dining room. Most of the officers seemed to take pride in the amount of rum they could drink. If they had to go to sea after lunch, they would have to have been drunk. When Earle would come to Montreal, he would always arrange for me to have lunch with him and Rene. We had one laugh after another. Their native language was French, but they always spoke perfect English when I was there—part of their Jesuit education. They sure were enjoyable to have lunch with.

Sporting Sponsorships

The Canadian Open was sponsored when I was at Seagram's, and at the time was considered as one of the best four or five golf tournaments in the world. Larry O'Brian, who reported to me, was in charge of the tournament. It moved around Canada. However, because of the advertising laws in Canada, we were not allowed to really identify with it. We also produced an excellent film to which we were not allowed to put our name. Another problem was that it took our salesmen off the road for about a week to work on the event. Costs also came out of our marketing budget. I spoke to Charles about dropping it, and he agreed if we could find a sponsor. Larry soon found Imperial Tobacco to take it on.

One of the years we were sponsoring the tournament, Larry O'Brian had me go down to the Tournament of Champions in Houston to encourage some of the great names like Arnold Palmer, Gary Player, Jack Nicklaus, and Sam Snead to come up for the Canadian Open. Going to these tournaments we would always take the two Canadian players George Knudson and Al Balding on the tournament circuit to dinner.

On this day, a Wednesday, Knudson and Balding had played the Pro

Am and we were waiting for them. Ben Hogan, only one of four professional golfers to win all four professional majors, was on the massage table.

When we were leaving he called out, "George!"

"Yes Sir?" replied George.

"Do you like golf? Has golf been good to you?"

"Yes Sir."

"Well get your hair cut. You look like a bum," came the response from Hogan, known to all as Sir.

George had long hair like a hippie. Before dinner we had to get to a barbershop and get George's long hair cut. Hogan went further after we left and called for the Golf Commissioner to come to the locker room. He told the Commissioner of the Professional Golf Association to, "Get all those caddies that look like a bunch of bums with their hippie hair to get their hair cut." He went on, "Golf is a gentleman's game and we're going to keep it that way."

The Marketing Experience at Concordia University

Talk about interesting experiences! While I worked at Seagram's, the Dean of Commerce at Concordia University approached me asking if I would teach a marketing course there. He had been aware that I had written the teaching manual for Thain and Leighton Canadian Problems in Marketing. David went on to be the head of the Banff School of Fine Arts, and the book was the leading marketing textbook in Canada at the time. I agreed after some thought. I was to teach the third-year marketing course in the evenings for two years. I felt I owed the system something. I was pleased that my classes were way over subscribed with students, and the class was standing room only. I was able to bring in new products under development, and we looked at different packaging, labels, and talked about price point, and a few months later they would see those products on the shelves. The class was between one and a half to two hours long, and we literally had to turn students away. There were people lined down the passage to get into the class.

I enjoyed it, but after two years with a young family and the extensive travel I was doing, I found myself considering stepping down. The trigger was when the students had an uprising and threw a huge IBM computer out the window. The students had said one of the professors was racist. They subsequently found out he was living with a person of colour, so clearly he was not racist. At the time, it was a disaster for the school, and it disrupted the university. The large IBM computer was a very expensive piece of equipment. I felt I had given back to teaching because I had a responsibility having been blessed with getting an education and receiving scholarships. With this though, I have always wondered why after I resigned from the Faculty of Concordia University that I have never heard from them since. I have written a couple of times to see if there is any sort of alumni magazine they can send me, and I still have not had a response from them. I did graduate first in my commerce class at Concordia. I guess I ticked someone off. I would have thought that they would be pleased with what I was able to accomplish.

One time I was flying from Montreal to Vancouver, and Canadian-American stand-up comedian Rich Little from California and his manager were sitting in first class with me. There was only the three of us and I spent my time marking exam papers. The flight attendant had no idea who Rich was, and he went on and on about the safety of the plane. I listened to this whole conversation while Rich pretended to be very concerned. He repeatedly asked how they could make the plane safer. All the while, the air stewardess tried to allay his concerns, not knowing for one minute that he was pulling her leg. He went on to ask them, "Would you consider attaching passenger pigeons to the wings of the plane? Would that help?" She was trying to get him to relax, and just took it all in. I laughed so hard; the ink from my pen was running all over the place. Rich was so funny; he sucked her right in. The students must have wondered what happened because I was marking their papers in red ink, and there was black and red ink all over their papers. I would have to say that experiences like these are sometimes quite memorable because they are so unexpected and sometimes so outrageous. They keep life interesting. I must say I do have a good laugh whenever I think of that incident.

Generational Forays

Going back to Seagram's: I remember Charles telling me he had an eightieth birthday party for his father at the Waldorf, and Charles and Edgar had been fighting over who was going to run the company.

Charles stood up to speak, and said as a birthday gift, he told his father, "Dad, I love you, and as a gift I'm going to tell you that I'm no longer interested in a senior job. So you're going to have two sons who love each other again." He continued, "I think Edgar should become CEO."

Edgar and Charles were his two sons, and Minda and Phyllis were his two daughters. The company was called CEMP, which stood for Charles, Edgar, Minda, and Phyllis. CEMP controlled the Seagram Company and Cadillac Fairview at the time. Charles had 30 percent; Edgar had 30 percent, and Minda and Phyllis each had 20 percent—but they always backed Charles. Charles had the votes; he could have booted Edgar out at any time. Charles is a great guy. He would have done well on his own. In later years he built some very successful businesses including founding the Montreal Expos.

Charles was the son of a rich man—he was a smart guy; he worked hard and cared about people. And I can tell you that the Seagram family would own and control DuPont and Seagram today if he was in charge. He would never have condoned what happened. I know the way he would think. And I've certainly heard from his best friend at the time, Blane Bowen, that Charles thought what they were doing was wrong, and that Edgar Jr. was pissing the company away. In fact, in a recent and rare interview in The Globe and Mail, Charles was quoted as saying, "It was a disaster, it is a disaster, it will be a disaster. It was a family tragedy."

When I was at Seagram's and Edgar Sr. came to Montreal, we all knew it because there was a lot of talk flying around the next day about his wild partying. The one thing Edgar insisted on was moving the office to 375 Park Avenue in New York from 1430 Peel Street in Montreal, to be housed in the world's most expensive skyscraper at the time when it was completed in 1958. I used to go down for a few days once a month to New York and stay at the Waldorf Hotel next door to the office to see what was going on in marketing. In those days, Air Canada landed at Kennedy Airport. You then took a helicopter downtown to the Pan

Am building, took the elevator down, and walked across the street to the Waldorf. That was a lot of fun.

Mr. Sam stayed in Montreal. Mr. Sam was battling the City of New York on municipal taxes because the Seagram Building, which was an architectural landmark in the city, was built well back from the street where there were benches and an open area plaza. However, the city wanted to tax him as though the building fronted right out onto the street. I don't recall how that turned out; however, in 1961 the City revised the 1916 Zoning Resolution, where developers were offered incentives to create open space arrangements—such as those fronting the Seagram Building. Just as the headquarters for Seagram's in the Montreal building now belongs to McGill University, the Seagram Building in New York is no longer associated with the Bronfman's today.

CHAPTER 2

The Big Mac

Life is full of trade offs and one gets exactly what one needs in every situation.

About six months to a year after I left Seagram's and came to Sudbury, George Cohon—the American-born Canadian founder and senior Chairman of McDonald's Canada, McDonald's Russia, and the Ronald McDonald House Charities both in Canada and Russia, as well as author of To Russia With Fries—called me to ask if I would like McDonald's for northern Ontario. This is hard to believe, but nobody had ever heard of McDonald's up north. George and I knew each other through YPO, and we hung around quite a bit with Ken McGowen—the "Mac" of Mac's Milk—and the Hasty Market. George and Ken were good friends and we often had drinks together. I told George I knew who McDonald's were, but didn't know much about them. And so I said no to George. I was way too busy and couldn't take it on. It so happened an hour after George called that my good friend Bob Gougeon, whom I had sent to Berlitz's to become Sales Manager for Seagram's in Quebec, called to ask me if I could find him a business. He really wanted to get into business for himself. He told me he didn't have any money when I asked him.

"How about hamburgers?" I asked almost jokingly.

He was a little taken aback, "What are you talking about?"

"McDonald's," I mentioned. When he admitted he didn't know anything about them I continued, "They have eleven or thirteen restaurants or stores, as they call them in Ontario. I'd like you to go to every one of them and tell me if you're interested."

And he did. He drove to every restaurant in Ontario and talked to the guys running them. As I mentioned, McDonald's was fairly new back in the day, however, in conversation with owners and operators, Bob was able to get enough information from them on the good prospects for the fast food concept and burgeoning fast food industry. Bob got really excited and I called George and said we'd do it. George was happy to move forward with us and so we did, although we didn't have too much to do with George after that as far as the business was concerned. Bob was the one working with McDonald's to get the store up and running. With much planning in location, Leo Gasparini, my partner in some industrial buildings, found the site for the restaurant up in Sudbury. Bob came to Sudbury and worked for a while at Pioneer, which was the construction business I owned and was running at the time we built the restaurant.

He also went to McDonald's Hamburger "U" for the intense weeklong training program. The university was originally opened in 1961 in the basement of a McDonald's restaurant in Elk Grove Village Illinois, and now has a 130,000 square foot campus in Oak Brook, a western suburb of Chicago Illinois. Known as the "Harvard" of the fast food industry, McDonald's university was touted as the first restaurant company to "develop a global training centre," with the focus to train managers, mid-managers, owners, and operators. Having had the experience of sales with Seagram's, Bob excelled in that, and he was also totally inspired and motivated with the management training in business and social skills. He got quite excited. With his strong desire to run his own business he could see the potential for incredible growth and future prospects; these days, the employment stats quote, "an above 99 percent employment rate immediately post graduation."

His brother Riki and I put up all of the money, $40,000, which we borrowed and signed the notes from the Toronto Dominion Bank. Bob lost $80,000 in the McDonald's restaurants in the first two years. McDonald's then changed their policy, came in, and told him this wasn't going to work; they didn't want anybody involved who wasn't operating the business. Ultimately, Bob had to get rid of his partners. So after the first two years, they put all the money up for him to cover his debt, and they bought us out. Riki and I received $80,000 to get out. We doubled our investment, which wasn't a hell of a lot; but it allowed us to pay off whatever we borrowed from the bank and put the same amount into our pockets as profit.

Well then Bob was just off to the races. He was back for one more McDonald's restaurant, and then two more of the same. He advertised the three of them, and they really started to do well. Initially when I had the business, I had everybody we knew go in there for lunch and breakfast for hamburgers. I thought hamburgers were going to come out my ears. We ate in there every day to help try to get the business going and talk to people about it. It's hard to believe today, because now all the years have gone by and you can only be an operator of those franchises for twenty years. McDonald's will only grant a license for that period of time; they make it easy for you to sell because they want to have young blood running their franchises. Bob's son didn't want to take over from him, so Bob sold the business. He and Dorothy retired and they've done extremely well.

Food Service Industry Operating Smarts

Bob was one of the best operators they had. I remember him telling me this story about being at a big McDonald's convention when he was asked to stand up because he had the highest order amount in Canada. In other words, the average person would spend eight dollars in Sudbury, where everywhere else, everyone was spending seven dollars. He was asked how that happened.

He said when somebody asked for fries the instructions were to ask, "Will that be a big fries?" If somebody asked for a hamburger they asked, "Will that be a big Mac?" If somebody asked for a soda they asked, "Will that be a large soda?"

Just by doing that, he was about 20 percent ahead on the average sale in Canada. He was a very smart, hard working, and well-liked person. I don't think he had an enemy in the world, and to this day he still doesn't. Bob's a wonderful friend and still is. As I say, he's now retired and moved to Toronto because his children and grandchildren are there. That's where his wife would like to be—closer to the children. He probably misses golf by the lake up in Sudbury, but life is full of trade-offs, and we get exactly what we need in every situation.

One time I was in Aspen, Colorado with Bob Gougeon and four other McDonald's store owners from across Canada—Halifax to Saskatoon. Bob had invited me to join him on this trip, and we were skiing in Aspen. We were dining at the Copper Kettle, a very fancy and famous old restaurant in the middle of the Colorado Rockies. It was well known amongst the very few restaurants in Aspen at the time, and was started by a group of friends who had been in the Foreign Service in World War II. They built a good reputation serving meals from the countries they had toured: North Africa, Italy, Germany, Northern Europe, and Near East and Central America. Each day the menu reflected a specific country; even the breadbasket related to the country of the evening. The Copper Kettle was designed originally by first-generation post-war architect Herbert Bayer, and sat in a three-story building at the base of Aspen Mountain at the site of an old tramway building that became the Tipple Inn, Copper Kettle restaurant, and Tippler bar.

It just so happened that the rest of the McDonald's owners, friends of Bob's, were all sitting together with us at the one table. A patron from the next table came over to ours when his wife had gone to the washroom. He explained that it was her birthday and when she came back they were going to bring out a birthday cake for her. He asked if we would sing happy birthday to her. These chaps, single and multiple McDonald's owner and operators, sang happy birthday every day—several times a day—so they were happy to oblige. They almost lifted the roof off the restaurant. Of course this patron and the other restaurant patrons did not know who these fellow singers were. Some of the looks were quite comical. Unfortunately the Copper Kettle is now closed, but that was certainly a memorable evening—we just got right into the spirit and the moment.

So that was my experience with McDonald's. Because I had the opportunity, I often wondered whether they would have touched me if I had taken all of northern Ontario at that point and with that kind of a setup. I could have kept it.

In 2010, through the commitment of eighteen owners over about twenty-six locations in northern Ontario, a pledge of $1 million was made towards the $34 million construction cost to build a new Ronald McDonald House in Toronto, which was slated to be the largest Ronald McDonald House in the world. Northern Ontario McDonald's owners and operators stepped up to the plate and did the region proud.

CHAPTER 3

YPO

YPO was always a great place and sounding board—a wonderful environment to go for help.

One of the things that played a big part in my life was YPO (Young President's Organization). When I left Seagram's, Charles wrote me a cheque that kept me going for six months when I didn't have a dime—when I didn't know where my next meal was going to come from. It sure kept me going. It wasn't a company cheque—it was one from him personally to say thank you, and I surely did appreciate Charles's gesture. He was a wonderful person. In addition, the greatest thing he did for me was to put me into YPO. When leaving Seagram's, Charles told me that now I was in my own business, I would qualify for YPO. At the time I didn't know anything about YPO. Charles told me it had been a good thing for him; he made great friendships and learned a lot, through education and sharing amongst members regarding leadership, business, and management, and connecting executives and leading companies. YPO is a global network with over 400 chapters and 21,000 young executives today. It was founded in 1950 in the States; actually near New York City, and Ontario became the first chapter outside of the States in 1956. One of the criteria is you have to be under the age of forty-five years, have the title president, chairman, CEO, managing director, or partner, with at least fifty full-time employees. Charles arranged for me to get into YPO. He thought it would be good for me, and mentioned he was going to contact Ontario YPO as a favour to me.

The Toronto YPO Chapter hadn't taken anyone new for five or six years. They decided to open the doors and let a few business owners in. Charles recommended me to Jack Carmichael of City Buick, who called me up. I came to Toronto and was interviewed. Gordon Sharwood, Fred

Eaton, and Irving Gerstein—now "Senator Gerstein"—were at the same meeting. The introduction to YPO was a very important thing that Charles did for me, and it paid off big time later on in terms of all the great connections I made. As a point of interest, Gordon Sharwood, who was interested in the challenges of family businesses, went on to lead a group of fourteen Young Presidents to form CAFÉ (Canadian Association of Family Enterprise).

With only about fifty members in Toronto's YPO, they certainly hadn't let anyone in from outside Toronto. I don't know if Murray Hogarth of Pioneer Petroleums from Hamilton was in yet. Len Savoie from Windsor and Sault Ste. Marie was running Algoma Steam Ships, and I think he came in later. Other than those two, I was the only person from outside Toronto. In any event, Jack Carmichael, owner of City Buick knew Charles introduced me. When he heard I was in Sudbury, he worked hard to help me get accepted. Another connection came up when we discovered that every year Paul Desmarais bought a new Buick for his father from Jack Carmichael, who in turn would send it up to Paul's father in Sudbury.

Friendships and Working Relationships

Gordon, Fred, Irving, and I became lifelong friends after we joined YPO. Dick Thomson, CEO of the Toronto Dominion Bank, was in YPO, along with Ted Rogers who joined later, and Monty Black. I can name thirty or forty people who became wonderful and long time friends of mine. You had the opportunities to discuss your business problems with YPO, and they sometimes put you together with people who could help you. You could attend YPO conventions and educational conferences, which we did from time to time. The intensive conventions were geared towards bringing together "the best and brightest leaders from the worlds of business, politics, finance, technology, philanthropy, social enterprise, and the humanities. Renowned resources, in-depth discussions exploring current topics, powerful networking opportunities and exhilarating social and cultural opportunities challenged and inspired attendees to become better leaders in their business, family, community, and beyond," is how the YPO Global Leadership Summit is described. The contacts were incredible. In fact, I attended a seminar at Harvard, and a couple of the teachers were classmates of mine.

Of course when I joined YPO I was running Pioneer Construction, and one time Irving Gerstein called me down to meet his father-in-law, Mr. Smith, of Smith Transport and Bramalea. Irving's wife was Gail Smith. Irving told me about a company available for sale. I believe it was called Milton Brick, which owned a lot of properties such as low rental apartment buildings. Mr. Smith had been on the company's board and it was going to be sold. My accountant and outside auditor Ted Coe, upon whom I depended a lot, had a look at it with me. Following me saying, "Okay," we received a call from Irving who said his dad Bert Gerstein would like to meet with me. At the time, the Gersteins owned People's Credit Jewellers, a large coast-to-coast Canadian jewelry company. Ted Coe and I travelled to Toronto to meet with Bert Gerstein and Irving for lunch at the National Club.

Bert scolded me, "My son's involved in the jewelry business, and what are you getting him involved in this business for? There's no way he's going to get into it." He dumped all over us, as if it was our idea; we just sat there and took it.

After we left, Ted Coe asked why I took all that. I had accepted Irving's father's remonstrance without any emotional response or reaction, fully understanding where he was coming from, and the need to just let it go. I replied, "Well, you know, if the deal was over it wasn't going anywhere, and Irving's a good friend, so why should I embarrass him? I'll just take a pass." It was just one of those things that happened that wasn't going to happen. Not every deal works out. Irving is now one of the best and most liked Senators up in Ottawa. To this day he is still a good friend.

I remember when I wanted to buy Edwards Sudbury Limited, Dick Thomson called me and said, "Peter, interest rates are about 18 percent, what are you going to do?"

Because one of Edwards' businesses was the mortgage business, I said, "I guess we'll have to pass it on." I wish to God he hadn't given me the money. I was buying the business for the wrong reason. There were six Edwards children and a lot of fighting in the family as to what to do. My wife convinced me to buy the business, which was primarily a mortgage portfolio—some buildings on leased Canadian Pacific Railway

(CPR) land owned by Marathon, CPR's land company, which at the time had some of the finest land in most downtown cities in Canada. Clearly I paid too much and at those interest rates, probably the highest bank interest rates ever in Canada. It put a lot of stress on me and my other business. It certainly was a character builder. And I did learn a lot from the experience: when, how, and why to invest in a business.

Banks, Banking and Business Expansion

Another time, we were up in Quebec City at a Canadian YPO convention, and Ted Rogers, now deceased, but past President and CEO of Rogers Communications invited me to join him because he wanted to go for a walk.

I remember it was evening after dinner, I don't know where our wives were, but he confided, "Peter, I'm under a lot of pressure from the banks. I have an opportunity to change banks; what do you think I should do?"

In response I said, "Ted, I recommend against changing banks. If you change banks, the new bank is going to put a lot of pressure on you. The bank you're with is probably doing you a favour. Try to work with them."

Anyway, he took my advice, and a few years later he thanked me for that. I always called him "Mr. Leverage" because he wrote the book on leverage. He was very good at it. God, he was a brilliant guy, and he had the greatest heart there ever was. Described as being the fifth richest person in Canada, Ted and his wife Loretta were extremely generous to the Toronto universities: the University of Toronto, and Ryerson University where the Faculty of Business was renamed the Ted Rogers School of Management for their generous gift, awards, and scholarships.

One Saturday morning I was walking up Yonge Street in Toronto, and around the corner near the Canadian Tire store was a luxury car dealer where I ran into Ted on the street.

I asked him, "What the hell are you doing walking around downtown Toronto on a Saturday morning?"

He said, "Well I was over at this car dealership trying to sell car phones, you know, cellular phones for cars."

"You know Ted, my son really thinks there should be a cellular phone service in Sudbury," I told him, and continued on, "because Sudbury is kind of spread out and business men really need them."

Ted told me if my son found one hundred customers, then they'd put cell phones up in Sudbury. He kept his word, and that's how the cellular business got into Sudbury. And that's how YPO worked.

African Safari

YPO organized many wonderful trips, and once I headed out to a safari in the Maasai Mara National Game Reserve in Kenya with a YPO group. Before we headed out, we were in Nairobi for three days meeting with business people and government officials. They were hoping that the YPOers would see some business opportunities.

We were staying at the Intercontinental Hotel. There were about ten floors in the hotel and my room was on the third floor. It was a lovely room with a balcony; however, I noticed that there was an armed guard sitting at the end of the hall. I asked the guard on our floor why he was there. He told me thieves would scale up the outside walls and rob the rooms. I told him I would pay him two dollars per night if he would move his chair and sit outside my room, which happened to be across from the elevators. None of these supposedly smart guys—I'm referring to my fellow YPOers—figured out why the guard slept outside my room in front of the elevators on our floor.

One evening we were invited out for dinner to the home of the Citibank manager for Eastern Africa. The man sitting to my right asked me where I was from and I replied Canada. I asked him if he was with the bank and he said no, he was the Minister of Finance for the Kenyan Government. The week before, Prime Minister Mulroney had forgiven a $70,000,000 loan that Kenya had with Canada. He thanked me for that but said we should have been a bit wiser and asked the then President Daniel arap Moi to match the amount from his Swiss Bank account.

CARE Canada, which I talk about later on, ran Eastern Africa for CARE International. Their offices were in a compound on the outskirts of the city. As chairman of CARE Canada, I had to go there occasionally, but I was in and out as quickly as possible. It was well known there were about 3,000 murders a year in Nairobi, and the police were never able to solve any. If they nailed you on a traffic violation, you paid them on the spot. They did not issue you with a ticket. This system was the way they earned a living because they were not properly paid.

Strategic Social Networking Events

One of the greatest things to ever happen to me was to meet Fred Eaton. He's a lifetime friend. He and his brothers have given to good causes across the country for years, and they still do. His brother Thor was never really in the Eaton business. Having always been a venture capitalist, Thor invests in deals. He and his brother George were partners with Michael Smith, and did extremely well in Michael's business, which was importing replacement parts and undercarriages for heavy equipment primarily from Asia. They were way ahead of their time. I know Thor's done very well in some junior mining companies. He's still involved in a few that I'm interested in. Fred was on the Board of Masonite, and as a big investor he did well there. When the dust settled a few years later, after Eatons went through its troubles in 1999, we all became friends again. I think they understood, whether I was right or wrong. I was trying to perform the role of a director in telling them what I felt.

One of the YPO experiences I had was with Fred before I was on the Eaton board. Not long after meeting him, he said that Dick Thomson was on his board, and he really didn't know Dick as well as he would like to, probably because Dick had become his main banker after Alan Lambert had been banker previously. So I suggested I could fix that. I arranged a YPO trip to northern Ontario. I told our members that most of them had never been north of Barrie, and they didn't really know where northern Ontario was. I organized an underground tour of Inco mine, and a tour of the Inco facilities—this was before it became Vale. It was absolutely second to none. They have the largest smelter refinery in mining operation in the world, and unfortunately most people in Ontario, let alone Canada, have never seen it. Most of the people in Ontario have never been north of Muskoka. A huge part of Ontario is really up there.

A Visit to La Cloche Island

I often still ask people if they know Manitoulin Island, and sadly they know nothing about it. As I have shared before, the lakes on the island are beautiful—full of fish—and not only can you see the bottom, since there's no pollution in any of the lakes, but you can also drink the water out of any of them. In any event, I told Fred I could orchestrate this trip, which I did. I invited our YPO chapter up to northern Ontario and to Sudbury.

From there we went to Great La Cloche Island (French for "Bell Island," named by explorers for the bell rock featured on the centre of the island), and by boat from Little Current to Killarney. We had lunch at La Cloche, owned by my late friend Cliff Fielding, a Sudbury entrepreneur.

You can drive onto the island, which is located south of Espanola on the way to Little Current, on the North Channel of Georgian Bay. It's bigger than Bermuda—over 30,000 acres in the North Channel of Georgian Bay, and very valuable property. Cliff bought it for $252,000. At the time, my uncle, who was the Assistant Deputy Minister of Lands and Forests, was bidding against Cliff on behalf of the people of Ontario, but the government would not go higher than $250,000.

The island has seven beautiful lakes on it and hundreds of miles of shore around the perimeter. It's just spectacular. In fact, Cliff told me he took enough timber off there in the first year to pay the $252,000 for the property. That's the kind of guy he was—very bright. In 1933 he worked at Inco as a car and locomotive repairman. He started out hauling lumber with a team of horses to build the tailings lines near Copper Cliff, and went on in 1935 building his transportation company and moving into the ready mix business—the first in Sudbury to supply ready mix to the mining and construction companies in the area. The company was called Wavy Industries.

The municipal, federal, and provincial governments required two bids on contracts. No problem. He created a second ready mix concrete company called Mallard Ready Mix in another part of the city with its own management. It was years before anyone knew that he owned them both. It was about twenty-five years before a real competitor was started, Rainbow Ready Mix.

During this period, Cliff found out he could buy a Canadian Pacific Railway British Preferred stock at the same price as a common stock. The shares had been sold in Britain many years before, and they paid the same dividend as the common stock; however, the English Preferred shareholders had five votes for every common share, and the CPR required their permission on some corporate changes if they wanted to make some. In the end, Cliff bought them all. Ian Sinclair, the CEO of CPR, invited him on the board.

After about a year, he and his wife Lil were invited to a board meeting at the Empress Hotel in Victoria, British Columbia. He asked some tough questions and Ian Sinclair said he was no longer welcome at the meeting or on the board. Cliff said the most embarrassing thing he ever had to do was tell his wife that they had to leave, and were flying home commercially. She reassured him, "It is okay, Clifford, we will get through this."

Several years later, Cliff's son Jim was invited on the board. It is estimated that when the CPR was unbundled and the various parts went public, Cliff's shares were worth a billion dollars. Cliff had an eighth-grade education. Cliff, Sam Bronfman, T. D. Edward, and some of the most successful people I ever met never finished high school, let alone completed university, or anything like that. The lack of an education should not be a barrier for anyone.

In any event, on this particular trip I made sure that Fred sat next to Dick on the plane, and for the duration of the bus tour. When we went to Killarney by boat; Dick and Heather were on the same boat as Fred and Nicky Eaton, and they were in same cabin down at the Killarney Mountain Lodge for the weekend. By the end of that weekend Fred, sure knew Dick Thomson.

Jim Jerome was there. He was the Speaker of the House in Ottawa, and happened to be a tenant in the building I owned in Sudbury, where he practiced law before becoming the Speaker of The House of Commons. Jim was a very funny storyteller.

We had some people talk to the YPOs about northern Ontario, and the future of northern Ontario. It was interesting at the time. I remember back then telling Bill Davis there were over 300 government boards in the province of Ontario, and to my knowledge there wasn't one person from northern Ontario on any of them. Northern Ontario generates huge amounts of money from the mining activities, and clearly did not have representation at the time.

The purpose of this story was to tell you about YPO and how it tied relationships and business together. We didn't have any female members then—now, of course, there are just about as many female as male members. The first woman chair to YPO and now merged World Presidents Organization (WPO) was elected in 2010. In the recent 2013 Global Leadership Summit, one of the company founders and CEOs presented on how hiring more women to executive ranks could increase company profits. So much is moving forward in significant directions for women in the organization and business. YPO was always a great place and sounding board; it was a wonderful environment to go for help. In fact, it was YPO that helped me to get into the door manufacturing business later on. Today, Canada boasts ten YPO Chapters with about 700 members, and eight WPO Chapters with about 650 members spread throughout the provinces with the majority sitting in Ontario.

Backtracking: Montreal to Sudbury and the Purchase of Pioneer

It came time to leave Seagram's, and I called Jimmy Hinds, a lawyer in Sudbury.

I said to him, "You know, Jimmy, I'd like to go work for myself. I'd like to buy a business. If you hear of anything let me know."

He responded, "Well if I do, I'll let you know." About six months later he called me and said, "I think Grant Henderson would like to sell Pioneer Construction."

"I can't afford it," I replied.

He suggested that just maybe I could find some backers. One thing led to another and I met the famous Lawrie Martin, who lent Paul Demarais his start up money. He lent me some money and I met with the Edward family who agreed to buy a piece of it. I bought Pioneer, which was a wonderful business. I bought out the Edwards, and finally a few years later I bought what was left of the family company, which included a hotel, some commercial buildings around Sudbury, and a mortgage business. Mr. Edwards had died, and the family wanted the cash. I knew Dick

Thomson, CEO at TD Bank, from YPO as I have mentioned, and called him to borrow the money.

Home and Away: Buying Pioneer

Lawrie Martin had moved on, and the new manager, Don Valentine, at the Royal Bank wouldn't even talk to me when I went to buy out my partners, the Edwards from Pioneer. He wouldn't let me go to Toronto to talk to anyone there. I found this out when I happened to be at a YPO university. Anyway, there I was at the YPO convention in Acapulco when they were opening the Princess Hotel. I was sitting around the pool talking to Jimmy Pattison, a member from Vancouver, when a hotel employee let me know I had a phone call. The call was from Ted Coe, my auditor, who informed me that the Royal Bank had turned me down. When I returned to the pool, Jim could tell something was wrong from the expression on my face.

He asked me what was going on, and I replied, "Well the bank just turned me down cold. This guy Valentine won't let me go to Toronto to see people at the Royal Bank head office, and if I can't then I'm stuck. I want to buy my partners out, and I said I could do it."

There we were on a Saturday, sitting by the pool in Acapulco, and Jim said to me, "Well I've got a friend, Ted McDowell, soon to be Senior Vice President of TD Bank in Toronto."

Jim obliged by making the phone call, and connected me with Ted McDowell. Jim got his start by opening a GM car dealership in Vancouver and grew to become the largest selling dealership in Western Canada. Today he is described as a business magnate and philanthropist, and ranked by Forbes as the third wealthiest person in Canada. I did appreciate Jimmy's introduction.

Ted McDowell called me on Monday and suggested we should talk. I went to Toronto with my auditor Ted Coe and met with him. It turned out Ted's uncle, who was at this meeting, was the credit manager at the bank. Anyway, the meeting went extremely well, and I was able to get the money from TD.

They asked me which branch I wanted to deal with and I said, "I should be dealing with the downtown branch, but the guy talks. Everybody at the golf club who deals with the bank knows everybody's business."

They promised to change that, and sent up one of the people who attended that meeting, and who turned out to be the best banker in Sudbury after the retirement of Lawrie Martin. He got a lot of business going. That all worked out quite well, and that's sometimes how things happen when one thing leads to another. I owe Jim Pattison a big thank you, and YPO a big thank you.

I met a lot of wonderful people through YPO, and it features later on in my life too. I stayed with YPO until I was fifty when they threw me out. I was the Chairman of the Ontario Chapter and chaired the split into two Chapters. Clearly one Chapter could hold all the people who deserved to be in there—a great resource for young people in business.

CHAPTER 4

Business Building

Over the years I think that I have been involved in many businesses, because I like the variety of knowledge and challenges in the diversity of economic endeavour.

I really loved the construction, mining, and road building business at Pioneer. I loved the work. It was interesting; it was a challenge as well as a gamble. A lot of equipment sat idle sometimes, and the amount of profit you added on might determine whether you were awarded the contract or not. We operated an open pit mine up at Geco, north of Wawa Ontario, for Noranda Mines. We were in the road building business; we had asphalt plants and gravel pits, and we also installed services for house and commercial building lots.

The excitement of the bidding was very interesting as to how much margin you would put on the bid. Sometimes in the spring you would look out at the yard and see the equipment under the snow and wonder if you were going to get any contracts at all. There were times when the other contractors were full, and you could pick up work at a higher margin. It was always a gamble.

I recently travelled to Sudbury to attend Emil Pidutti's funeral. He was in his early seventies, and died prematurely after battling cancer for about ten years. His father was a hairdresser, and Emil started out in the same business. When he was about twenty-eight he began building fourplexes, and then moved up to building apartments with a hundred units. Emil wound up owning at least 4,000 units in Sudbury, Saskatchewan, Barrie, and Toronto.

While he was building them, he tried to leverage them as much as possible until he could get the lowest possible final mortgage. When his CIBC bank manager moved to Saskatoon, Emil moved his banking with him, although he lived mostly on the Lake in Sudbury, and kept an apartment in Barrie and Toronto.

Pioneer would do the rockwork and the paving for him, and he would tell you he was unable to pay for the work until the job was complete. And that was fine, because our estimating department always built a little interest in to the price. Emil always paid when said he would. He owned many strip malls, and if you drive through Barrie, Ontario, you will see the commercial plazas and developments, store after store, which were built by him. He always kept his head office in Sudbury, and because I had helped him, he gave his life insurance business to my son.

Emil had a great sense of humour. One time we were standing in front of an apartment building discussing when it would be ready for paving. A gorgeous real estate sales woman, Ursula Van Der Kamp, drove up in her big Mercedes to talk to us. After a couple of minutes Emil instructed Ursula, "Get out of here." She asked him why. "See all those bricklayers and drywallers looking at us?" he asked. When she looked around and said yes he continued, "They would all like to make love to you, and they have stopped working. That's costing me a lot of money. So please take off."

On one occasion Emil's external tax accountant, Andy Sostarich, told him he had to pay a large sum of money immediately to the tax department. Emil felt the amount was totally unfair, and so he decided to head to North Bay, then the tax headquarters for northern Ontario. He arrived there with a cheque. Emil had let his hair grow but then shaved it all off. As he handed the cheque to them he took off his fedora, and dumped all the hair on the counter saying, "You have taken everything else—you might as well take this too."

We used to have coffee from time to time. I laughed when he told me the story—never thinking I would use the idea several years later.

The President Hotel

I also owned the President Hotel in Sudbury, which had about one hundred rooms. It was where all the students hung out in those days; there wasn't a bar at the university. And as a matter of fact, when Quart beer first came to Sudbury, we bought up the first several weeks' supply of every quart in the brewer's retail store. If anyone wanted to drink Quart beer they had to come to the President Hotel. They used to serve Quarts in Quebec, but they never served them in Ontario. We had an incredible university crowd; we also had the union NDP crowd in the other part of the building. The hotel was very successful, and usually full. We had a contract with Air Canada, which was quite a profitable business for some time.

A little more competition came to town when Laurentian University opened their own pub. Of course, universities do not pay taxes, and hotels pay a higher rate of tax than the average business. With the university opening up pubs, things started to work differently, and that affected the hotel.

The Business of Bids and Distractions

The hotel business was different and sometimes presented me with interesting challenges to deal with. One time Lou Spracklin, the hotel manager, was home in Newfoundland on vacation, and our assistant manager Richard De Diana phoned Judy Robertson, my secretary at Pioneer.

Judy came into the engineering room when we were working on a bid, and said, "Peter, you'd better talk to Richard."

I replied, "I can't. We're right in the middle of a bid; we have a car warming up waiting to take the bid to Toronto."

On highway bids the Ontario government would have three people, each with a key to the lock on the bid box, and they opened their lock in front of witnesses. They wanted to make sure there was no corruption, and believe me, if it wasn't there by 4:00 p.m., then the bid would not be considered.

Anyway, Judy came back in and insisted I talk to Richard, stressing it was absolutely urgent. So I went to the phone and asked him what was going on.

Richard reported, "I've got a chap here from Human Rights." When I asked what his issue was he responded, "They told us we fired so-and-so because she was black."

I asked, "Who is she?"

He said, "Well, you know the woman in the coffee shop? You told us that you wondered how a woman working in a coffee shop could afford a mink coat. So we hired a private eye to watch her, and caught her stealing big time. So we fired her."

I asked, "And you've explained this to the guy from Human Rights?"

When he said yes, I questioned again, "Can you please ask him again if he thinks the reason we fired her was because she was black, and that we're prejudiced?"

I could hear Richard asking, "Mr. Crossgrove would like to know if you think we fired this lady because she's black and we're prejudiced?"

The guy from Ontario Human Rights said, "Of course, that's why I'm here. We want you to rehire her."

I asked, "Well, if we were prejudiced, was she black when we hired her?" My response put an end to that story. It was not that I was attempting to be smart; rather, I was under so much pressure to get back into the bid room and get that bid completed.

Petrik

One day when I was just starting the Pioneer business on my own in Sudbury, I ran into Riki Gougeon on the street downtown. Riki was a very good friend of mine; his brother was a much better friend. His father had died and hadn't bothered to pay his income tax for years. He owned Gougeon Insurance forever, and now Riki's daughter runs it, and it's a very large and successful business. Anyway, there was Riki downtown crying that he didn't know what he was going to do because his mother needed money. She was working at the company and earned one hundred dollars per week; that was what he was paying her. He needed $5,000 to keep the business going otherwise he would have to close it. He'd been in to see Lawrie Martin at the Royal Bank of Canada, and Lawrie wouldn't give it to him unless he got another signature.

I asked Riki who Lawrie had told him to get, to which he replied, "Anybody."

"Let's go," I said and went in with him and signed that note for $5,000.

Eventually, Riki and I had a side business going. We financed insurance premiums. We were borrowing money at 6 percent and lent it out at 12 percent. We created a little company called Petrik, which controls all those companies today. Petrik would borrow the money from the bank at 6 percent, and loan it out to pay insurance premiums for gas stations, and all kinds of small businesses who couldn't pay their insurance up front. We'd finance them and then deal with the insurance company. We had an arrangement with these small businesses regarding missing one of two payments whereby we would notify the insurance company. In the end, we still got all our money back, so it was a very lucrative business. When I went to London, Ontario to attend the MBA program at Western University, I was released from my guarantee at the bank, and walked away from that interest with Riki.

In Business: A Helping Hand

Sometimes in business you are given an opportunity to help someone get a business started by just lending a small hand. I first met Bernie McDowell when I was selling retread tires to used car dealers in Sudbury. That was between undergraduate and graduate school while I was trying to make some money.

Both Bernie and his twin brother were car salesmen on a used car lot. Both of them were alcoholics. Bernie had six children. I gave Bernie a ride home one day because he was too drunk to drive. When he went into the kitchen I asked his wife Aileen how she got by, and she told me by working night shifts at the hospital as a nurse.

Several years went by and I received a call from Bernie when I owned Pioneer Construction. He asked if he could come and see me. He did and he explained that he had quit drinking for a year and wanted to get into the construction equipment rental business. If he did, he wanted to know whether we would rent equipment from him. I said sure as long as his rates were competitive. I asked him how he would finance it all and he responded by saying he would sell his house in downtown Sudbury and buy a small house with about twenty-five acres on the edge of town.

Peter Edward, a well-known Sudbury businessman, was going to mortgage his new property and lend him some additional money. Peter's primary business was lending money, although he was a graduate of the McGill School of Agriculture. Peter was very conservative and a careful lender; however, his father was an alcoholic, and I think he made an exception in this case.

Bernie got set up and when he was ready to go he came to me to ask if he could rent the Cadillac I was about to trade in. I agreed. He and his friend Quinto Amadori, who weighed about 300 pounds, hit the road. Quinto owned a wrecking yard but wanted to see the province of Ontario. They travelled from Thunder Bay to Noranda calling on contractors and small mines. Business started to build up initially with road contractors, then a few years later with the mines. In the first two years they put 600,000 miles on the Cadillac.

I was a director of the Ontario Road Builders Association, and at the annual meeting we always had a supplier's day. I took Bernie to the supplier's day and introduced him to Silvio "Sil" Bot, CEO of Bot Construction, and Kingston "King" Beamish, CEO of Beamish Construction, and Syd Cooper, CEO of C. A. Pitts Construction, along with several other folks. When the construction companies were working in northern Ontario and needed a compressor, drill, loader, backhoe, and so on, they called McDowell Equipment.

I sold Pioneer and moved to Toronto and from time to time when visiting up in Sudbury, I would have lunch with Bernie. He always insisted I go and see his equipment yards. By then he had hundreds of acres of used equipment and spare parts. He also had a huge repair and paint shop, and a new office building, although he still ran his office out the basement of the house. He like Seymour Schulich and others steered his insurance and group business to my son, who now has over 6,000 clients across Canada and operates out of Sudbury, because he likes it and wanted to raise his seven children in the lifestyle there.

A few years ago, Bernie called and asked when I was going to be in Sudbury because he needed to see me. When I arrived at his office he was drinking red wine. He told me he had taken money out of the business for his wife, to ensure she lived well for the rest of her life. Several years before he had bought his wife a home on Lake Ramsey, which is quite beautiful. I asked him what his problem was, and why he was drinking. Apparently he had given the business to his four sons, and the son running the mining section was fighting with his brothers. No one would work for him and the division was dying.

I told him what I would do for him and instructed him to get his auditor Andy Sostarich—probably the smartest accountant I have met in my life. Andy came down with the statements, and the earnings and value of the company blew me away. I met with each brother individually with Andy as witness, and asked all three if they wanted to buy their brother out. They all quickly agreed and the fourth brother was brought in, told he was being bought out and what the terms were. He quickly agreed. Part of the deal was a no-compete clause, which he ignored. A few days later Bernie bought in a small competitor in the mining equipment business with excellent management. The company has grown in leaps and bounds, and sells equipment and parts all over the world.

Bernie was not able to get off the booze, and it no doubt shortened his life as it did his twin brother several years before. Bernie was a good person who needed a hand. I am sure there are many people like him, and if you can, you should stop and help.

Flying the Skies of Northern Ontario

Travel was then what it still is now in remote areas where exploration and mine development is still carried out, and can be related to business. You must be properly prepared, anticipate potential problems so you can bank on the turns, and negotiate the highs and lows to find your way.

During the period that I ran Pioneer, we had some pretty close calls on aircraft flights. Riki Gougeon and I owned a Beechcraft Model 18 aircraft, and I often found myself flying the skies of northern Ontario. Pioneer was running a big rock backfill mine for Geco—part of the Noranda Group in Wawa, up north of Lake Superior. From time to time, our management people and I would go up to visit the operation.

The gravel landing strip in Wawa could be interesting to negotiate depending on the wind because the strip was on a slope. We had a couple of part-time pilots, but only used one at a time. On one occasion, a couple of our people left Wawa in bad weather in the plane. The pilot finally decided he was lost and he called for help. Two US Air Force jets from a base in Sault Ste. Marie, Michigan appeared on either wingtip and guided the plane to safety.

On another occasion we were flying from Wawa to Sudbury, and it seemed to me we had been flying for a longer time than we should have been. George Moore was the pilot. At this point I asked George where we were.

"Honestly, I don't know," he responded.

I told him to get below the clouds. As we did, I could see a highway and I told him to follow the highway. We finally saw a water tower and town, but were unable to read the name of the town on the water tower. We saw a gravel airstrip and we landed. I went over to a pit where they were crushing gravel nearby, and when I asked where we were, they told me we were in Cochrane Ontario. There is nothing east of Cochrane. We'd probably have run out of gas and crashed if we had missed Cochrane. We were about one hundred miles east and 300 miles north of our destination of Sudbury.

One other time we were flying from Sudbury to Toronto. Donald Plaunt was the pilot, and he was lost. So he decided to drop down to find we were over a farmyard. The plane was flying so low; the surprised ducks were scurrying everywhere. Thank goodness there was no water tower. Donald saw Highway 400 and figured out our location.

Waterlogged Floats and Flips

The worst incident I ever had in a bush plane was trying to fly from Lake Simcoe to Lake Muskoka. It was on May 23, so the ice was not long off the lakes. I had been attending a YPO executive scheduling and planning meeting for the coming year at YPO member Peter Levy's cottage on Lake Simcoe. I had arrived there in my car and the meeting was Thursday night and Friday morning. Ron Besse, a neighbour in Muskoka, was there with his plane. He suggested I fly up with Lorne Barklay, (another neighbour in Muskoka), and have one of the students, who were helping Peter open up his cottage, drive my car to Muskoka. I agreed.

The plane was beached overnight and there had been high winds with waves washing over the floats. The floats have plugs you have to open up and pump out because they can leak. Ron clearly did not check the floats, and obviously the wave action had filled them with water. When we were in the middle of the lake after taxiing out there, he powered up the plane to take off. The nose came up. Therefore, the tail and most of the back part of the pontoons were well under the water. It looked like it was going to flip ass-over-teakettle. He told us to get out of the plane and Lorne and I jumped into the frigid water. Ron ran to the front of the floats and stood on them and the plane started to level. In the meantime Lorne got caught in the guy wires at the back of the plane. By the time I was able to get him untangled, the plane had drifted away as it was extremely windy and the waves were high.

A Close Call

Ron was fine but we were in big trouble with hypothermia. Fortunately Peter Levy was down on his dock with the two university students who were helping him with his boats, and one launch had its motor running. One of the two ladies, who had been serving meals and drinks to our group, was watching the plane take off with a pair of binoculars. They both saw what happened and ran down to tell Peter that we were in the water. Peter headed out with the two students at full speed. Lorne told me that he didn't think he would make it. He told me that if I made it, he wanted his wife Rosy and his children to know how much he loved them. I could not feel anything at this point but the sweat in my armpits. We were close to cashing in. Peter and the students arrived with the boat; Peter jumped right in and helped us, and the students pulled us out. There is no doubt they saved our lives.

When I arrived back at Peter's cottage I went right to the shower with all my clothes on and turned on the hot water. Clearly my veins and arteries had contracted, and as I warmed up, I started to bang against the shower walls. I wound up with a lot of bruises.

What should our pilot have done differently? First: pump out the floats. Second: when we were in trouble, he should have told us to put life preservers on and run the plane up on shore. And when he stood on the floats he might have also sent us a rope. I guess he panicked. There are many plane accidents in northern Canada that are never reported, because the pilots are afraid to lose their license or become uninsurable.

I have to say, when you have the unfortunate experience to brush with death, you really appreciate what you have. Life takes on a whole new meaning and perspective. I know I sure was thankful to be alive after that episode. I am sure Lorne felt the same way when he thankfully did make it through.

Life Changes and Letting Go

I did love the work at Pioneer. That was one business I wish I could have found a way to hang on to. It went because I went through a humongous divorce, which after Gordon Lightfoot's, was the largest settlement in Canadian history. They really didn't take into consideration income taxes in those days. The legal fees and everything else just killed me. It was the first case Patrick Le Sage had ever heard as a judge. None of the Sudbury judges would hear it. Most of the lawyers and judges from around town sat in the courtroom every day listening to the whole proceedings. This often bothered me because it was none of their business.

When the divorce was settled, one of my children lived with me, and two lived with my wife. By the time I paid the lawyer's bills and I paid all the taxes, I had to sell something, and it was around that time that Syd Cooper, who was running C. A. Pitts in Toronto, came along. In fact, his general manager was Wally Barrie, who I had played football with and lived with in the Phi Delta Theta fraternity house at McGill. Actually, Syd and I were on the Board of the Ontario Road Builders Association (ORBA) at that time, and the board members were all much older than me. I was the token member from northern Ontario.

At the next ORBA meeting, Charlie Armstrong, who was sitting beside me, asked, "Anything doing?"

I told him Syd Cooper had approached me to purchase Pioneer.

"Watch out. He will negotiate the price and you will think you have a deal, and then he will come back and change it," he warned.

And that's exactly what happened. It was Alan Beatty, who was senior partner of a major law firm in Toronto on Syd's board, who actually came up to see me after I thought we had a deal. Alan had also been raised in Copper Cliff and I knew him. His father had been President of Inco, and I also knew him through the Eaton family.

Alan was the lawyer and also Vice Chairman of the Eaton Company, and Chairman of the Board of the CFTO TV network that the Eatons wound up owning. Baton Broadcasting was actually 70 percent Eaton owned and 30 percent Bassett owned. Over time, the Eatons bought the Bassetts out because Johnny F. Bassett Jr. had started the Toronto Toros and Memphis Southmen professional and football teams, and he needed money to support them. He sold his 10 percent share to buy the two teams. David Bassett, his youngest brother, took his money and went offshore to the Bahamas. He had it well invested. CIBC managed it for him, and he turned out to be a very wealthy man. Douglas Bassett became the CEO of CTV when his father retired. I think he eventually sold his interest to the Eaton family though, so they wound up owning it all. In any event, Alan came up and tried to negotiate the price on behalf of Syd Cooper.

The Sale

In the meantime, I used to have breakfast with Cliff Fielding, the Sudbury entrepreneur whom I mentioned earlier; he was one of the largest shareholders in the CPR. He was in the concrete and cement block business in Sudbury. He also had several gravel pits and shipped Inco slag across Canada for railway ballast. I have also said he had two ready mix companies, Wavy and Mallard, so people thought they were getting competitive prices. Another member of the breakfast club was Benny Cecceralli. Benny supplied the smaller grocers with fruit and vegetables, and in the fall brought in boxcars of grapes, which he sold to the Italian community to make homemade wine. Boxcar Nurmi owned the Pepsi Bottling franchise and a couple others, and we had breakfast every morning at between 6:30 a.m. and 7:00 a.m. at a hotel on Highway 69. It was after I'd been up to my office and all the crews had gone out. We sat and chatted about different things, and had coffee while talking about hunting and fishing amongst other topics of interest.

In any event, I told Cliff that I was selling Pioneer to C. A. Pitts. He told me he would like to have a shot at it, and I informed him I had signed it up. Anyway, they came in to try to renegotiate and I wound up selling to him. I thought then I should never have sold it. I was just going through a very difficult situation at the time, so I did sell it. Sometimes you've just got to let go, follow through, and knowingly take courage, and trust that something greater is just around the corner. If you have common sense, integrity, and you are prepared to work hard, then there will be other opportunities. I had to let it go.

CHAPTER 5

Running for Politics

I really believe in politics and I believe you get the government you deserve. You don't go out and just work and not support the democratic process.

While living in Sudbury I became involved in Conservative politics. Not in a big way. As a matter of fact, my family were all Liberals. Mr. Edward told me we needed a Conservative in the company. So I became a Conservative. As a believer in the democratic system, I have always supported all parties. Some members of the NDP and Liberal parties were big patrons of the beverage facilities of the hotel I owned.

When I mention Bill Davis, I have to tell you that I've known Bill a long time, and I'm very fond of him. I think he was a wonderful Premier and a wonderful person. I had an opportunity to talk to Bill from time to time. Bill was the eighteenth Premier of the Province of Ontario at the time, and held this position from 1971 to 1985 when he resigned. I knew and liked him and I still do. Bill was a good guy and a good Premier in spite of the fact that he didn't allow the completion of the Allan Expressway. The decision to not permit continued construction of the remainder of the highway to downtown Toronto came soon after he took office as premier. Much of the Rosedale community was against the highway, and the section of the road south of Lawrence Avenue in Toronto became known as the "Davis ditch."

Whenever I had the chance, I would raise northern Ontario issues with him. I told him that in order to get doctors in northern Ontario we needed a medical school. Today we have an excellent medical school, the Northern Ontario School of Medicine, hosted by both the Laurentian University in Sudbury, and Lakehead University in Thunder Bay (over 1,000 kilometres apart). It became the first new medical school in Canada in over thirty years. I also told him we needed a four-lane highway to

Sudbury, similar to the one on the Michigan Peninsula, because far too many people were being killed on Highway 69. In addition, a highway would bring tourists north. It's interesting that he extended the four-lane highway to where his cottage was at the Severn River. One of the other things I mentioned was the reality that over 300 boards and commissions in Ontario were without any representation from northern Ontario. Bill started to change that almost at once.

An Invitation to Run and My Acceptance

The head of the political side of the Conservative wing of the party at the time was Ross DeGeer. I had been on a committee that had raised money for the Conservatives. Bill Kelly was in charge of fundraising for the Conservative party in the province of Ontario, and it was he who invited me to join the fundraising team. My recollection of the team was that Bill Kelly was the chair, and the members were John Eaton; Joe Barnicke, J.J. Barnicke Limited; Dalton Bales, Ontario cabinet minister, lawyer, and Attorney General of Ontario in 1972; and I believe Alan Eagleson. I'm unable to recall a meeting Alan attended that I was at.

In some way, they had me in charge of the Parry Sound to Manitoba border as my area of focus, as if it was ten miles wide. Most of those people had never been to northern Ontario, like most other people living in Ontario who have never been to northern Ontario. Before we really got going, an election was called in June of 1978.

Ross DeGeer, the top political advisor to Bill Davis, called me both to inform me and ask, "Peter, we're desperate. There are only thirty days to the election, and we don't have a candidate for Sudbury. You need to help us. Would you run?" I told him no, and that I was too busy. He asked if I would think about it.

Bill Kelly then called and asked me. "Oh okay, alright," I responded.

There was no chance of winning, because no one could remember when the Conservatives had even run second. Sudbury and Nickel Belt were the two ridings, and they were either Liberal or NDP both provincially and federally. The incumbent in Sudbury where I would run was Bud Germa, who was the sitting provincial NDP member. Bud had previously run federally, and was the last Federal member of the Communist

Party in Ottawa to be elected to the House of Commons. I decided to run, since there was no hope of winning.

Team Effort and Funding

I did not have supporters, a campaign team, or money for the campaign. A couple of days after I decided to run, with only twenty-eight days until the election, my first call was to Ross DeGeer. I told him I needed some money for this campaign and asked him how much money he had for Sudbury.

He replied, "Well because it's you Peter, I can tell you the truth: we've written off Sudbury. We have no money to support a candidate in Sudbury because we know we're unable to win, but we needed a candidate. So you're on your own."

Well that really ticked me off. By that time I had arranged to have Bob Demarais, Paul Demarais's brother, to be my CFO (Chief Financial Officer), and like his father he was a lawyer and a Conservative. Bob later became a judge. I gave him a list of people to call in Toronto, because Conservatives could not raise money in Sudbury. They can now. I asked Bob to call the list including my YPO friends. I told him to tell them that the only way to beat the growing NDP and Liberal parties was in northern Ontario.

As an aside: I recently sent a letter to our Prime Minister suggesting he appoint a Senator from north eastern Ontario. If you want to speak to the Federal or Provincial representative in northern Ontario, you must speak to an NDP or Liberal, and that's how they get re-elected. I called some of my friends like Fred Eaton, Monty Black, and others, and told them if they're ever going to beat the NDP, they've got to beat them in Sudbury. They responded big time.

What the government doesn't realize is the NDP has a strong hold in northern Ontario along with the Liberals, and if the Conservatives are going to make any headway then they have to find a way to get some representation in the north. Anyway, I raised something like $60,000 more than I was able to spend, because all the advertising time had been sold; it was just too close to the election.

In any event, we now had money for the campaign. With about twenty days to go until Election Day, we found out our opponents had purchased all the time for radio and TV ads. Our slogan was, "It's About Time."

On the Campaign Trail

I really enjoyed campaigning, going door-to-door, and debating. In fact, I ran into many interesting people doing the door-to-door trail; many people whom I had gone to school with and a number of my parents' friends like Mr. Demarais, Paul's father. We had a long talk. I told him I had to keep going there, because people were getting ahead of me in the apartment building, knocking on doors, saving more time to meet people. I ran into Bob Rodgers, a fraternity brother, who I went to McGill with and played football with. He was a professor at Laurentian University and was campaigning for the NDP. In two weeks I lost over twenty pounds and I wore out two pairs of shoes.

I ran on the idea of having a four-lane highway from Toronto to Sudbury. As I mentioned earlier, of course Bill Davis got the first part of it done as far as his cottage. Ernie Eaves extended the next section, when he was Premier, to Parry Sound—his riding. Mike Harris then extended the four lanes on Highway 17 from Huntsville to North Bay, which was his riding. That should never have happened in my opinion. They are now working on the rest of the four-lane highway from Parry Sound to Sudbury. It's a good thing, because there are far too many fatal accidents. The section from Sudbury has much heavier traffic, with all the traffic going out to Western Canada. Huge trucks come up Highway 69 through Sudbury, and it's extremely dangerous on that two-lane highway. It will be done, but probably not within my lifetime.

Of Loss and Relief

I lost the election by only 1,000 votes. It was an incredible result. What I learned was how important it was to get your vote out. If I had won I don't know what I would have done. But it was an interesting experience, and one that everyone should have. I got right into the campaign. The amazing thing to me is when you ask someone how they're going to vote, they'll tell you right at the door. At the time, I thought it was nobody's business, but the NDP knew everybody who was going to vote for them. They sent cars around with several hundred volunteers driving their voters and seniors to the poles to vote. They didn't fool around. If we had done that, we would've won. Thank God we didn't win though, because I could not afford it.

We had $60,000 unspent in campaign funds after the election. The first call was from Bill Kelly asking if we would send the money to Toronto and they would manage it.

"No," I said, "the money will stay in Sudbury and help fund the next Provincial campaign." Bill had John Eaton call me, and I explained to him why the money was not going to Toronto. He apologized for making the call.

This political race was an interesting side experience in my career. I was trying to be a great citizen. I really believe in politics, and I believe you get the government you deserve and it is important to support the democratic process. I made a donation of one hundred dollars to buy NDP incumbent Bud Germa's campaign. I was the owner of the President Hotel in Sudbury and the NDP guys all drank there. My hotel manager wanted to make a donation, so we made a donation.

Losing was extremely hard on the campaign team. When we conceded there was a lot of crying. People work so hard on these campaigns and become quite emotionally involved. We had nothing to be ashamed of, because our results were fantastic. So my brief political career ended there, and it could be chalked up to yet another interesting aside to my life experiences. You really have to put yourself out there into the public eye. And what interested me as well was the personal interaction with community citizens, getting to know more of what they were looking for to improve on in their daily lives, and how best I could support them as a representative. I am happy to have been involved in the entire political process. It gave me some valuable insights, and I felt I could contribute much to the development of the region when speaking from the platform that was created. I also feel that experiences such as these no doubt contribute to the skillsets required for making a good and fair boardroom delegate.

PART TWO

CHAPTER 6

Toronto, City of Opportunity and Business

Meeting as many people in business is very useful. The term is having a "large Rolodex." It's nice to be able to pick up the phone and call someone for advice, or to have them make an introduction for you.

I moved to Toronto in 1980 after Sudbury. I initially went to work for Coopers and Lybrand as a consultant doing turn-arounds for the banks, which were major lenders to some companies that sometimes turned out to be in extremely bad shape. I knew Dick Thomson, and through Conrad Black, I had been introduced to the CIBC. However Dick Thomson, CEO of TD Bank, and Russell Harrison, CEO of the CIBC Bank, both felt that I had to identify with a consulting company rather than work solo, because if anything happened to me, they needed backup to continue dealing with problems where their client was in trouble. This made sense to me. I took the advice and went to work with Coopers and Lybrand's consulting division.

York-Hanover

My first client was the Bank of Nova Scotia, and I wound up only working on their problems. My largest client was eventually the York-Hanover Company, owned and controlled by Karsten Von Wersebe. Karsten was a fellow from Germany; he was a very ambitious and highly leveraged guy. He was brilliant, but he was just about five or ten years ahead of himself. Karsten owned all the land south of the 401 Highway at the airport, which is all industrial park now. He must have had 200 acres there of the finest prime land in the country. Like a lot of Germans, he fell in love with Niagara Falls, and had a lot of property down there. In addition, we had an office in New York and several properties in the US.

Karsten had vacant space in buildings he owned, and in order to lease out the buildings, if he needed a meat market, he'd go into the meat market business. Or, if he needed some sort of a retail store, he would be into that. Karsten spread himself right across the commercial board, and was into all kinds of different businesses. And he had a lot of good assets across the country—excellent buildings and good development properties. However, he was always over-leveraged. He owned the Skyline chain of hotels and the Four Seasons in Calgary. He was always on to the next deal, and subsequently had a lot of his properties highly mortgaged. He was very bright and energetic. It's just that real estate hit a terrible period in early 1980, and some real estate companies that have become quite successful today almost went under—and several other companies did.

Castor Holdings

Karsten had an associate company that he borrowed from—a company that invested European funds and Canadian Pension funds. The company was called Castor Holdings. Castor Holdings, which meant "Beaver" in English, was a company that had been started in New Brunswick for tax reasons. Castor was run by Wolfgang Stolzenberg and loaned money to York-Hanover. They had different year-ends that allowed them to move assets and debt around. My job was to go in, clean up York-Hanover, and try to get the Bank of Nova Scotia loans down or more secure, which we were able to do to a large extent.

Peter Widdrington, a good friend of mine, had just stepped down as CEO of Labatt's and was invited on the Board of Castor. I told him I would not touch it with a ten-foot pole. So he resigned after his first meeting. Castor Holdings took a few pension funds for hundreds of millions of dollars, and Wolfgang used to fly around in private jets, and had a big yacht and the grand lifestyle. I think the company went bankrupt, and I don't think they ever caught up to Wolfgang. The auditors and directors were sued, but I couldn't tell you the end of that story.

While at York-Hanover, we had a hotel division. We owned the Skyline

Hotels in Ottawa and Toronto, the Sheraton, and a couple of small hotels in Niagara Falls. We leased out the Four Seasons hotel in Calgary.

I received a warning that the tax department was coming to our offices at 110 King Street West with the intention of closing down the hotel division. I remembered Emil Pidutti's deal with the tax department, which I shared with you earlier while I still had Pioneer. I went to all our employees and asked them to give me all the keys they had, and I put them in a big box. When the tax guy arrived, he advised me he would be shutting the hotel division down.

"Here are all the keys," I said as I handed him a box full of them. He did not really look at it, because they were mostly car keys. "I will have to notify about 10,000 employees they have no job," I continued, "so if you will excuse me I will get right on it."

"Are we not able to work something out?" he asked me. With that, he provided us with the time and terms, and over a couple of years we got things cleaned up.

ITCO Properties

I left York-Hanover and I don't believe it ever went into receivership. I went to work for Starlaw Holdings to run ITCO Properties Ltd. The company charged with turning around the bad loans that had been made by their Trust companies in the US and Canada. Because I was able to get the Bank of Nova Scotia's money out of York-Hanover, someone at Clarkson and Gordon—now Ernst and Young—approached me to go into Starlaw Holdings.

I did some work for the McConnell family. The McConnell family from Montreal controlled several trust companies: International Trust, Yorkshire Trust, and they were the founders of Morguard Trust. I believe they were the largest individual shareholders in Canada Trust. They had lots of good assets, and were the largest third-party money managers in Canada at the time. The family was third generation at this point. The McConnells were also a very generous family. They had the largest foundation in Canada, and I think my recollection is that it was about $700,000,000.

I went to work for them in the late 1970s, when the real estate market was still in bad shape. When real estate goes to hell, it becomes terribly illiquid. The McConnells had loaned out money from various entities all over the place: in the States in Denver and Florida, and of course all over Canada in BC, Alberta, and Ontario. My job was to attempt to collect the money by rearranging payment or foreclosure. The vehicle was ITCO Properties, and I was the CEO of ITCO Properties. In a couple of years, we had things in pretty good shape.

Toronto as Home

I enjoyed living in Toronto. I lived at 61 Crescent Road for many years. It was a block from the Rosedale Subway station, and a block and a half from Yonge Street—close to some very good restaurants. I kept a car at the house and one downtown at the Royal Bank building where I worked. That meant I could walk to work and take the subway home, and during the day, if I needed a car to go out to meetings, I had one. It was very convenient. On weekends, we headed out to Beaumaris on Lake Muskoka in both summer and winter.

We had a lot of friends in Toronto both through YPO, business, and old school chums. Our house was eventually sold and knocked down to be part of Gerry Schwartz's Rosedale mansion.

Of Doors and Power Companies

In order to build a business you've got to invest capital in it.

The McConnells then suggested that I look for a company we could buy together so I could get back in business where I had ownership. Of course I liked that idea.

A short time after that, I was at a YPO meeting and mentioned if anybody heard of any businesses available, I was interested. One of the fellows suggested there was a little door business out in Mississauga with sales of about five million dollars. The owners wanted 2.5 million dollars for it. The company was called Interior Door, and after looking at it, I recommended it to the McConnells. They said we should buy it if I put up 20 percent of the money, which I did. We bought another company—a shelving company, which manufactured shelving for drugstores. It was a marginal business, and initially it was so tough that I had to go out there and work on afternoon shifts to help them out. We wound up selling that business.

Interior Door

Jim Fish, who was running the door business, sold it to us. He owned most of it and had a couple of small partners, with 5 percent shares of the total shares. We bought them all out. Jim had another business on the side—designing and building office interiors that I wasn't aware of at the time. But he was the President and CEO of Interior Door. Anyway, one time I went out to see him and he wasn't there. I found out he rarely ever showed up, only to pick up his cheques, which wasn't too good.

So I started to get more involved and I met Philip Orsino. Philip was the auditor with Hillborn, Ellis & Grant, and a graduate in commerce from the University of Toronto. He was fairly young, and it was quite an honour to be an audit partner at that age. I asked him what he thought of the door business, and he really knew a lot about it. The more I listened to him, the more he sounded like a marketing guy rather than an accountant. He said his father-in-law had been in the door business at one point, and he was the auditor for Interior Door. I asked him how he'd like to run this door business, called Interior Door. He said he'd love to run it.

So I believe Philip was twenty-six or twenty-seven years old when I hired him. I spent a lot of time with him, probably half of every day, five days a week, and we talked constantly. We were exceptionally close and became extremely good friends, and still are. We laughed because I told the McConnell family that I thought I could get the sales to $50 million in five years, and in less than five years we were more than $50 million in debt. The McConnells could come up with their money, but I couldn't. We had to keep leveraging so I could stay in the game. That was a tough company to build. I don't know how many times we mortgaged the plant out in Mississauga. Fortunately the real estate values were going up, so we were able to increase the mortgage at the time, and that helped.

Florida Power and Light

We heard that the Florida Power and Light Company was getting out of a bunch of ancillary businesses that were being badly run. They owned a door company that had plants in Alabama, Florida, and Virginia. The head office was in Tampa, Florida. We leveraged that whole deal. We borrowed the money from a bank in New York, and after Christmas one year, Philip and I had taken our wives to Florida for a holiday. We'd been working very hard and felt we should spend some time with them.

We had to leave our wives in Florida, go up to New York and sit in the windowless bank lawyer's boardroom on about the fortieth floor of the Empire State Building for three days. We negotiated with Irving Trust trying to get money. We had been using a bank at that time in Michigan, and we couldn't get any more money from them; we couldn't get anything from Canadian banks at all.

As time went on, we just kept adding businesses to that whenever they came up for sale. I believe at that time they were all in the US. However, the acquisition of the Florida Power and Light Division was a big and important deal. It became a very successful acquisition.

Century Wood Door Limited and Other Companies

It was also about that time we changed the name of the door company from Interior Door to Century Wood Door Limited, because we were also now making exterior doors. We added another door business based in New England, and we picked up small door companies here and there. Some of the people in the door business, who had started building doors in their garages after the war, were cashing in on the businesses they had built up. For them it became time to get out and retire. It was good timing for us. And we took advantage of it and purchased the businesses being offered.

We did try the garage door business. We bought a company in Mississauga that turned out to be a disaster, so we got out of it pretty quickly. Our doors were all sold directly to retailers, whereas garage doors were sold to installers. A lot of installers were thieves—they'd work with your inside people, effectively stealing doors and keeping all the money.

It was a whole different distribution set up that we weren't equipped to manage, and we couldn't accomplish what we were trying to do. So we took a hit on that, sold it and focused on the non-garage door business.

About that time, Philip's people came up with a "fast-fit," which included the doorframe, the door, and all hardware for the door, including the inserts, which were cut and complete. It used to take a carpenter about two days to install a door. This way, a labourer could install a door in an hour, instead of a carpenter taking two days. Everything was registered, so we were protected—the Fast-Fit name was protected. It was all shrink-wrapped, so all of a sudden we were getting Lowes and Home Depot business. Philip was a wonderful marketer. He would do anything for a sale. He pushed his people hard. They respected him, and they all made a lot of money.

The Merger of Premdor and Century

In the next stage, Saul Spears, President of Seaway Multicorp Limited, a door-making business, renamed his Toronto-based company Premium Forest Products (originally launched in 1979 as Premdor), in 1986. He came along to see if we would consider merging the two companies: Century with his company Premdor. We thought that was a good idea. Premdor was public with most of their sales in Canada, and we were private and much bigger in the States. It turned out to be a really good fit.

With the proposed merger between Premdor and Century, Philip would run the company as president and CEO. Initially Saul would be the chairman, I would be the vice chair, and we would have an executive committee. But things never really changed. I still stayed in touch with Philip constantly and we talked a lot. After a couple of years I became Chairman of the Board of Premdor. It was a good relationship. That company grew to become the largest door manufacturing company in the world, and we eventually sold it for $3.2 billion to KKR (Kohlberg, Kravis, Roberts & Co).

Premdor Beginnings and Shareholders

More about the merger of Premdor and Century that eventually became Masonite: The first person to talk to me about a merger was Joe Rotman. Joe was a major shareholder in Premdor through his holding company Clairvest. Joe did not know that Philip Orsino and I had been talking about a merger with Premdor, and had decided we needed to build Century further before merging it with Premdor – a public company.

Joe was sitting behind me at the annual meeting of the Toronto Hospital Foundation and he tapped me on the shoulder. He suggested we talk about a merger. I said we would in one year, and we did. We merged a year later in 1989 and subsequently changed the name to Premdor. Joe stayed on the board and made a great contribution until we sold to KKR several years later. Joe is a very bright guy and extremely generous. He funded the Rotman School of Business at the University of Toronto, and he recently became the Chancellor of The University of Western Ontario.

Another major shareholder in Premdor was Rick Moran, the founder of Swiss Chalet, who lived on a huge sailing vessel, which was always parked in a warm climate. Rick was available to attend board meetings. Frank Hori, the CFO, was also a large shareholder who sold out and re-tired shortly after the merger. Saul Spears had a large position at Premdor as well, and stayed on the board until the KKR sale.

There was only one other major shareholder, Al Lieboff, from London, England, who played an active role in the negotiations. Shortly after the merger, Lawrence Bloomberg who was the founder and CEO of First Marathon—an aggressive investment bank (and who worked out at the same time I did at 6:00 a.m. in the morning at the Cambridge Club), told me, "Al Lieboff needed to sell his shares for another deal he was investing in," and he asked if I knew anyone who could help.

I said that I did—Philip Orsino. I gave Lawrence Philip's name and contact information. The introduction started a relationship whereby First Marathon raised all the capital for Premdor-Masonite to grow into the huge and successful company it became. The two other directors were Howard Beck, a brilliant lawyer and a founder of the law firm Davies, Ward, and Beck and John Berton, a wise old fox who represented the

Starlaw Holdings. During this period, Philip became CEO of the Year in Canada in 2003, which was a well-deserved honour.

Lawrence Bloomberg sold First Marathon to the National Bank of Canada where he is still a director, and for the past many years has been Chairman of the Board of the Toronto Mount Sinai Hospital. He has also donated many millions of dollars to worthy causes.

Masonite

Masonite was a division of International Paper Products of the United States. Masonite made door skins, which are the outside skin of the door made in moulds under high pressure from sawdust and glue. We were buying over $400,000,000 in skins per year from Masonite. We were their largest customer and they were our largest supplier. When we signed our last purchase agreement with Masonite, Philip wisely insisted on a first right of refusal if Masonite was sold. When International bought another forest products company, the banks made them sell something; so Premdor bought Masonite, changed their name to Masonite, and listed on the New York Stock Exchange. Masonite was a well-known name. It was a brilliant move, and the sales margins improved immediately.

The interesting thing was that when we were selling the company to KKR, the board was not keen to sell it. Philip was the one who said it was time to sell. I asked him what he was going to do.

He said, "Well they want me to run it." He had just been made the CEO of the Year in Canada, and made an Officer of the Order of Canada.

I responded, "That's BS. They don't want you to run it. They'll get rid of you because you're a builder."

In order to build a business, you've got to invest capital in it, and the way KKR operated, it was pretty clear they would cut every cost they could, try to get the profit to the bottom line short-term, and then quickly sell the multiple earnings. So they would cut any cost to get the earnings higher. The higher the earnings they would get, the higher the sale price. They had no interest in growing the business and investing cash and expense. I told Philip they would never hire him. He insisted I go down to New York and meet with them—and I did. They had a lovely dinner for me; I think there were about five members of KKR's executive team.

They had the finest wines—the finest of everything. They told me how much they wanted the company and Philip.

When I returned to Toronto, Philip enquired of me, "What do you think? They're really good guys aren't they?"

I said, "Well yeah, they're good guys, but they're not going to keep you."

"Oh, they're going to keep me," was his comeback.

How Smart is Smart?

In about two weeks they fired him of course. They didn't want him at all. When we were selling the company, it was very difficult. Our stock had grown from about $2.00 to about $42.50, and our shareholders felt that at $42.50, we weren't getting enough money for the company. Everybody on the board who was a major shareholder—a serious shareholder—knew it was a good price. I knew I would go with Philip to see the major shareholders. I met with the head of the CNR Pension Fund, for example, and I went out to meet with a fund that said he owned 10 or 12 percent of the company in Regina. In the end, it turned out they owned about 3 percent. Everybody lied, which was another interesting thing.

I also went down to New York at Philip's request and had a meeting with the representatives—about fourteen hedge funds; they had only owned the stock for about three days. They said we should borrow $42.50 a share, dividend that out, and leverage the company—just like KKR would. They referred to me and the board as being too old to be involved in the business, and that we didn't know what the hell we were doing. They went on lecturing me, and talked about having Harvard and Yale backgrounds and everything else. They let us know who they were—all with an average age of about twenty-eight years old. I just got up while they were talking to me. I turned around and walked out. I didn't say good-bye. I didn't say anything.

Philip chased me into the elevator, "What are you doing?"

"To hell with those guys," I said, "They're a bunch of assholes. They don't know one thing from another. All they're trying to do is make a quick buck. They don't care about you, they don't care about the company, they don't care about the employees, and they don't care about our shareholders." I continued, "They probably own 10 percent of the company and they think that they're able to call the shots."

I had a one-on-one with Michael Dell, the founder of Dell computer. I explained to him the rationale for selling, which was the high price for the stock and the cyclical nature of the business. He owned about 10 percent of the stock. When I finished he said, "It makes sense to me and you have my vote."

The next day in The Globe and Mail, there was an article that reported a big "brouhaha" in New York the previous day with Masonite. And indeed there was. That's all there was to it—me walking out of the meeting. Anyway, we sold the company, and two weeks later Philip was out the door. I think he was heartbroken. I feel it was the biggest mistake they ever made because two years later they were in serious financial trouble.

Reflections on the Door Business

For the couple of years Philip has been back in the business as CEO running Jeld-Wen Holdings Inc., with over 20,000 employees, they became Masonite's largest competitor, and they also may be the largest window manufacturers in the world. You can bet they are knocking the daylights out of Masonite; however, they are private.

The door business is cyclical, as is the housing business. Everybody's finally learning that. However, the home renovation business expands when new house building is drying up and people then start to work on the interiors of their homes. In addition, when homes get flooded, the doors expand and have to be replaced. Doors are relatively inexpensive to replace, and they make quite a difference in appearance. The average house contains twenty-eight doors.

We were always in different countries. We were manufacturing in Turkey, Israel, Ireland, France, Chile, Costa Rica, South Africa, and Mexico, and Philip was moving into India and China. As these markets developed, he was the first guy in the "door" (no pun intended), with the business. If things were slow in the United States, they were fast in Europe, and housing was picking up in other countries. Philip was right on top of it. He's a brilliant person. That's what was going on at that time, and is basically the background of Masonite.

Masonite was sold in 2004, and while CEO of Masonite, Philip, served on the board of University Health Network before he became Chair of the Board of Trustees of UHN until 2009, he raised and donated millions of dollars for leukemia research.

Philip Orsino's Triumphs

Perhaps the contributory factor to Philip becoming involved with UHN was as a result of his bout with leukemia—his own personal experience trauma and miraculously overcoming the disease in his fight for survival. And it started with an observation. Dr. Alan Hudson, Philip, his son Joey, and myself were playing golf at the Devil's Pulpit Golf Course in Caledon near Toronto in a fundraiser for the Princess Margaret Hospital. Joey, who was about seventeen at the time, was far and away the best golfer.

At dinner, Alan commented, "Philip, there is something wrong with your face. Come in to the hospital tomorrow, I would like to have some-one see you."

Indeed something was wrong. Philip was not well, and it turned out in the end that he had the three deadliest forms of leukemia.

Three highly regarded oncologists told me that Philip needed a bone marrow transplant. As a prospective donor in what is known as an allo-geneic bone marrow transplant, and being a family member, Joey's bone marrow was the best match in Canada according to his tissue, which was the same genetic type as his father's. Based on three criteria, while Joey's bone marrow matched, Philip was not eligible for a bone marrow transplant in Canada because he would not survive. The hospital required at least six matches. I was told that we should start to look for a replacement for the Masonite CEO.

Philip was very aware of what was going on. He made me promise that he would not be replaced as CEO. I gave him my word that he would not, that since he had kept me fully up to speed I would become more active.

In the meantime, one of the doctors at the Princess Margaret Hospital heard that there was a marrow donor program at the University of South Carolina, in Columbia, South Carolina. Philip decided the only option was to try the program. With the initial screening and process, they just about kill you. Philip did not have a hair on his body and he was pasty white. When he was ready; they injected Joey's bone marrow. Philip was back to full speed within six weeks.

Surviving this illness is a testament to Philip's incredible willpower and determination. He has given back to the health system. I put him on the UHN hospital board. He chaired the audit and finance committee and eventually the board. Philip and Dr. Alan Hudson, world-renowned surgeon and CEO of the University Health Network and others, also figured out a way to finance all those UHN buildings on University Avenue in Toronto, and to replace the outdated Bell Wing on University Avenue. It was brilliant and we all are the beneficiaries of their actions. He has also given to and raised millions for the hematology division of the Princess Margaret Hospital.

Philip has been made an Officer of the Order of Canada in 2003, and an FCA (Fellow of Chartered Accountants); both awards were well deserved. It is now about fourteen years later, and as far as I know Philip is in excellent health. I recently ran into Gerry Schwartz, the CEO of Onex Corporation—a Canadian equity investment firm—which controls Jeld-Wen, the largest door and window company of which Philip is the CEO. Gerry said Philip sure works hard. That's no surprise to me.

A couple of years after Philip's experience at the University of South Carolina, the mismatch unit was closed for lack of success.

Downtime: Travelling Interludes, Tales, and Interesting People

When in business travel becomes a necessity as does finding balance for downtime. Balance in life is important, especially when the work schedule is constantly booked. It's quite extraordinary though as I have mentioned before—the relationships, friendships, and adventures that can occur through random meetings—sometimes in the most unexpected ways. You just never know. Even in playtime, life will open doors and introduce you to many people who will become business associates and lifetime friends. I almost came to expect the surprises as well as to enjoy meeting many wonderful and interesting individuals.

I was at a spa in California called Rancho La Costa in Carlsbad. And while there I happened to be on the same pool water-ball team with William Holden, the American actor who starred in the movies such as Sunset Boulevard, The Bridge on the River Kwai, and The Towering Inferno, his highest grossing movie of his career. Water-ball was part of the daily exercise routine.

After we were finished, he asked me where I was from and I said, "A place you have never heard of—Sudbury, Ontario."

"Isn't that about eighty miles north of North Bay?" he asked.

"How did you know?"

He told me when he was on honeymoon, his wife was working on a movie being filmed in Timiskaming and he had nothing to do all day, so he flew around northern Ontario with the bush pilots to pass the time of day.

We had lunch and dinner together along with Stefanie Powers, whom he was with at that time. I used to go out for the morning walks with her because he had a bad knee and I was there alone.

William told me he had been an alcoholic, and what saved him in terms of living a decent life until he got his act together was the movie The Bridge on the River Kwai. His career peaked after this film. Instead of being paid a large lump sum, he received $50,000 a year for the rest of his life. Otherwise he would have been a bum on the street. When he met Stefanie he stopped drinking and they worked together to found the Holden's Mount Kenya Game Ranch in Kenya. They had been in a nine-year relationship and when William died, Stefanie followed her interest in wildlife welfare and created the William Holden Wildlife Foundation at the Ranch. The Foundation still runs today with educational programs that serve over 10,000 students per year. The educational programs' objectives are to create awareness, build respect, and build appreciation for wild and natural life, understanding that "nature is a renewal resource but only if we assume responsibility of its protection." The Foundation teaches conservation, and programs support libraries built for the education of local students. It was through Stefanie's "long relationship with actor and conservationist, William Holden, whose many years in Kenya motivated his conservation activities—long before the notion of conservation was embraced by popular culture." The dedication and work of both William and Stefanie has ensured that a number of East African species have escaped extinction.

William also told me that they would be making the movie Network in Toronto and showed me the script. This was in 1976. When he arrived in Toronto he called me and I flew down and had lunch with him. Out of Network William was nominated and won awards for best actor and in a leading role. He was a wonderful person. However, I believe the booze got him in the end.

On one of my first trips to Aspen, I was there with Duff Scott, Vice Chairman of the Toronto Investment Banker Greenshields, and John Eaton, Chairman of Eaton Canada. They brought ladies whom they eventually married. There were not many restaurants in Aspen then and so we looked to trying the best one, which was The Shaft. We arrived without reservations for dinner to a long lineup. John went up to the front of the line and gave the maître d' twenty dollars to see if we could get in sooner.

A chap near the front of the line said, "Listen, you asshole, anyone in the line can do what you are trying to do. You're crazy. So get to the back of the lineup."

When we got into the restaurant, we wound up at the next table to this fellow who was with his wife and another couple. We started to chat and after quite a few drinks we were invited back to their condo, which they were renting at the bottom of the first lift of the ski hill, and which you could have bought for $100,000 with $10,000 down. It was large with three bedrooms. I became long-time friends with both couples.

One couple, Tom and his wife, were the Sibleys from Sibley Illinois—a small village in Ford County. He was a Harvard graduate, a huge corn farmer, and also had a herd of buffalo. He was the mayor of the town of Sibley. I used to go down to Sibley (which was noted in Ripley's Believe It or Not! as the largest corn crib in the world before being demolished in 1965), for the July 4 parade and I would sit on the viewing stand with him. It was great fun. I had Tom up to my place on Manitoulin a few times and he introduced me to the Ocean Reef Club in Key Largo, which his uncle Harper had developed and it is also where I have had a house for over twenty years.

The other couple was Buzz and Betsy Norton who lived in Lake Forest, Illinois. Their business was based out of Chicago. He was a big antique dealer with a store in the Merchandise Mart in Chicago. He later started an auction house run by Leslie Hindman—the one-time host of Home and Garden Television Network (HGTV). Buzz helped Leslie set up the business and he arranged her financing. The auction house is known as the largest in the mid-west States. Buzz used to call me if they had a fight and I would go to Chicago to sort things out. Buzz searched all over Europe for antiques. He always said, "One man's junk is another man's treasure. I only want a little in-between."

Buzz and Tom had two private railway cars—one was a sleeper, and the other was a dining and parlour car, which were both staffed and were attached to railway trains. One was called Hiram after Tom's grandfather who was a Baptist minister. We travelled across the country in great style to attend several Super Bowls. Hiram was the last car on the train, and it has a viewing platform. I particularly remember a couple of trips to New Orleans. I would fly to Chicago to catch the train. It was a lot of fun when the people from small towns came out to wave, thinking we were celebrities. The train was packed, so someone would go up and find a bevy of ladies and ask them if they would like to come back and meet Robert Redford. Of course, he was not there but usually they stayed and partied. In New Orleans, the railway cars were parked across the street from the stadium. By game time I would have flown back to Sudbury or Toronto to watch the game on TV when I was all partied out and I had a better view of the game from the television anyway. There were many trips to Miami, Denver, and Los Angeles.

Every year, the railcars would be sent up to Canada a few days before Mother's Day weekend to Algonquin Park for a fishing trip. Most of the fellows had gone to Camp Pathfinder in the Park. The outfitter for the tents and canoes was Don Swift, who they all knew because he had gone to the camp with them. The canoes, tents, and cooking utensils had been prearranged and dropped off by "Swifty" wherever we wanted them. I would get on the train in Toronto. The railway cars would park on a siding in Algonquin Park, which had originally been used to pick up lumber in the park by the Northland Railway Company. We were trucked to wherever the tents and canoes were as we took different routes through the parks every year. The first night we would usually spend at a cabin so we could drink beer and play cards. We would go paddling and hiking for three or four days. Sometimes our travels would take us portaging from lake to lake, and sometimes travel down fast moving rivers that were enjoying the spring run-off with high water. The trip was always Mother's Day weekend as the ice was off, no black flies yet, and on the north side of the hill we could find ice for our whiskey sours. We were always very careful to take all our garbage out to conform to Park regulations. Whisky bottles would be taped with electrical tape so they would not break, and we could make whisky sours before dinner with dry mix water and whisky.

There were many college students who were in the park at the same time, all Americans as far as I could tell. They would be graduating that year and having fun with their friends before they went their separate ways. It was a riot because we had everything organized for one trip over the portage, as they could be half a mile. However, the students had to make two trips. We were organized and they were not. We saw many moose on our trip and a couple of times they came in to see our campfire at night.

Buzz Norton always had a fishing line out and caught speckled trout. Patrick Hodgson, who had moved from Buffalo to London, Ontario, was the cook. Pretty well everything was fried—Klick, Spam, potatoes, and some veggies that were dried and could be brought back to life with water. Patrick owned a company in London that produced mixers for cement trucks and snowplows. One time I stopped in and there he was welding along with his employees. He has been in Toronto for many years and is well known as a very shrewd investor. Along with Buzz, Tom Sibley, and Patrick, Brent Baird was a venture capitalist, Bill McGivern an attorney, and George Morris was head of Buffalo Blower and Forge. They were all from Buffalo. Gage Bailey was from Boston and owned a graveyard. Wilf Dinnick, a stockbroker from Toronto, and I were the two token Canadians. One year we arranged through Len Savoie, a fellow YPOer who ran The Algoma Central Railway, which is owned by the Jackman family, to send Hiram through the Agawa Canyon in Algoma Country, north of Sault Ste. Marie, to see all the fall colours. All this never would have happened if John Eaton had not offered twenty dollars to the doorman at the Shaft Restaurant in Aspen. Those trips were highly memorable.

CHAPTER 7

The Camreal Dundee Merger: Negotiations, Turn-Arounds, and Obligations

The most capable executive I have ever met: bright, a great strategic thinker, works seven days a week, respected by his peers and employees, and a man of great integrity. His word is his bond. I see these qualities in all good CEOs. They're good leaders and they're good to their people.

Camreal was a real estate company that had previously been known as Lehndorff. The company was well offside. This means that the rents were not covering the interest on the mortgage loans with its lenders; the name, management, and board were changed. The shareholders were primarily from Germany. Germans seem to have a real affinity for Canada. They like the people and the country. Some time back, Lehndorff was a relatively large real estate company in Canada for several years, and the majority of the investors were based in Germany. The company owned many good and varied properties across Canada including the Sutton Place Hotel in Toronto.

They were over-leveraged and the market at the time had several real estate companies facing the same problem. The company was in deep trouble and basically illiquid. Some of the people working at the company had bought properties from the company, which I thought was strange, and still do. It was just a disaster. They had real estate all over the place, with no coordination, and improperly managed.

In any event, Lehndorff was in trouble and Alfred Apps, a lawyer at the law office Fasken Calvin (now Fasken Martineau), was brought in to become the CEO. I was asked to be the non-executive chairman based on my experience as former CEO of York-Hanover and ITCO Properties, having turned them around with a new board put in place to clean it up. A new board was put together for Lehndorff, which included four well-known businessmen from Germany representing the German investors, as well as some Canadian directors. The company's name was changed to Camreal.

My first trip to Germany to visit the German shareholders was quite interesting. There were about 400 shareholders in the room, and it seemed each shareholder had a lawyer with them. I travelled to Germany with Alfred to update the shareholders as to what actions were being taken. The meeting went on and on. The shareholders were very upset because they had seen their shares tumble from over twenty dollars to less than one dollar. Alfred had just started in on fixing the problems; however, one by one they unloaded their frustrations and the meeting continued for hours.

Decisions to Merge

A few months or so later, Alfred told me he was approached by Michael Cooper, who had been a classmate of Alfred's at law school and was the CEO of Dundee Realty. They decided the two companies should merge. Alfred thought it would be a good idea to put Camreal and Dundee Realty together. When we looked at the numbers it made a lot of sense. I still had not met Michael, but I knew and was very fond of Ned Goodman, the Chairman of Dundee Realty. I was sure if we put them together Michael would be the CEO, but Alfred said they were classmates, Michael had other things to do, and he wasn't going to want that. I suggested we should bring the idea to the board, and we created an independent committee, which I chaired.

This committee included Detlef Bierbaum, who was managing partner in Oppenheimer in Cologne, which is one of the largest private banks in Germany. There were some other substantial people from Germany, including Dr. Gunther Bautz, a bright and experienced lawyer. Bill Dimma, former Chairman of AE LePage, was on the board. It was a very experienced board and had good board members.

Negotiations

We had a meeting because Alfred had negotiated the deal. In my view, it was a pretty good deal for the shareholders of Camreal. The Germans were anxious to get their shares liquid, having dropped from about $20 to almost nothing. If the deal went forward, this would get their shares liquid at about $2.45 or thereabouts. The deal was stuck at an offer of $2.15 per share for Camreal and was going nowhere. There was a lot of arguing back and forth, and Ned Goodman called me to ask what it was going to take to get a deal done.

I said, "$2.65."

He asked, "Are you sure?"

"Yes," I said, "$2.65. I talked to the Germans, they trust me, and I feel that's a fair value."

He agreed that if I could get them to agree then we had a deal. And so it was agreed. I met with the four German directors and told them what the final offer was. They asked me what I would do. I told them I would take the deal. Alfred recommended it too. They asked who would be CEO. Alfred said there were going to be two co-CEOs, he and Michael, whom I still had not met.

Miscommunications and Misunderstandings

Communication in business is key and the lack of it can lead to very different outcomes than first anticipated. A couple of days later, Alfred came back and said he wanted to back out the deal when he found out he wasn't going to be the CEO, and he called a meeting in a downtown hotel. Michael said there must have been a misunderstanding because there was to be one CEO—and it would be Michael. I called Germany and the four German directors flew over to Toronto. We had a meeting at the King Edward Hotel with the four German directors, Alfred, and the lawyer Alfred had retained. Alfred wanted the merger called off.

After a lot of discussion the German directors turned to me—led by Detlief Bierbaum, who as I mentioned was from the largest private bank in Germany. He then reported to Carl Otto Paul. Again they asked me what I thought they should do.

I said, "Take the deal."

Even though I never met Michael, I knew Ned was extremely successful and did not suffer fools gladly. Needless to say, Alfred has never spoken to me since, and some unkind things he has said about me did get back to me. Dr. Gunther Bautz, Detlief Bierbaum, and myself joined the Board of Dundee Realty. A couple of years later, Dundee REIT was spun out, and Dundee REIT was formed. Dundee REIT has been paying a 6 percent dividend for years and is worth north of thirty-seven dollars per share.

Michael Cooper's Successes

Michael Cooper very quickly spun the income properties into a REIT. Michael, like all dedicated executives, does a really good job. He is one of the most capable executives I have ever met. He is bright, a great strategic thinker, he works seven days a week, is respected by his peers and employees, and a man of great integrity. His word is his bond. I see these qualities in all good CEOs. They're exceptional leaders and they're good to their people. Michael Cooper is all of that; he's absolutely brilliant. He's just a straight shooter from the word, "Go," and he is smart as hell. He's the type of person who would do well at anything. He also has a great sense of humour.

The spinning out of the REIT was interesting. We had to form an independent committee to review the deal. The directors had to be independent and the majority had to be Canadians. The only independent directors were two Germans, an American, and myself. The committee had to have an investment bank give them a fairness opinion. Ned Goodman told Peter Godsoe at the Bank of Nova Scotia that they would get the work. Being the chairman and only member of the independent committee, I decided to put the assignment out for bids. The Bank of Nova Scotia, Bank of Montreal, the CIBC, and National Bank bids were all between $900,000 and $1,000,000.

I then received a call from someone who had been on the Board of Gentra with me, telling me The Royal Bank would like to bid. I said that was fine but they would probably be too high.

One half hour later, Tony Fell of RBC called and said to me, "I hear you said we would be too high."

When I responded in the affirmative, he asked, "Can we have the rest of the day?"

I agreed. Their bid came in at $350,000 and they did a bang-up job. After that I would see Peter Godsoe at Barrick board meetings and other places, and he always called me the "Committee of One." The real fact is that I invited Detlief and Gunther to all my meetings as advisors.

Ned Goodman and Dundee REIT

Michael has recently started Dundee International REIT in Germany and Dundee Industrial REIT in Canada. He is able to attract good people and you can be sure these ventures will do well.

Ned Goodman was the Chairman of the Board of Dundee Realty. When Camreal merged with Dundee, it became Dundee Realty, and then Dundee REIT. It split off from the Realty Company because you can't have non-income properties in a REIT. Ned and Michael made the Realty Company private, and it is still going very strong in the development business. Now Dundee REIT has split off the industrial properties into Dundee Industrial, and that will be a great company too. I just bought a bunch of stock in that company and I'm very happy with what will happen there. That's Dundee. It has been a wonderful experience—an ongoing experience that I'm still involved in.

The Eaton Company of Canada

There is no other business that I have ever seen that cared so much about their employees and suppliers.

At the time I was invited on the board, the Eaton Company of Canada was the largest private company in Canada with approximately 38,000 employees. Not only did they own the largest retail company in Canada, but they also owned one of the largest real estate empires, including large pieces of the downtown Eaton Centre and the Yorkdale Shopping Centre both in Toronto, and the Pacific Centre in Vancouver. They owned major downtown properties as well as in Montreal, Winnipeg, Edmonton, and Calgary, plus substantial real estate properties in smaller cities and towns across the country. Eaton was a Canadian icon and known in every household across Canada. Timothy Eaton, originally from Northern Ireland, started the company in 1869.

They were innovative pioneers in the day, introducing the mail order concept with their catalogue in 1884. In addition, they owned Eaton Credit and most people had an Eaton credit card. They were into the credit card business very early on. If you bought something at Birks or The Brick, it went through the Eaton Credit Company. They also owned 17 percent of the Laurentian Bank.

Signy Eaton, mother to the Eaton brothers and a very bright lady, was on the board, as was Dave Kinnear, who upon retiring as CEO of Eatons of Canada, was replaced by Alan Marchment. Both were professional managers until finally Greg Purchase—a brilliant merchant who had worked his way up the ranks and had started with the company in Winnipeg—came on board as the new CEO for Eaton. Greg was CEO prior to me joining the board, and still held the position when I came on the board as a director.

There are four brothers who owned the company with equal share when I became involved. They were: John, Fred, Thor, and George. Greg Purchase became too ill to work, and when Greg died, Fred went in as CEO, and his brother John was chairman of the board. Fred was the first family manager in many years, and the company was doing extremely well. This changed the company from a professionally run company to a family run company.

The company was very profitable at the time, and Conrad Black who was also on the board gave them excellent advice: that they take the retail company public and privatize the CTV broadcasting company, which they privately owned. I thought that was very good advice, which they ignored.

Keeping Up With Changes in Marketing

After a couple of years, Fred Eaton became the Canadian High Commissioner to the Court of St. James—a job he was very good at—and his younger brother George took over as CEO. George is very bright but severely dyslexic. However, just as his brothers, he had not worked his way up through the business, and was dependent on people he surrounded himself with. And they were generally ass-kissers. Thor was never involved in the business. I asked him why, and he said too many family members were involved in it already. Thor is one of the brightest and most well read people I have ever met. He has been a very successful venture capitalist and generous philanthropist along with his wife Senator Nicole Eaton.

It is hard to believe, but at the time, no one—not even the bankers—ever saw Eaton statements. When Fred took over, he invited Dick Thomson, CEO of Toronto Dominion Bank on the board, not too long after the bank started to see things were declining and started initiated restrictions. The Eatons went on to woo Matt Barrett, CEO of the Bank of Montreal, but he was having nothing of it. Shortly thereafter Peter Godsoe, CEO of the Bank of Nova Scotia, called me and asked me how he could get some of the Eaton business. I gave him George's private phone number. I believe when Eatons failed, the bank did get all their money back.

It was not long after that at an Eaton board meeting when having looked at what was going on in retailing in the United States, I suggested they focus on the major Canadian locations like Montreal, Toronto, Yorkdale, Edmonton, Calgary, Winnipeg, and Vancouver, and sell off about sixty stores in places like Huntsville, Sudbury, and Medicine Hat. The suggestion was they should get out of hardware, sporting goods, outboard motors, and so on.

The board meeting was on a Thursday and as I was walking down the street with Conrad Black and Dick Thomson after the meeting, someone said, "Thank God someone said it."

To which I responded, "We will see."

On Monday, there was an Eaton's chauffeur at my office with a letter from John saying, "Peter, if you feel that way, clearly you have resigned from the board." Needless to say, that hurt.

When the company failed, George called and said they needed an independent committee. I suggested two bright but busy people—Joe Rotman and Philip Orsino. The third person suggested by Fred was Brent Ballantyne, who was let go from Maple Leaf Foods when McCain Foods took over. Brent became chairman of the board and hired someone who had just been let go as CEO of the Hudson's Bay Company. The new CEO did not want to reduce the number of stores—and the company failed. With business and commerce changing so rapidly these days, it is important to keep abreast of what the current trends dictate. The company could not be saved. The model no longer worked.

The Toronto Santa Claus Parade, touted the largest in North America, was sponsored by Eaton from 1905 to 1981. When it was announced in 1982 that Eaton would no longer sponsor the parade, George Cohon of McDonald's Canada and twenty corporate sponsors were able to save it. The Eaton brothers still continue to support many charities because they fortunately did not have all their eggs in one basket.

Family Antics

I recall a funny story when the Eatons were on a fishing trip. We were fishing up near Ungava, which is all flooded now by Quebec Hydro. The fishing was spectacular because with every cast you'd catch a fish. Sometimes you'd catch a salmon, and sometimes you'd catch a pike or a trout—either lake or speckled trout. It was incredible fishing, and we enjoyed wonderful short lunches. You would never experience that again in a lifetime, but there are still places up in northern Canada where there is wonderful fishing.

The only one who wasn't present was John. George, Fred, Thor, and some of their children were there. The oldest child was about thirteen—that would be John David; Henry and Fred Jr. were also there. George—who had been a Formula 1 and A driver (racing cars in thirteen World Championship Grand Prix around the world as Canada's leading racing driver with a full-time seat in Formula 1 and inducted in the Canadian Motorsport Hall of Fame in 1994) before Gilles Villeneuve—was telling the boys about racing in different countries: Brazil, Monaco, California, and all over the place.

One of the boys asked, "Uncle George, where's the nicest place you've ever been?"

"A whore house in Acapulco," was his response. I'm pretty sure he was kidding.

Ontario Store Fixtures: From Private to Public to Private

It just goes to show that doing the right thing for the shareholders regarding some board considerations is not always easy.

My first involvement with Ontario Store Fixtures (OSF) was when it was a private company. OSF was a designer and manufacturer of display units, fixtures, and shelving for retail stores, as well as supplying fixture displays for financial institutions among other commercial applications.

OSF had the contract for the Eaton store in the Eaton Centre, which was being built in downtown Toronto. They also had the contract to fixture most of the other stores being built in the Centre, which were then owned by Eaton Canada and Cadillac Fairview.

Two brothers, Milton and Harry Shier, owned OSF. Harry was a good friend of the Eaton brothers and myself. We often hunted and fished together, and Harry was the best fisherman I ever knew. If there were fish there, he would catch them. His cottage was located west of Parry Sound in the same area the Eaton brothers had their cottages.

I would boat down from Manitoulin on some occasions to fish and party. After fishing we would have a few beers and a sauna that Harry had built on his dock. The Ministry of Natural Resources would never let you do that today. They would probably say no to the dock and the boathouses too. Harry also had a tennis court that we enjoyed.

In any event, OSF was over-leveraged with this major Eaton Centre, and the Bank of Nova Scotia had sent in a monitor and chartered accountants—Clarkson Gordon. Harry Shier asked me to attend the weekly meetings, which I agreed to do with the urging of Fred Eaton because they needed OSF to stay in business. I would fly down from Sudbury to attend the meetings that were always held at 2:00 p.m. The bank monitor would chair the meeting, and I can never recall him being sober. When I saw the monthly charges from the bank for the monitor as well as Clarkson's, I am amazed that they survived—but they did.

OSF continued to grow, and had to become a public company to raise equity in order to expand. They were recognized as the best store fixture company in North America. They did all of The Limited stores and Victoria's Secret Stores, which were only in the United States at that time.

When they went public they needed some outside directors: Alan Marchment, CEO of Guaranty Trust Bank; Duff Scott, Vice Chairman of Merrill Lynch; Monty Black, Chairman of Standard Broadcasting; and I were the outside directors. Milton Shier, a wonderful man who none of us knew well, and Harry Shier, whom we all knew well, joined the board and it went public.

The company was public for a few years and then they decided to take it private again because they thought being a public company was a pain in the ass—and it can be. The stock had done quite well; it had gone from about two dollars per share to about twelve dollars per share. When they wanted to go private, all the independent members of the board became members of the independent committee. We had a legal advisor and an investment bank advisor. I believe we thought that a fair price to buy out the public shareholders was fourteen dollars per share, but they had twelve dollars in mind. The deal went through at fourteen dollars.

However, Harry, who worked out at the Cambridge Club with Duff, Alan, and I, did not talk to us. Alan and Harry both had black belts in karate and worked out in the same karate class. Monty never believed in working out. After a couple of years we became friends again, but it was never the same. Harry and Monty have since passed away. It just goes to show that doing the right thing for the shareholders regarding some board considerations is not always easy. Nevertheless, sometimes in making the unpopular choice you hope you don't lose the friendship of colleagues and associates—hopefully not for too long anyway!

The Royal Trust Fiasco

Directors have vision, understanding, and foresight regarding future issues arising; they determine the best direction and course of action required in the best interests of the company.

Gentra was the name given to Royal Trust as it worked its way out of receivership. Brascan was controlling Royal Trust, who got into serious trouble because of the real estate bubble and crash of the late 1980s. Royal Trust was in the lending business. It was a stock that everybody had; every grey-haired person in Canada had that stock as a safe investment that paid dividends. Brascan gained control of Royal Trust and it wound up going into receivership a few of years later in late 1992. The name was changed and the new company was formed in 1993.

The court took it over and was going to appoint a board with Fraser Fell appointed as chairman. He phoned me to ask if I would serve on this board and I said no. I was far too busy and just couldn't do it. A couple of weeks later I was reading an article in The Globe and Mail regarding the Board of Directors of Gentra, which was the Royal Trust, and I saw I was one of the directors. I called Fraser to ask him what he was doing. He told me he needed me.

It's hard to say no to Fraser. He's done so much for so many people for so many years. He's one of the most incredible people and the nicest person I've ever met. I'm not saying that because he's married to my first cousin Margot Crossgrove. He was the managing partner of Fasken and Calvin, one of Canada's largest leading law firms at the time, and also served as a director and sometimes chairman of the board of some major Canadian companies. He had a major involvement in not-for-profit institutions and still does. He has, along with Margot, a large and very successful family. I don't think there's a businessman in Toronto who knows him who wouldn't say the same thing. He's done so much good in his life.

We had some interesting experiences at Gentra coupled with a lot of hard work. In the first year we had seventy-six board or committee meetings, and I was on the credit committee, which of course was the busiest committee. We had a chap (I don't recall his name), who had just retired as credit manager at the Royal Bank who was outstanding, and boy, did he know the ins-and-outs of credit!

Lawyers, Lenders, and Loans

At our first meeting, a group of about eight Japanese lenders showed up; all of them were with their lawyers. They had demanded to come to the first meeting of the board. They wanted to know how we were going to fix things when we hadn't even had a meeting yet. I couldn't believe it. The lawyers were all looking a little sheepish. I guess they were all told to be there and they were. It was the dumbest meeting I've ever seen. There we all were in this small room with eight Japanese guys, eight major Canadian lawyers standing behind them—not enough space for everybody—and they were dumping all over us. The court had just appointed us; we had nothing to do with the mess the company was in.

I think at that point Brascan had a couple of people on the board: George Myhal, Director and COO of Brascan; Trevor Eaton, Chancellor of McMaster University; and Mel Hawkrigg, Chairman of Orlick Industries—the Hamilton auto parts manufacturer. We had to deal with a lot of bad loans and messes all over the place—not only in Canada—but the United States and Europe as well. We got to work cleaning them up.

Turning the Company Around

Shortly after we had started with Gentra, I attended the first annual meeting at the hotel by Queen and University. The predecessor company Royal Trust had been around forever, and with about a thousand people attending, there wasn't one of them who didn't have grey hair—if they had hair at all. I was sitting in the front row with Mel Hawkrigg who had run London Life, which was another Brascan company at the time. Someone got up to the microphone and commented that he could see only two board members held stock in Gentra.

I turned to Mel, who was sitting beside me, and I commented, "Yeah that's me and you. And I got mine for twenty-three cents, and you got yours for twenty-two bucks."

I thought he was going to piss his pants; it was so funny. Eventually the twenty-three cents turned into $3.60 and having bought a fair bit of stock, I did quite nicely with the company.

Things started to clean up very quickly because we were trying to get bad loans sorted out and the cash back, initially to pay off the Japanese bondholders. We had some people who came from Brookfield, a Brascan real estate company, and they were very good people who worked awfully hard. Even the West Edmonton Mall, which everyone knew was a disaster, we got cranked around and sorted out. We had properties everywhere including overseas, which we gradually cleaned up. As this happened and the debt came down, Brascan was entitled to more directors, so they appointed Heather Reisman and Bill Davis, former Premier of Ontario, who of course I knew very well.

Director's Obligations and a Note to the Shareholders

Regarding director's obligations, Heather and Bill came on board. Then Brookfield, the real estate section of Brascan, wanted to buy the Stock Exchange Building, which is part of First Canadian Place. I said no problem, and suggested we put it up for tender. That's not what they had in mind, but it's certainly what I felt we had to do. About a week later I had a note from Trevor Eaton telling me I was not going to be put up for the board of directors that year. I called Fraser Fell, who was Chairman of the Board of Gentra, and told him.

Fraser was a bit upset and he said, "Peter, I think there's a way to fight this." He continued when I asked how we would do that, "This is clearly about your position on the Toronto Stock Exchange Building. If you ask as a director, they have to send a letter to all the shareholders, and then you can tell them why you think you're leaving the board. Just stay one more year, please."

I was pissed off and at Fraser's suggestion, I called Trevor telling him, "Trevor, I just want you to know that I'm going to be sending out a letter, which I'm having drafted by a solicitor. It's going to all the shareholders and you'll have to send it."

He said that was fine; of course, he didn't believe for a minute they would have to do that. Well then he did his checking and called back an hour later and said, "Peter, we would like you to stay on the board for another term."

And so I did. By that time I didn't really want to be there. I was doing it for Fraser. It was interesting how it all worked out. Brascan eventually bought all of Gentra. Because of the strong hard working board and the excellent management team, I believe the shareholders, including Brascan, avoided going bankrupt. The shareholders at least retrieved some of their investment, and as far as I was concerned, that was a good thing.

PART THREE

CHAPTER 8

Mining Boards: Local and Foreign Adventures

It was a big lesson in boards. I learned that on the hospital boards; I saw it again there, and I've seen it since. Some board members either like the prestige or they need the money. They don't want to lose their board seats because they only care about the seat and not the best interests of the shareholders.

During this time on Gentra's board, I'd also been on Placer Dome's board, which was a large mining company specializing in gold, other precious metals, and copper. Their corporate headquarters were in Vancouver, British Columbia. I have been involved in mining for all my life one way or another. Mining is a business I know quite well. I have been on the board of several companies: Detour, Kiena, Sigma, and Campbell Red Lake. In 1990, I went out to Vancouver to run Placer Dome. I had been representing the Placer Dome board on Placer Pacific and went out to visit Australia every quarter for several years.

Australian Travels

When I served on the Placer Pacific board—a company that was listed on the Australian Stock Exchange—it was public, but Placer owned 85 percent of the float and I was the only non-Australian director. I travelled from Toronto to Sydney frequently over those several years I was on the board. There were no direct flights in those days to Australia. Flights originated from Toronto to Los Angeles with a three-hour layover, and then we'd fly Quantas to Sydney, which was a fourteen-hour flight. Depending on the wind, we sometimes had to land in Fiji or north of

Sydney in Australia to take on fuel. The airline model 740 400 eliminated that problem.

We would arrive in Sydney at 6:00 a.m. Monday morning and I would go to the hotel, which is now the Four Seasons, have a shower, and then head off to the Placer Pacific offices, which were about one hundred yards away. When the meeting was over, I returned to the airport and headed back to Toronto about 5:00 p.m. Sydney time. The plane arrived back in Toronto late Monday afternoon, and I came in to the office Tuesday morning only having missed one day of work. At that time, I was CEO of ITCO Properties.

On My Travels: Meeting Jeremy Soames

On one of the trips to Australia between Toronto and Los Angeles, I noticed that the fellow in the seat next to me was reading Barbarians at the Gate, written by investigative journalists Bryan Burrough and John Helyar. It had just been published in 1990 about the fight that F. Ross Johnson and KKR, a multinational private equity firm, had with respect to the takeover of RJR Nabisco (tobacco and food product giant), in what became the largest buyout in history up to that point in 1989. I asked the gentleman how he was enjoying the book and we started to chat. He told me he was with Rothschild's Bank, and I mentioned that I knew their top person in Australia. We decided to have dinner together during the three-hour layover in Los Angeles.

"You look extremely familiar, yet I am unable to understand why," I commented at dinner.

"Some people say I look very much like my grandfather, Winston Churchill," he responded. Jeremy Soames and I became friends, and we still are. I recently sat beside him at a dinner that Ned Goodman was hosting in Toronto. It was interesting that Ned had no idea that we knew each other.

The Australian Walton Family

When travelling to Australia for Placer Pacific board meetings, I some-times took a few extra days and visit with my friends John and Josie

Walton. I had met John in Africa on safari. His father owned a chain of department stores in Australia and the family was well known. They are great people. John was a graduate of the Stanford Business School.

He told me the story about walking into his father's office and of his dad saying, "I have good news and bad news."

John asked what the good news was, and his dad said, "As of today you are the CEO of the company," continuing when prompted by John for the bad news, "and I sold the company today to Alan Bond. I didn't think we should have our money and your job at risk at the same place."

Josie, John's wife, had come out from England and had originally married an older chap, who was a good friend of John's and had a 25,000-acre sheep and cattle ranch in central Eastern Australia. He was a fair bit older than Josie; they quickly had two daughters and then he died suddenly. His partners in the operation were two Canadians: Maurice Strong and Paul Desmarais. One of Paul's sons worked on the ranch when on summer vacation. Josie was able to buy them out. Josie's daughters were going to school in Sydney and John would take them out to dinner. John and Josie eventually married and they had a son, John.

I used to love going to Miller's Creek, which was where the ranch was—approximately a five-hour drive from Sydney. In the evenings, we would go out horseback riding and see these huge kangaroos in the bush, and twenty-five white parrots or red parrots in a tree. It was truly beautiful. Their neighbours, who were farmers, would drive over for dinner perhaps forty miles or so. I wondered how they made it home.

John also had a 5,000-acre sheep farm west of Sydney. I remember going there and arriving with the farm manager waiting for us, telling John that several sheep had black hoof disease. As we were walking through the fields he was slitting their throats. It was awful.

A few years later, I found out that the Australian boards' directors get paid for years of service. In my case it was about two years' fees that I was not expecting. Along with meeting some extremely interesting people, a few who became good friends, I made some excellent business contacts.

I believe I was able to make a bit of a contribution to Placer Pacific as a director. Granny Smith, a gold mine in Australia, is still going. Placer Pacific was going to take a pass on it because they couldn't make the numbers work. I suggested they contract everything out—the crushing and the mining. When they did, the numbers worked. Then several years later, they took over the operations themselves and the mine is still going.

Mines and the Primitive: Papua New Guinea and Solomon Islands

I remember going to the Porgera Mine in Papua, New Guinea. New Guinea was pretty primitive. The people still had bones hanging out of their ears, there were a lot of murders, and life expectancy was about forty-two then. They were very primitive people. I remember meeting the Prime Minister, Paias Wingti, in the capital Port Moresby and he told me his father had been a headhunter and his grandfather had been a cannibal. He looked rather wild himself.

It was a very difficult country to do business in because you just didn't have the skills, the trades, or the infrastructure. It was a good thing Porgera had such rich ore because we had to build about one hundred miles of roads and power lines to open up the mine. We created an un-anticipated problem by bringing the road in, and of course bringing beer in, which the local populace was not used to and couldn't handle. The men and women wore skirts made of leaves and went about barefoot. They used to get high from consuming betel juice derived from a nut that grows in the tropics of South East Asia. It would leave a pink residue in their mouths and was used for stress reduction—a stimulant providing a mild euphoric effect.

We built another mine on Misima, an island that was part of Papua New Guinea, off the eastern end of the mainland near the Solomon Islands. When we got there we did a lot of good work in Misima, because the people there were suffering from malaria from the mosquitoes. We were pretty well able to eradicate the malaria, which was a type that caused severe brain damage.

I remember going to the mine opening and there must have been a thousand girls about the age of sixteen all bare-breasted and dancing. We tried to figure out which one had the most beautiful breasts. They were all wonderful, just wonderful people with big smiles.

It was a much different business down near the Solomon Islands. The locals there were a different type of people. The Porgera people are rather aggressive and they would start a fight at the drop of a hat. Their villages were known to fight amongst each other. They lived in grass huts and there were times when someone would go over to a neighbouring village and light the huts on fire. Sometimes we travelled across by helicopter. While flying over, you could see the walking trails that people used to go from village to village. The trails were clear and quite evident. These people travelled miles in bare feet. It was quite fascinating.

Taking Over as Placer Dome CEO

Coming back to Placer Dome, the board wasn't happy with their CEO and they asked if I would take over as CEO. At that time I was really busy with Masonite, but I agreed to do it because I liked the mining business, and I thought the company wasn't being really well run. I thought I would really enjoy the opportunity to try to turn the company around as well as have a significant amount of shares. I knew it would be difficult since I realized I did not have the support of some of the directors from Western Canada. There was lots of room for improvement because there were far too many people in management, which led to a slowing down of the decision-making process.

The first thing I did was take out about two floors of management because there were too many people involved in the decision-making process and decisions weren't being made—this was not only frustrating but also expensive. This is not uncommon in large companies, particularly when there has been a merger of companies. I went to the first management meeting where we looked at a project. I asked for somebody from finance and I was told the individual was against the project and therefore not attending. That was the last meeting we ever had without everybody present. Fortunately I was quite familiar with the properties, since most had come from the Dome side of the Placer Dome merger.

Detour Mine: Fitting In

The experience at Placer Dome was interesting. There were certainly numerous problems because the stock hadn't done anything for a few years. So I was spending a lot of time marketing. I called in the management group at one particular meeting and it was reported that they were running out of ore at Detour Mine. I had been involved on Detour's board in a separate company—I flew in when I could get in by road, except in the winter when the ground was frozen. I think Campbell Mines might have owned a piece of it. It's funny now because I'm co-Chairman at Detour. There I was, being told Detour was running out of ore and would have to be shut down.

I suggested we send some exploration geologists up there to look at the property. Exploration geologists look at things much differently than mine geologists. Two weeks later I asked if the exploration geologists had been there and the answer was no—the mine geologists were doing the work. Another two weeks went by and we had another managers' meeting. I asked what was happening at Detour. There was silence. I asked if their exploration geologist had gone up there to look at it. Again they said no. I called out the fact that I had asked to have that done. Again there was silence.

And my response, "You guys better have that done. We're now in the FIFO program—either you "fit in or fuck off"—and I'm not going to tell you this again. While we're at it, we have the finest engineering group in mining—probably in the world in-house—and they're building all these new mines." I continued, "I want to send the engineering group to places like Campbell and Dome to change the hoisting capacity and see if we can change the way we're doing things." The results were incredible; I think we doubled the production in some of those mines.

In the meantime, they found more ore at Detour, put in permanent roads, and it became quite an operating mine. I also asked for the exploration geologists to go down to Timmins to look at our property there where they had been mining for about eighty years underground. They discovered the huge Dome Open Pit on surface.

Decision to Walk Away

Placer Dome walked away from Detour again several years later, and now it's about to be the biggest gold mine in Canada. Placer Dome walked away from Gibraltar, a copper mine in British Columbia, which still operates as a mine and makes a lot of money. In my view, they did one stupid thing after another. They really had an opportunity to build the gold business in Australia at that time, and they should have expanded in Australia, which is a good mining environment. They were certainly having the first look at all the good properties at the time. They were also the first Canadian mining company in Mexico, because they needed a Mexican partner who owned 51 percent, and this made things difficult.

I was able to double the stock price the year I ran the company, but I had trouble with the board. First of all, I don't think any of the western directors had ever run anything. They were mostly professional types of people, having never run their own business. They didn't look at the world in quite the same way I did. Secondly, I think they all felt I was going to move the head office back east. The third thing is the chairman for the search committee for the CEO had visions of getting rid of the chairman and CEO and becoming the chairman himself, which he was able to do. About twenty-two years later, the company Placer Dome was sold to Barrick at the same stock price it was when I left. This wasn't much of a deal for the shareholders.

The Long and the Short

I turned down a deal with Russia, but John Willson, the new Placer Dome CEO, revived it after I left and within months wrote off $27 million. John Willson, who came in as CEO had been running a small gold company in north west United States called Pegasus, which filed for bankruptcy in 1998 after real cyanide heap leach disasters in their Montana operations. This massive superfund clean up was one reason Montana produced such strong anti-mining legislation. I believe the company went bankrupt within three weeks after John left it to join Placer Dome.

I thought about going into Indonesia and Tanzania. I turned the project down for Placer for a lot of good reasons. Although I was able to double the stock in one year at Placer, I sold half my position in Premdor to buy it. I made a lot of money on it, and I had some options.

Women in the Kiena Mine, Donations Out of Success, and New Realities

Lionel Bonhomme, a well-known Timmins prospector, recently came into my office. He brought greetings from a man who was the mine manager of Kiena Mine when I ran Placer Dome several years ago. To my knowledge, Kiena was the only mine with women working underground in Canada or anywhere else at the time.

They were equipment operators. They operated scoop trams and trucks. It was a mine where everything was mined by a ramp from surface rather than a shaft. Apparently Raynald Vezina, Director of Richmont Mines Inc. and mining consultant (who also worked in various management positions for Placer and Falconbridge), had requested a $10,000 donation for the Val-d'Or Hospital in Quebec and I said no—I would get approval for a $100,000 donation, because we were making our shareholders a lot of money at that mine.

Some news came to light recently in a report regarding Kiena: the company is suspending mining activity at the Val-d'Or mine after having been cited by the owner company as not currently being economically feasible. The mine will cease its gold production mid-June 2013 as stated on Newswire from Wesdome Gold Mines in March who reported the mine was "facing decreasing recovered grades, persistent industry cost pressures, and uncertainty in the Canadian dollar gold price."

Newmont and Placer Dome That Never Was

Another time while running Placer Dome, I had two meetings with Sir James Goldsmith, who was the controlling shareholder of Newmont, and because of all the synergies, he wanted to put Newmont and Placer Dome together. He would give us a 30 percent premium, which would have been on top of the 100 percent increase we had achieved in the stock price in the last ten months—the first price increase since the mergers of Placer, Dome, Campbell, et al. I would run the company and Placer would have the majority of the board members.

I met him in Paris and in London, and he wanted to go ahead. He gave me a handwritten outline of the deal. He would not make a hostile proposal. (Hostile proposals are an attempt to acquire a company sans approval from the board of directors of that company. These are done in two ways: they may try to purchase enough shares in the company to gain a controlling interest in the company, or secondly, persuade shareholders to vote in a new board of directors who will accept the takeover bid.) He had done that with the BF Goodrich Rubber Company on the suggestion of his advisors and it was a bad experience. I even handed out his autobiography to our board.

I told them, "This guy was a good guy," and we would control the board.

I reassured them they didn't have to worry about their seats. The board didn't believe they would have board seats. They were more worried about their board seats than they were about the company. It was terrible. It was a big lesson in boards.

I learned that on the hospital boards, I saw it again there, and I've seen it since. Some board members either like the prestige or they need the money. They don't want to lose their board seats because they only care about the seat and not the best interests of the shareholders. I have always been a shareholder if I'm on a board. I get ticked off with guys who are on boards and don't own shares. Even as directors, they could take all of their director's earnings to buy the stock initially—whether they can afford to or not.

Eleventh-Hour Negotiations

The challenges of commitment as a board member came knocking on my door between Christmas and New Year's prior to leaving Placer Dome on January 1. The board gave me permission to spend up to $200 million for 50 percent of a Chilean property and the operating rights, owned by the Outokumpu copper mining company in Finland—partially owned by the Government of Finland as well.

I asked the board if we got the property, what would we call the mine, and director John Nichols said, "I just bought a lama and I called it Zaldivar." It seemed appropriate for the new mine given the Chilean-South American connection.

We were in Miami negotiating and I was with Sandy Laird, VP of mine development, and Jay Hyland, VP of the South American operation. I handled all the negotiations and I was aware that Outokumpu was under a lot of pressure from the government to get their balance sheet in order by the end of the year.

The meeting went on for two or three days. They started at $250 million and I finally negotiated the price to $70 million. Jay and Sandy were nervous wrecks because they thought I would destroy the deal, but I knew they needed the cash. I knew some of the Finnish words, and unbeknown to them, I understood what they were saying. Jay and Sandy were pacing outside and I kept coming out as we negotiated right through the night. They desperately wanted the property. It turned out to be one of the best copper mines in the world. No retiring board member would have taken on the commitment of negotiating for a mine in the eleventh hour of his or her tour of board duty. I felt a responsibility on behalf of the shareholders and board of directors to get this done, although I had lost respect for them because I felt they had been self-serving.

Several years later, VP of Operations at Barrick, Peter Kinver, was saying he wasn't getting enough production through Zaldivar. I suggested he get a bigger screening plant through the system that bypasses the crusher, siphoning off the fines, which tend to jam and clog the crusher, and reroute them back onto the belt after. He thanked me for the suggestion, which increased production and reduced the power usage.

Zaldivar, Eskay Creek, which is in British Columbia, and Goldstrike, were among the three most profitable mines in the world. Eskay Creek was Canada's highest-grade gold mine and the world's fifth largest silver producer before it was closed in 2008. The remaining mines are Zaldivar in Chile and Goldstrike in north eastern Nevada, owned by Barrick—the largest gold mine in North America. Both are still very profitable mines.

Placer is Bought by Barrick and the Transition

Shareholders want dividends. They do not want the company to issue stock for long-term projects that are billions over budget and years late.

When I left Placer Dome on January 1, I sold my stocks and options for twenty-four dollars per share with gold at $330 per ounce. The interesting thing was twenty-two years later, the company was bought for twenty-two dollars per share by Barrick and gold was $1,800 per ounce: the stock was still exactly the same price as when I left, and there were no stock splits. In other words, if you had one share, they split it in two. That's very interesting after all that length of time—you tell me the shareholders didn't get screwed! I was told that Rob Franklin who was chair, as well as directors of the independent committee of the Placer board set up to negotiate with Barrick (presumably to get the best deal for the Placer shareholders) were somehow the only Placer directors invited onto the Barrick board. Now what the hell has that got to do with anything? How does that help the shareholders on whose behalf they are negotiating? At the time, there were two other suitors—Newmont and Goldcorp. There were other directors on the Placer board with large stock positions.

I felt the two best directors and the two who had the shareholder's interests at heart were John McDonald of Canada's largest electrical contracting company Black and McDonald, and Alan McFarland, a founder of McFarland and Dewey—a New York Investment Banking company. Both John and Alan had a significant amount of shares. However, at the end of the day, they were overwhelmed by the politics, and along with Fraser and myself, they were gone.

When Barrick bought Placer, no one on the committee looking at the deal for Barrick spoke to me. I knew the assets very well. Barrick needed Canadian properties for tax reasons, and they had been far better off taking Campbell Red Lake and the Timmins operations, than to have to build a mine in the Dominican Republic when their resources were stretched building Pascua-Lama. It would have also reduced their country risk exposure.

Barrick had first choice of the assets. Goldcorp took the rest; it was a sixty-to-forty split in Barrick's favour. Barrick let Goldcorp have Campbell Red Lake, which would have reduced their country risk and increased their much-needed income from Canadian investments. Campbell Red Lake is one of the most profitable gold camps in the world. Its very high grade is extremely profitable and they continue to find more very high-grade ore.

I like most mining people. There are some bandits in mining because there has been so much money flying around, and excellent moose pasture has been highly promoted for exploration with no basis in scientific data. Of course, the investment bankers and the promoters make money. The bad deals seem to attract the capital as easily as the good deals, at least as long as the metal prices were going up, and that is now changing. You have mining executives who have been pissing money away by the millions and billions of dollars to build bigger, not better, companies.

The Placer Dome board formed a search committee to replace me. This was probably because of the Jimmy Goldsmith and Ned Goodman deals that I proposed and they turned down. Those two deals were phenomenal deals. The committee was composed of Rob Franklin, Vernon Taylor from Denver, and Bart Ryan from Sydney, Australia. Rob found himself as chairman of the company—in my view he was the most unqualified chairman they could choose. Bart thought he had a deal with Rob to be vice chairman—this was not to be. After becoming chairman, Rob decided he did not need a vice chairman. Fraser Fell, who had appointed Rob to the board in the first place, was kicked out and put out to pasture. Many people think that Rob ran the company for the next twenty years.

Most of the people I spoke to felt Rob was in effect the CEO of Placer until it was sold to Barrick. Fraser Fell had put Rob on some boards that eventually became Placer Dome and, without Fraser, Rob would never have been involved.

When several companies (including Barrick) were approaching Placer for takeover, Rob chaired Placer's independent committee. What finalized the deal was the independent committee of Placer joined Barrick's board: John Crowe, Don Carty, and Rob. I am not sure what benefit that was to the Placer shareholders.

Rob sat beside me the first Barrick meeting and told me that Peter was too old, and that some of the other directors had to go. I am sure he was gunning for Peter Munk's job as chairman, and although I was the only person on the board with a history of operating mines and exploration, I knew he would find a way to get rid of me. He became the chairman of the nominating committee very quickly. He had to approve the hiring of John Thornton who replaced me.

Early Barrick Days

In the early Barrick days, Barrick Gold was originally called American Barrick so it would be listed higher in the newspaper stock pages and easier to find by investors. The original company was United Sysco and the CEO was Bob Fasken. Bob's COO was Bob Smith. I knew them both well. I used to fly up with them in the company's Turbo Beaver to Griffith Island, an island off Wiarton in Georgian Bay, to shoot pheasant and chucker partridge. We were members of the Griffith Island Club in Georgian Bay.

Bob Smith had been a miner all his life having been raised in the mining community of Cobalt, northern Ontario; whereas Bob Fasken was an investor. The public company United Sysco had a couple of small gold mines in northern Ontario and northern Quebec. The mine manager was Louis Dionne. At the time the price of gold was about $300.00 per ounce.

Unfortunately Bob Fasken had some real estate investments in Mississauga that had become illiquid. I ran into both of them in the Royal Bank tower after they had just been told by the Royal Bank to find a buyer for the mining company, since they were running out of money. They asked me if I knew a buyer and I said I would approach David Ferguson, CEO of Starlaw—the McConnell family holding company. David quickly said no because they didn't know anything about the business.

In the meantime, both Peter Munk and David Gilmore, who were electrical engineering graduates from the University of Toronto, had previously started a public company in Canada called Clairtone, which without a doubt made the finest sound systems in the world at the time. They decided to expand their manufacturing facilities in the Maritimes with a government loan, and after they started to build the plant, the government changed the terms of the deal; the economics did not work and I believe the company went bankrupt.

That's when they headed to Australia to launch their hotel chain—a series of small hotels, which they had successfully built up in Australia, Fiji, and Papua New Guinea. When Bob Smith and Bob Fasken were looking for a buyer of the mining company, Peter Munk, David Gilmore, and their accountant Bill Birchall had just returned to Canada from Australia, where they had sold the small hotel chain.

Peter, David, and Bill were looking for something to invest in. I think they originally invested in some oil and gas deals with Gary Last (professional engineer, vice president of production, and consultant in the oil industry), which did not work out too well. Then they heard from the Royal Bank that a small mining company might be available. They did some homework and saw that the stock price of gold mining companies was quite lucrative; for example, at the time Campbell Red Lake's stock was selling for twenty-eight times its earnings.

So I believe with some initial financial help of Adnan Kashoggi, Saudi Arabian businessman, they did the deal with the Royal Bank. Bob Fasken left and Chief Operating Officer Bob Smith remained.

From Entrepreneurial to Professional Directors

Initially when I went on the Barrick board, they had people like David Gilmore, one of the co-founders. David is certainly entrepreneurial; he founded Fiji Water as well. Angus McNaughton was of course a brilliant guy who had retired as CEO of Genstar, a huge company he and his partner created. These chaps started to drop off the Barrick board, including Joe Rotman, who everybody knows is a very strong and independent businessman. I probably should have dropped off—but I didn't.

The board was changing dynamics, towards what I would refer to as being prolific with professional directors who don't necessarily understand the business. Most of the directors of Barrick have never been to a mine, and if they did, they wouldn't know what the hell they were looking at. I felt very strongly about this issue and said so.

The Positive Impact of Bob Smith

Bob Smith, the Chief Operating Officer and Director of Barrick, convinced me to stay on the board. Bob knew how to build a mine. He was a wonderful person and very experienced operator and mining engineer. He was really the one who built the company and figured out how to mine Goldstrike in Nevada. This was a very difficult mine to operate because of water and potential environmental problems. It has become one of the largest gold mines ever developed.

Bob wanted to make Barrick an international company. At the time I joined them as a director, they were only in Canada and Nevada. He wanted to start expanding the company outside of North America to South America, over to Africa, Australia, and elsewhere. However, the opportunity in Tanzania came first, but the government kept changing the tax base and it was a difficult deal to put together. There was no infrastructure and it was hard to train a workforce because many were sick with malaria and AIDs. Barrick had to build and operate a hospital and even so, many trained employees missed a lot of work time.

I knew a lot about Africa through my work with CARE, and I knew that it's extremely difficult to do work over there long term. The people are so poor and many of the governments are so corrupt. The company made some money in Tanzania. Bob worked very hard at it. Initially they had trouble with the recoveries of gold out of the ore. Another problem was that someone was actually stealing shiploads of concentrate.

It was a great tragedy that Bob had to retire early due to health issues and died shortly thereafter. He had Peter's ear and the respect of the board. He was also focused on building the best gold company—not just the biggest.

The Bre-X Mining Scam

And then there might be the occasion to come up against a scam. Bre-X was probably the biggest mining scam in Canadian history and perhaps in all mining history between 1995 and 1996. Investors lost billions of dollars. They invested in a gold play in Indonesia and there was no gold.

It started as a penny stock out of a stock promoter's office in Calgary, Alberta. It grew from pennies per share to several dollars per share within several weeks. The results appeared to be so good that all the majors were looking at it like Barrick, Placer Dome, Inco (now Vale), Newmont, and Freeport-McMoRan Copper and Gold Inc. Several companies were lining up with various members of the Suharto Indonesian presidential family because it appeared you had to have a political in to get a deal done.

Barrick looked at it and made a bid in the billions of dollars. Everything was subject to due diligence of course. I was the only board member to vote against it. The reason: the diamond drilling was as I recall twenty-five metres, and they were getting the exact same results at the same depths on every hole. In my experience, this was not possible.

Bob Smith at Barrick asked me to go and visit John Lydall, one of the best-known and respected analysts on the street who worked for First Marathon, and who had just returned from the property. I went over to see him; he showed me the maps and said he had seen the diamond drill core. I said that I had heard they had been sending their ground-up drill core to Australia for assaying (the process of determining the quality or content of a metal or ore), and that they thought the gold in the sample was placer gold (it had been panned from a river or creek).

The difference is that the placer gold is rounded off from the water and the diamond drill core samples have sharp edges. I had seen pickle bottles full of placer gold in Papua New Guinea for sale in grocery stores. Papua New Guinea is the other side of the island of Indonesia. John said he had heard that there had been some trouble with an Australian lab, but a reputable lab in Canada was now doing the assays.

I followed up with Bob to report that I was not convinced. About ten days later, coincidentally I landed in Jakarta on CARE business and I saw the Barrick airplane on the tarmac. And about two weeks later, we were having a Barrick board meeting in London at the Claridges Hotel, since Peter Munk was over at his home in Switzerland for most of the winter. We were told that our geologists were to go to the property in Indonesia to do due diligence. When they arrived in Jakarta they were not allowed to go to the Bre-X property. This explained the plane I had seen. We decided not to bid any further and just drop out of the bidding because we did not want to offend the government in case we were wrong.

After the board meeting, Peter Munk asked me if I was staying for lunch. I said no, and that I was heading to Charlotte, North Carolina for a United Dominion board meeting there. He said I had to come to lunch because King Hussein of Jordan's sister was coming to lunch only because I was there in order to see if CARE would launch a program in Jordan. She was a lovely lady who looked exactly like her brother. I put her in touch with the right people and I was flown to Charlotte in Barrick's jet and able to make the meeting.

The bidders dropped away and the Government of Indonesia forced Freeport-McMoRan to make a bid subject to due diligence as they had a large copper and gold mine in Indonesia. They drilled a few holes parallel to the Bre-X holes and found nothing. It was a hoax.

A few days before this, I had been walking down Richmond Street in Toronto near the old Hy's Steakhouse and Cocktail Bar, and I ran into David Weldon and his son. David ran a large brokerage house and his son was a broker. David was on the hospital board with me. His father Colonel Weldon was Chancellor of the University of Western Ontario. They were a London family and very generous supporters of Western. He asked me what I thought of Bre-X since they and a lot of clients were in it. I told him in my view that it was a pile of crap and I explained why. I ran into him about a month later and he thanked me, because they had been able to get out of it at a profit. It became a penny stock (a very small company with highly illiquid shares involving a high risk of loss generally trading below five US dollars per share), and then went bankrupt in 1997. Over time and especially in the mining industry, you come to discern what is good and what might seem dubious. I guess I have been lucky because of my extensive experience and background in mining. It always pays to do your due diligence and not rush head long into the costly and uninformed excitement that others may generate.

International Geopolitical Risks, Global Management – Corporate Structure, Operations and Strategic Challenges

Barrick tried to sell African Barrick to the Chinese; however, after doing their due diligence, the Chinese withdrew their offer. That's about all. Billions of dollars have been tied up for years; plus, a lot of good people were sent over there and left the company because they felt stranded.

I understand that the Chief Financial Officer has recently left African Barrick, along with the chairman of the board, when they were advised of the results of the Chinese due diligence. The new Chairman is Kelvin Dushnisky, a senior VP. He is a lawyer and in my view, he is probably the best person to handle Government relations and community social responsibility in mining. He is extremely bright, but very busy on Barrick CSR problems around the world. I do not think he has the time or experience to run a $3 billion company.

Barrick would be much better suited if they had an independent member of their board who knew something about mining. But of course, they do not. Much in the same way as I represented Placer Dome on the Board of Placer Pacific, when I was an independent member of the Placer Dome board. Barrick have $3 billion invested in African Barrick, but no one from the Barrick board is on the African board.

Highland Gold and Management Stretched Thinly Around the Globe

When I think about management in the mines being stretched thinly over the globe, it reminds me of the time we were reviewing the annual exploration budget of Barrick at a board meeting—about $300 million. I asked where Alex Davidson, the VP of exploration, was because I wanted to ask him some questions. Apparently he was representing Barrick on the Highland Gold board, a Russian company based in London, but operating in Russia.

I believe Barrick owned 27 percent of the company. Again, if there was anyone on the Barrick board who knew anything about mining, they should have been on the Highland board, because the management people with properties all over the world were very busy and already travelling constantly. Barrick eventually sold out their position at a loss.

Corporate Structure, Operations, and Strategic Alliances

The other thing I objected to was the corporate structure at Barrick. I always felt that the last person Chief Operating Officer Peter Kinver, who was running the mining division before I left, was exceptional. Bob Smith was exceptional when he ran the operations, but they were much smaller. Peter Kinver really improved operations; he improved the safety records, the environmental conditions, and the community social responsibility. They just leapt ahead, and the production numbers were great. He had twenty-two mines. I know the guy running a mine wants to talk to the boss pretty much every day if there's an issue. It would take maybe a five-minute phone call and he would make that phone call.

The problem Peter Kinver had on top of it was building these humongous mines in difficult areas with altitudes of 13,000 or 14,000 feet. For example, Pascula-Lama is probably almost $3 billion over budget and two or three years behind schedule. It was based on $1,200 ounce gold. I don't think they'll ever finish Pascua-Lama, and there is a lot of country risk associated with the property. Peublo Veijo in the Dominican Republic is way over budget and also behind schedule, and I understand they have metallurgical and power problems there, as well as now being asked to renegotiate profit sharing. My sense is that they're going to have social problems.

Local Over International Geopolitical Risks

A major consideration in mining is the local over international and geopolitical risks. I don't know why Barrick, other than Hemlo (Barrick's mine north of Lake Superior) is not more in Ontario and Quebec. I think they should've looked at Detour, which would be Canada's largest gold mine and based in northern Ontario to balance their country risk instead of overbidding the Chinese by a substantial amount to buy Equinox (whose main assets were sub-Sahara Africa).

My understanding is that Peter Munk and Nat Rothschild, a director, were big proponents of the deal. I was not involved in the discussions. Because of my involvement with Detour, it was a conflict of interest for me. In any event, I'm not on the board anymore, so I shouldn't have much to say, other than I think that people who are looking to invest in mining companies should look at the geopolitical risk of the company. Not just look at cash costs and ounces, but all in costs and risks, and country risk as well.

Fortunately they have been unable to go ahead with Donlin Creek and Cerro Casale because their partners put the brakes on. If they had, think of the mess they would be in. Their shareholders want dividends. They do not want the company to issue stock for long-term projects that are billions over budget and years late.

Present and Accounted For

I pushed to have a separate board committee where there was a senior executive VP of construction who reported to the board committee regularly on costs and on the timetable. They would have to know something about the business because, other than myself, most had never worked in mines and prospected. I had done both. I was not able to make this happen. Bill Birchall is really the power behind the throne, and it was my belief that he felt the committee would interfere with management.

Peter Munk goes to Switzerland in the winter and likes to go to Montenegro in the summer. Even though he's on the phone every day, there's no doubt about it—it's just not the same as being present. Peter doesn't visit the mines. He did not have time because he was running Trizec, had real estate interests in Europe, and was building a huge yacht basin in Montenegro on the Mediterranean with some Russians and Nat Rothschild. He maintained an apartment in New York and Paris, and controlled the Clark Oil and Refining Corporation. He had a lot of balls to juggle.

Nobody else really visits the mines. Bill Birchall goes to one maybe once a year; he used to go with me to a mine every year because I chaired the safety and CSR committee of the board, and requested we visit a mine every year. I know how important it is that the board shows up at a mine. We also invited the rest of the board but they never came. They don't even show up for openings. It's a great opportunity to have the government present.

I don't understand the way some things get done anymore. I wish Barrick well, but I'm not sure that they're home yet. Jamie B. Sokalsky is a wonderful guy; whether Bill Birchall and Peter will have him for lunch is debatable.

Dismissing Experience

One interesting thing is that when Peter kicked me off the Board of Barrick, he told me it was time for younger people like the new member from Goldman Sachs. When you are dismissing experience, what are the requisite capabilities you will be replacing it with? Peter is ten years older than I am and would not know a swede machine from a slushing machine, or a drift from a stope, or a diorite from a piece of granite. Steve Shapiro, chairman of the audit committee, is excellent. Brett Harvey, the CEO of Conoco, knows something about mining coal, but is extremely busy running the largest coal company in the United States. Howard Beck, who is older than I am, is able to cool Peter down when his emotions get out of hand. Howard is also a wise man. From an investment point of view, Barrick is one of the worst investments I have ever had. In my view, they need at least one mining person and one exploration person on their board.

Recently, Peter Munk called me and told me that The Globe and Mail were publishing a negative article on Barrick, and Barrick had to go the highest sources to find out that I have given them an interview, which was utter bullshit. I have not talked to The Globe and Mail in twenty-five years. I told Peter that I would phone Philip Crawley, the publisher, because this was not true. I told Peter that I would sue anyone that said I had. He said he would pay for the lawyer and I responded that I would sue Peter for defamation of character. The article came out the next morning and there was nothing in it that Peter or Jamie Solasky had not said publicly. I felt he was trying to bully me. I called Peter the next day and didn't receive so much as an apology.

When Peter asked me to resign from the board after twenty-two years, he called from a car he was being driven around in in Austria. This was a relief because he was listening to other people whose views I disagreed with. I was damned if I was going to feed his ego.

And Today's News...

Currently, news reports have indicated that Barrick has had to halt its construction on Pascua-Lama in Chile as a result of allegations that the project is polluting the groundwater and rivers in the Atacama Desert. Not only is this region the driest in the world, but both the gold and silver projects are in close proximity to ancient glaciers.

Mining reporter Pav Jordan of The Globe and Mail recently wrote, "Less than a year ago, Barrick raised the development price tag on Pascua-Lama to more than $8-billion, compared to estimates of around

$3-billion when the company launched the project in 2009. A significant portion of higher costs was attributed to a year-long delay in building the mine."

Indigenous groups have filed complaints with the Chilean courts, and it could take months to substantiate the claims of environmental degradation and non-compliance of regulations regarding protection of the land and waters. The board meeting was held recently and daily reports of investigations into Barrick and the upper hierarchy seem to have come under close and intense scrutiny. We shall see how shareholders will react to the debacle that is unfolding daily.

It is interesting to note that while Barrick stock is around nineteen dollars—currently down from forty-two dollars earlier in the year—the directors have increased their pay from approximately $120,000 per year to over $220,000 annually. I have made this statement repeatedly because none have any mining or geological experience.

Barrick recently sold their gold assets at bargain price—the lowest gold prices in years. It is a good safe environment and, when gold prices move up, in my view this will have been another dumb move.

Many people thought that Peter Munk would retire at the annual meeting this year, but in my view I don't think he has any intention of stepping down. He keeps himself in good health. I recall after Tom Bell, the chairman and CEO, stepped down at the mandatory age of sixty-five, the phone then stopped ringing, and people were not calling him for lunch or much of anything else. You lose a great deal of power and prestige, as well as the use of the corporate jet, the day you retire.

Most of the directors have never been to a mine let alone Pascua-Lama where they have so many problems. Winter is arriving now with snow, severe cold, and extremely high winds at one of the highest points in the Andes—where both the machinery and the employees struggle with the lack of oxygen.

In twenty-two years I can only recall one meeting with the advisory board whom I believe meet one day a year and are paid $100,000 per year. Peter Munk did me a big favour because the day I left, I sold all my stock and it is probably down by 70 percent now.

What do I think Barrick has to do to recover? First of all I would say they should find at least three directors who know the operating side of the business and form a technical committee. A Chief Operating Officer should be appointed to report to the committee monthly and to the full board quarterly, so developing situations should be formed on a timelier basis. I suggest the chair, vice chair, and board members' salaries be cut by 70 percent. They should only allow the COO the use of the corporate jet, and get rid of the advisory board, which is a large expense and should be deleted.

The biggest mistake I ever made was not reversing my decision to join Barrick's board and instead join Seymour Schulich's board. They have fun—no egos. They want to be the best not the biggest, and they have knowledgeable people of the board who understand the fundamentals of the business. They backed Randall Oliphant, the CEO of New Gold, which was just listed as one of the best-run gold companies. It must rankle Munk because he fired him after a very short period. Randall got thrown under the bus just like Aaron Regent.

Since I started writing this book, Barrick decided to sell their oil division, which they bought about five years previously right after Placer Dome. The idea was to offset the increases in oil prices. When we were told, Rob Franklin commented, "Here we go again." Placer merged with the group of companies controlled by Dome Mines including Dome, Campbell Red Lake, Detour, Kiena, Sigma, Dona Lake and Musselwhite, which were being readied for development. Placer also had a petroleum division operating in south eastern United States. Placer owned Gibraltar, a copper mine in British Columbia, Kidston a gold mine in Australia and were just starting to develop Porgera, a gold mine in Papua, New Guinea. With the merger, we inherited an oil division at Placer. The oil and mining industry are totally different businesses, and at times the oil business seems to require a lot of capital. I do not recall any discussion where the board was advised that the oil division had been purchased.

We then received a memo from the chairman that Peter Kinver our Chief Operating Officer would run it. I immediately fired off a memo to the chairman and all of the directors saying this was the dumbest thing I ever heard. Peter knew nothing about the business; he was running twenty-two mines around the world and was building two new huge ones. The chairman listened and had Jamie Sokalsky, who was their CFO at the time, take it on. It has recently been sold at a loss of several hundred million dollars.

Barrick directors are paid an average now of over $215,000 per year. Who would leave that? Rob Franklin has said there has to be changes to the board and he chairs the governance committee.

A little over two years later the environmental committee, which I chaired, visited the site. I asked when Jamie visited it last and was told about two years previously. The division was recently sold for a loss of several hundred millions of dollars. At the moment and for some time now Barrick appears not to have a Chief Operating Officer. This is quite an unusual situation in my view and from the perspective of a fully functioning and present board.

CHAPTER 9

Mining and Country Risk

The rules are there—they're clear and there are many very experienced mining people in the country.

I have been involved in running businesses in many countries—not only in mining, but also with Masonite and in real estate. Some countries clearly are high risk particularly in mining. The capital costs of developing a mine are extremely high. In some cases you have to build the infrastructure as well, like hydro, roads, schools, housing, and hospitals. At the same time fuel, tires, and equipment prices have increased dramatically, and in some cases availability is an issue.

Then sometimes the country and states change the rules when they see an increase in the price of the commodity, but do not allow for the tremendous increase in costs. They raise taxes or royalties, or take a larger piece of the project. They share none of the risk, even though living conditions around the project, and often throughout the country, are improving because of the jobs created by the resource development.

It's also becoming more and more apparent that Indigenous communities on a number of continents are coming forward with complaints to the courts regarding the possible attendant issues of environmental degradation; witness Barrick's woes in Chile right now.

Eden Roc, Cote d'Ivoire, and Corruption

Eden Roc was a company that I ran in Cote d'Ivoire in Western Africa. Rick Paprazian, a friend of mine, was the Toronto manager of a New York investment bank. He asked me to go in and run the company to sort out the problems. They had put a lot of their clients in the stock and it was a mess.

It was a "heap leaching" operation, which means oxide ore was mined and excavated from a pit, then crushed and put in a pile on a heavy duty rubberized pad that collected fluids. A chemical was sprayed over the pile and leached through picking up the gold; the fluid was cleaned and the gold removed, and the chemicals recycled. This was the most economical form of mining there is, however, unfortunately most ore is not oxide, and has to be treated in a much more complicated and expensive way. The gold was extracted from the fluid by electronics. On one occasion we had a large robbery where the gold was removed. We eventually found out that the local police were among the thieves.

On another occasion, the Cote d'Ivoire Minister of Finance's office called me to see if I could meet with him in Paris. I told them it wasn't necessary because I was on my way to Abidjan the capital, where his office was. His assistant insisted that the Minister wanted to meet me in Paris. One of our issues was that our equipment was to come into the country duty free, since we were exporters and creating jobs in the country. This ruling applied not just for the mining industry but also for all others. However, they were charging us duty, saying they would give it back to us later. Of course they did not. They often didn't have it to give back. That's what I thought our meeting was about.

What he wanted was for me to help him set up a Swiss bank account and then we would get our money—or some of it. He left me with a huge hotel bill for booking the biggest suite, and for wines and clothing. When I arrived back in Toronto, I resigned. It was unfortunate that the country was so corrupt because it was right on the equator with excellent soil where everything would grow. They had so much going for them.

Diamonds in Botswana and Hard Work

I ran a diamond exploration company in Botswana for South African Minerals. At the time, this country had the best diamond mines in the world. The country was about 80 percent Kalahari Desert. There was only one tribe, which was good as well because you did not have to worry about tribal warfare. They were mostly cattle farmers and lovely people.

The government officials were well educated; many of them were in Canada and they were totally honest and above board. They had a great infrastructure, good schools and hospitals, and a well paid police force. Unfortunately we did a lot of drilling and found diamonds, but not commercial grade or value. We used labs in Johannesburg and Cape Town. South Africa is the next country south.

One time I was flying in a small plane to South Africa over the Kalahari Desert in Botswana. When we crossed the border, the terrain turned into beautiful farmland. That sure showed me the value of water and hard work. The land just transformed from desert to farmland. It was incredible.

Internationally Speaking: Chile, Philippines, Australia, Tanzania, and Russia

At Placer Dome we were building a mine in Chile called La Coipa. It was a challenge because it was at about 4,000 metres. Our 40 percent partner was an Eike Batista company called TVX Gold Inc. Ian Telfer, who is a very bright man and a gentleman, ran it. In Chile the mining laws and labour laws are very reasonable and very clear. The people work hard and are quite well educated. I thought that part of it at least was the effect the Catholic Church had on their lives.

The same can be said for the Philippines where I was on the Board of Philex, a gold mining company, where the people worked hard and respected the safety rules as well.

Australia is a great country to be involved in the mining industry. It's much like Canada and Nevada. The rules are there, they're clear, and there are many very experienced mining people in the country. There are also "punters"—people who will invest in risky mining ventures.

I had turned down the opportunity to invest in Tanzania while I was at Placer Dome. However, some former Placer people picked it up and sold it to Barrick after I arrived on the Barrick board. I voted against the purchase because the government was poor, corrupt, and kept changing tax rules and other things. There was no infrastructure, and aids and malaria were prevalent. It can become very expensive when operators are too sick to work and equipment is sitting idle. I think I was the only one who voted against the acquisition. Upon reflection it looks like I might have been right.

Russia was the deal I turned down just before I left Placer Dome. They wanted $27 million for the property. However, there was a fight between the federal, state, and municipal governments over whom, from the government's point of view, controlled the property. A couple of months after I left Placer, John Willson convinced the board to buy it. About six months later they wrote off the entire $27 million.

Excellon Mexico

I am currently involved as temporary Executive Chairman and CEO of Excellon—a small silver, lead, and zinc producer in Durango Mexico. It is the richest body of ore in Mexico. We are mining mantos (Spanish for "blankets"), which means the ore is in big bodies versus veins, which you mine and have a lot more dilution. The result is we are shipping high grade to the mill, not associated with rock that would normally be removed at the mill, and sent to the tailings. We are currently looking for the source of these mantos, which should create a very large mine. Just recently we have some excellent drilling results that hopefully are leading us to the source. We have approximately 50,000 hectares of mining rights.

In Mexico it takes time to make things happen. It takes a while to realize that tomorrow does not necessarily mean tomorrow. It just means not today. Mexico has a long mining background with trained geologists and mining engineers. They have labour laws and environmental laws every bit as good as Canada has. One thing we are not used to is that they have about two deemed holidays a month. They sure love to party, so their holidays are important.

To my knowledge, Placer Dome was the only Canadian mining company in Mexico. In those days, 51 percent had to be owned by Mexicans. After I left Placer, they got out of Mexico. Barrick were never there. Many Canadian companies like Goldcorp and New Gold have done very well in Mexico. There are also two huge mining companies in Mexico with a much larger market capital than Barrick: Penoles and Groupo Mexico.

First Silver and Holding the Reigns of Control

In approximately 1996 I joined the board of a company listed on the Toronto Stock Exchange called First Silver Reserve, now part of First Majestic Silver Corp. It owned and operated the San Martin silver mine north of Guadalajara, Mexico. The CEO and controlling shareholder was Hector Davila Santos. I had joined the board at the request of Tim Ryan, who was an investor and a long time friend of mine from my MBA days at the University of Western Ontario.

Tim, Jim Hendry (a mutual friend of ours), Steve Leahy (the CEO of North American Tungsten at the time), and I, all joined the board at approximately the same time. Our goal was to raise more money to really develop the mine. We bought Hector three pretty good deals and he turned them all down because he thought the price was too low. In retrospect, he did not want to lose control.

We were having trouble with the financial information, and were always after him for explanations and more material. We were also concerned about how work was handed out to contractors. We felt the process was flawed. One of my recollections was that he controlled the trucking contracting company. We started to attempt to make sure the proper processes were in place.

The Controlling Shareholder's Overthrow

In June 1998 prior to the annual meeting, we asked Hector if there were any unexpected issues that might come up at the meeting, and his response was, "No." At the annual general meeting an hour later, Hector announced that he was the controlling shareholder and that "Ryan, Crossgrove, Hendry, and Leahy would not be elected or re-appointed to the board." He then appointed three people at the meeting who were unknown to us and any senior people we knew in the mining business.

It was a good day for us to get out of there; however, I think it was a bad day for the shareholders other than Hector. I don't think we were ever going to convince him as to how a public company listed on the TSX should be run. He did not want experienced directors who took their responsibility seriously. So there I was kicked off another board.

When we were voted off the First Silver board, the group voted off included Alan McFarland. Because we were all substantial shareholders, we could not sell our shares quickly without disturbing the market. So we all agreed to have John Ing, the CEO of Maison Placements whom we all trusted, to sell our shares when over time as we saw fit. He did and he gave us a cheque based on the number of shares we each had several months later. We all felt that he treated us fairly and honestly.

Tim Ryan is Excellon's audit committee chairman, and is amongst the most experienced, smartest, and finest audit committee chairmen. Our shareholders can rest assured they are extremely well represented when Tim signs the statements.

What You Put Out and Comeuppance

News from the Financial Post and First Majestic Silver Corp. recently reported, "after a lengthy trial, the Supreme Court of British Columbia ruled in favour of First Majestic with respect to the previously reported litigation against Hector Davila Santos ('Hector Davila')."

The action came about in 2007 when Davila, who held the positions of Director, President, and CEO of First Silver Reserve, failed to exercise fiduciary duty in the acquisition of the Bolaos Mine in Mexico and pro-cured it "for his own personal interest." With a US $89.6 million ruling, Davila's counterclaim has just been ruled upon by a judge in the Court of Appeal for British Columbia ordering that he post US $79 million in security prior to proceeding with his appeal. It has been reported on Street Wire that, "Mr. Davila has no assets in BC that First Majestic could pursue except $14.85 million locked in a trust account, the judge found."

The saga has continued with Stockwatch News stating, "First Majestic Silver Corp. has defeated an appeal by Mexican businessman Hector Davila Santos, who was attempting to have an $89.6 million judgment against him overturned. (All figures are in U.S. dollars.) The Court of Appeal for British Columbia has dismissed his appeal not on its merits, but because Mr. Davila did not obey a prior court order. A judge had previously directed him to post $79-million in security for his appeal, citing the lack of assets he held in B.C., but he did not post the security."

It was a good thing we were not re-elected to the board. Davila actually did the three of us a favour. This story highlights the premise of one the prime motivations for corporate boards: shareholders place their stocks and positions entrusting a collaborative and unified board to work on their behalf for the highest and best overall. Dirty laundry eventually washes out.

Investing in Canadian Mines

There is very little country risk in investing in mines in Canada. I am co-Chairman of Detour Gold, which is in pre-commissioning at the moment. Detour is being built on time, will open on time, and is on budget. It will be Canada's largest gold mine. Every senior employee from the CEO down is an ex-Barrick employee. The mine is located north of Cochrane and south of James Bay—not an easy environment. Since they have 720 square kilometers of land that the mine sits on, I am sure the output and mine life will grow. This is the same mine that I was on the board of when it was a small fly-in-fly-out underground mine, and that was about thirty years ago. This is the same mine they wanted to close when I was running Placer Dome. I insisted they send in exploration geologists and they found more ore. About ten years later they did shut it down.

Pelangio Exploration: A Professional Board

Ingrid Hibbard, who grew up in Timmins and became a lawyer and is the daughter of a prospector, inherited the property from her father. When Placer walked away, her father re-staked it. Ingrid formed a company called Pelangio Mining (now Pelangio Exploration). She sold a majority to an exploration geologist Gerald Panneton, who had previously been with Barrick. Her company kept a large interest in Detour. Just after that I came on her board.

I was interested because they have an excellent property just across the border in Ghana from where I had worked in Cote d'Ivoire, plus a couple of her directors were friends of mine from Sudbury. Ghana, a former British Colony, is a safe and good country to operate a mine in. There are several large mines operating there. Ingrid's company owns most of the property on a geological trend between two of them. Eric Kallio, who was working for Pelangio on the Detour property, said the approach was wrong. He said the mine should be a large open pit mine. He was right. Eric is now the Chief Geologist for Lake Shore Gold in Timmins.

Not only is every person in the management of Detour a former Barrick employee, but the board technical committee is chaired by Louis Dionne and with Graham Wozniak, Robert Doyle, and myself. And all of us have been involved with Barrick. The committee meets monthly at the project manager's call. The project manager is Pierre Baudoin from Barrick. These meetings force the contractors and management to fully assess their monthly status and to add horsepower when required. Pierre uses it as a management tool with his direct report and that of the contractors.

The CEO Gerald Panneton is more passionate than Peter Munk, and I didn't think anyone could be. I really didn't know him when he was at Barrick. He is very bright with a Masters in Geology from McGill. He's a motivator who is well liked and respected by the employees because they know how hard he works. Many on the Board of Directors of Detour are experienced in the operating side of the mining business.

Lake Shore Gold Corp: Timmins Ontario

My involvement in Lake Shore Gold Corp. came through a long association with a company called Band-Ore Resources Inc. Thor Eaton came on board a few years before Band-Ore merged with West Timmins and was running low on funds. Band-Ore was merged with West Timmins and eventually West Timmins was merged with Lake Shore Gold. Thor funded West Timmins by buying the majority of their equity issues and flow-through share issues when no one else would because he liked and believed in Wayne O'Connor. He did this so they could continue to explore. After about twelve years he eventually had a pay-off and made some money when the merged Band-Ore/West Timmins was sold to Lake Shore Gold. I was on their board for about twenty years. Band-Ore sure had its highs and lows. The stock varied from twelve dollars to only pennies depending on what they were hitting on in their exploration drilling.

Their work was in the Timmins area and the late Wayne J. O'Connor the CEO (Chairman and Director of West Timmins Mining Inc. since 2006 and Director of Lake Shore Gold Corp. from 2009 to 2010), and Bob Duess the geologist and project manager for West Timmins prior to its acquisition by Lake Shore Gold, worked hard and had a lot of good hits, but the ore in major segments eluded them.

Flow-Through Shares

Exploration was funded by flow-through shares (FTS), of which Thor Eaton, another long-time director, always took a big chunk, which helped get the underwritings done. Flow-through shares were originally introduced by the government as a tax-assisted strategy to generate exploration and development funds with the intention of allowing share investors, primarily in the mining sector, to deduct these expenses against otherwise taxable income. In a written agreement, the shareholder pays for the shares with the corporation agreeing to transfer certain expenses to the shareholder. Flow-through shares are the right to buy a share or stock of a mineral resource company where tax deductions flow through from the company to the investor.

West Timmins Mining Merges with Lake Shore Gold

About five years ago, Band-Ore Resources merged with West Timmins Mining, a Vancouver company run by R. Michael Jones with Darin Wagner as his chief geologist. The Chief Financial Officer was Frank Hallam—they were all very bright people.

After a couple of years, Lake Shore Gold offered to buy West Timmins because they were starting to come along with some good results on property that tied in to the Lake Shore Mine. At this point West Timmins shareholders decided to merge with Lake Shore, so they had a couple of good bumps in their stock which effectively had gone from pennies to over four dollars. The purchase took place in 2009 with an all-share deal of $424 million. Frank Hallam and I were invited on the Board of Lake Shore.

Mike Jones now had more time to focus as President, CEO, and Director of the Platinum Group—a company they are getting up and running in South Africa. Frank Hallam is the CFO and Corporate Secretary of Platinum Group. Darin Wagner has gone on to create a public company called Balmoral Resources, which has some excellent properties in the Timmins and Abitibi area in Quebec.

The major shareholder in Lake Shore was Hochschild, a major Peruvian mining company, who had been brought in by Daniel Innes (the previous President and CEO of Lake Shore), who is a brilliant geologist and mine-finder. Lake Shore attributes much of their success to Dan for his contributions to the company. Dan left Lake Shore to become CEO of Pembroke Holdings—a private company that invests in mining projects both in Peru and Canada. Tony Makuch took over as CEO of Lake Shore in 2008 from Dan and Hochschild eliminated their investment in Lake Shore, having doubled it in a few years.

Quirks and Quarks of Mine Expansion: Leasing Equipment, Technical Committee Reports, and Transparent Bids

In talking about the quirks and quarks of mine expansion, detailed consideration is paramount regarding leasing equipment, the technical reports, and transparent bids. Lake Shore quickly went on an expansion program. They have been way over budget, not on time, have not delivered the gold or grade promised, and the stock has dropped to thirty-three cents as I write this. It was clear they were not going to complete the project with current finances; the cost of going to market and the dilution it would cause made it out of the question. The price of gold is not helping either. Therefore as a member of the technical committee, I suggested they go out and arrange to lease their equipment—whatever they could. It looks like they will raise enough money to complete the expansion.

I then pushed to form a technical committee of the board to review everything on a monthly basis because the board receives information at a minimum on a quarterly basis and often later. This has been done with three very experienced board members who have built several mines and found ways to control costs. The committee's job is not to run the mine, but to make suggestions to the CEO and COO who are under a daily pressure and do not have the luxury of doing more than reacting. Now the CEO and COO can tell the people reporting to them what information they require reporting to the committee. Approximately one month ago, Mr. Makuch changed the person in charge of grade control and underground geology. There is already a change in the ore grade and this will improve the production of gold ounces and re-establish the company's credibility, which clearly has been lost and is difficult to regain.

One additional thing that I am insisting on is that all tenders by outside contractors are opened in front of those that have bid. There are rumours around the north that it is no use to bid on Lake Shore's work because it always goes to their friends. It costs contractors money to bid and they will not bother if they feel they do not have a chance. Therefore, you may not get the lowest price. It does not even matter if it is true or not—if the contractors think it is, then they will not bid. That is clearly the perception among the contractors around the north at this current moment. It will be interesting to see where the Lake Shore stock will be in a couple of months' time from the time of writing. My guess is that it will be more than double.

Mining's Future

So what should we be considering for mining's future? Should we be buying gold and not US dollars? The Chinese are quickly exchanging their American dollars for gold and oil and other strategic assets. Brian Mulroney sold off our substantial gold stockpiles at $230.00 per ounce at a time when Canada was among the largest gold producers in the world. Other countries followed suit. The first thing Peter Munk had him do as a Barrick director was travel around the world to convince central banks to hold on to their gold.

Perhaps the future of gold mining can be understood from the analyst's recent insightful comments having been quoted as saying that basically gold production will continue to slow. As reported in the Financial Post recently, "Global gold production has reached record highs in recent years, but analysts at National Bank Financial said that investors should not get used to it. They are convinced a 'production cliff' is looming around 2017 in which senior gold miners will begin to undergo a sharp production decline. That will create investment opportunities.

"Analysts Steve Parsons, Paolo Lostritto and Shane Nagle think the reasoning behind the 'production cliff' is simple: too few large deposits have been discovered to sustain current production rates. The fact that miners are delaying or canceling projects because of cost pressures and other constraints has accelerated the move towards the 'cliff,' they noted. 'We contend that (constrained production) is already reflected in the shares of these companies, not because the issue is well understood, but because investors have simply responded to the side effects: capex pressures, project delays and eroding margins,' they wrote in a note."

Costs are rising, and more Mergers and Acquisitions (M&As) are expected to consolidate the industry. Companies can realize efficient margins, so current production rates can be maintained, keeping costs down, and maintaining their production levels and profit margins.

It's interesting to see how gold production will fare in the near future. In order to do so, these mining companies cannot overbid for assets. They must have people who know how to operate mines and understand geology from experience at a high level so that mines are built on time and on budget—and money is not wasted on greenfield exploration. I have never met a geologist yet who did not want to drill one more hole.

PART FOUR

CHAPTER 10

Philanthropy, Hospital Boards, Mergers, and Other Stories

I believe to this day there should be more volunteer work in communities and on boards, and I feel that I certainly inherited that as a value.

My parents clearly learned a lot from their parents because my father and mother were both big givers of time to the community and war effort. My mother was always knitting toques and socks for the soldiers. My dad was a volunteer at the curling club draw; he ran the community hall and he was the Library board chairman. He did much for which there was no remuneration.

Back then, people on the school boards and the town councils weren't paid. They didn't have secretaries, and they didn't have offices. And of course things got done much quicker and more professionally from a business perspective because there was no money involved. Non-paid voluntary work attracted certain people who just wanted to do the right thing. I think things ran more efficiently and a lot better. I believe to this day there should be more volunteer work in communities and on boards, and I feel that I certainly inherited that as a value.

My father never had more than a glass of scotch in his life. He would often get a call for help at least several times a year from his friend Harold Bruce, who was head of construction for Inco and head of AA for Copper Cliff. My father would head up to one of the bootleggers in Little Italy to find someone because a call would come in from a wife or bootlegger about that person. Everyone in town knew my father as being an Inco executive, and though he was six foot five, he had a very gentle way about him. Over the years he had done so much for the community that people listened when he talked. He was always able to get the drunks home or to the hospital. The interesting thing is that I don't believe anyone in town knew about it other than those directly involved.

People often ask me why I have done so much in the volunteer area. My view is one that my parents instilled in me: you should leave the country and the institutions you've been involved with in better shape than when you inherited them. If you have that kind of philosophy and you work for a hospital, or if you're involved with the school, or whatever you're involved with, I believe you want to make sure you're making a contribution that moves it ahead or at least maintains the institution in the fine shape you inherited it in.

The Toronto Western Hospital

It started with a call from Fraser Fell, Chairman of the Board of Toronto Western Hospital, who asked me to join the board where I quickly became the vice chairman. It was very hard to say no to Fraser, but it was obvious to me that Fraser wanted me to take over as chairman within a year or two, which I did. I knew we had structural problems at the Western; the newest building was built in 1938. We had wonderful talent: Charles Tator, a neurosurgeon; Bill Tatton, a neuroscientist; and Tirone David, arguably the world's best cardiac valve surgeon. Herbert Ho Ping Kong was Chief of Internal Medicine of Toronto Western. We had stolen him from McGill. Toronto Western had a lot of great doctors but we didn't have a dime in the Foundation to support research and teaching. The plant was very tired and the management had all been promoted by seniority. The CEO tended to run it all out of a drawer; if he liked a doctor, they got money, or if a researcher needed money and he was a favourite, he received it.

I decided I was going to have a look at it all and make some changes. Our first priority and the first thing we did was build the new building, which became known as the "Fell Wing." And the reason was because we tried, and when we couldn't get anyone to give us any money, finally Fraser Fell found somebody out of Barbados who gave $1 million anonymously. So when it came time to name the wing, I said we were calling it the "Fell Wing." That was the largest single donation Toronto Western had ever received. It was at a time we made management changes and Carl Hunt became CEO, and he removed the bureaucracy, which was based on seniority, thereby reducing the number of incompetent people.

The Ontario Government didn't have the money to give us to build the Fell Wing because they did not want the loan on their books. So we borrowed the money from CIBC, had the government guarantee the loan, and we put on a couple of extra floors without telling the Government of Ontario. Jim McCutcheon was chairman of the building committee and he did a wonderful job. The building was completed on budget and on time.

When it became apparent our Foundation at Western had no money, the next challenge was to figure out how to move forward. Carl Hunt had just taken over as CEO because we'd done a proper search. He was a very qualified person—an outsider with no history or biases.

An Innovative Idea

There were a lot of good things happening at the Western Hospital. I recall hosting a reception for the 500th kidney transplant done at the Toronto Western Hospital. People who had transplants came from all over the world. The occasion and feeling in that room brought tears to my eyes.

We had all this talent but we were about to lose it because we had no foundation money to speak of. Money was hard to raise because, at the time, the hospital was located in a very low income part of Toronto over on Bathurst Street. We sent all of our obstetrics division over to Toronto General Hospital because we no longer had the money or space. Carl Hunt, the new CEO, then approached me to inform me he'd been in talks with Vick Stoughton, CEO of Toronto General Hospital, and that maybe we should merge the two hospitals.

Both hospitals were running cardiovascular, cardiology, and orthopedics departments. And you may know, Western is where arthroscopic surgery was being developed. Carl asked if I would consider putting the two hospitals together and I absolutely agreed. Of course I knew Alf Powis who was Chairman at The General and CEO of Noranda, and Fred Eaton, the Vice Chairman of Toronto General—we were all friends. I suggested we have a meeting with Vick Stoughton and Carl Hunt, Fraser Fell, Fred Eaton, Alf Powis, and myself. We met for dinner at the York Club, and in determining how this should all work, and what the savings would be, we concluded the savings were going to be huge.

The Toronto Western and Toronto General Hospital Merger

My first serious lesson about board dynamics came after we determined the only way in which we could make this happen. I knew our board would never go forward if they lost their board seats.

There had been just so much duplication and administration everywhere you turned: in human relations, public relations, and general management. We had duplicate labs working on the same programs, and all we really needed was one. Eventually in the first full year of the merger, we saved $80 million. I had previously spoken to a couple of our senior board members who were very well known businessmen, and whose sons were good businessmen too.

I both stated and asked some, "We have to reduce the average age of the board members. Would you mind stepping down and I'd see that your son will be elected to the board in your place?"

The response came unanimously, "No way."

I knew from the response that unless we accommodated both boards it would never happen. I then suggested we merge both boards, and if the CEO came from one hospital, the chairman would come from the other hospital. This would get us around the social issues.

We all agreed to that plan. I thought that Vick Stoughton would quit and go back to the States—he was an American from Boston. The rumour was that he was going to leave. Just the opposite happened. As we were putting this together, Carl Hunt, the Western CEO, became the CEO of a chain of nursing homes across Canada. The boards of both hospitals recognized the value of the merger; however, the staff sure didn't. I had a meeting with all of the medical staff in the auditorium at the Western and some of them used some very choice four-letter words because they were absolutely against the merger.

When we were trying to merge the Western and General, David

Peterson, the Premier of Ontario, called a meeting in his office with Alf Powis, Fred Eaton, Fraser Fell, and myself. David said Tom Bell, previous chair of the hospital, just left his office and was against putting the two hospitals together, and that I was destroying both institutions. David told us that he himself had been born at the Toronto Western Hospital. I knew David extremely well. We were in YPO together—he had been to my summer cottage. We were and still are personal friends. I love his wife Shelly. He's a very funny guy and his brother Tim is also a good friend. So I just laid it out telling him all the reasons why we were going to do it. And David confirmed that it made good sense to him.

The Deed is Done

Doctors are so focused on what they're doing that sometimes they don't see the bigger picture. That's probably why they're good doctors. Frederick Lowy was the Dean of Medicine at the University of Toronto and was the only person on both hospital Boards of Toronto Western and Toronto General. I just arrived back to my office after speaking to the medical staff in the Toronto Western Hospital auditorium (trying to convince the staff that the merger was a good idea), when Fred called and said, "Peter, I hear you should've been wearing a flak jacket."

It was terrible—the nurses were wearing black armbands, people were making threats about my life, and it was not pleasant. Fred was the only person on both boards who was a great help to me in trying to merge the two boards, because the doctors were really fighting the merger. If you were chief at one, you were not necessarily going to be chief at the other. That was the concern. However, Fred was very useful in talking to the doctors, and so was Robert Stone, chief of surgery at the time. We had recruited Robert from Mount Sinai Hospital and Irving Gerstein, (Senator) who was the Chair at Mount Sinai, called me up to complain that we stole Dr. Robert from Mount Sinai. Of course, I was not involved in recruiting.

It is actually quite interesting how much resistance comes up when people feel either their lives or livelihoods are threatened; it is almost as if there is a default switch in the human mind in perceiving the negative before the positive outcome of an event or change of circumstance. The fear of going out of one's comfort zone is a normal reaction I suppose. Time and patience to quell the ungrounded fears; it was indeed a matter of perseverance, and so we continued to push on.

As we merged, Carl Hunt had taken the job as Head of a big chain of nursing homes, so Vick Stoughton became CEO and I became the Chairman of the Toronto Hospital. We had about fifty-three members of the board. I asked Monty Black to be chairman of the governance committee, and over the next couple of years he worked the board down to about twenty-six members. We made sure we had wide representation: Chinese, Portuguese, Italian, Jewish, Christian, and Black. The community at large was represented because Western had a lot of immigrant population. It was important we do that. The smaller committees did a lot of the work.

As chair of the Toronto Hospital, I was summoned to appear at Premier Rae's appointment's office. I was the volunteer and the woman was a paid civil servant. The Toronto Hospital was incorporated under its own Act, and the donors to the hospital appointed the board annually. They always supported the board-nominating committee's recommendations.

This lady told me they had determined that we had an elitist board, which did not represent the community. I told her we had representatives from the following communities on our board: Portuguese, Italian, Chinese, Indian, Black, French Canadian, Jewish, and wasps.

"If you can tell me one other public board in the province of Ontario with that kind of representation, I would be interested in hearing about it," I told her. I also said that we were, "able to do this in spite of the fact that the city and University of Toronto had three representatives—the selection over which we had no control." She said that she would get back to me and she never did.

Moving Forward, Action Steps, and Results

In moving forward, the board met and we started to identify savings. In the first year we saved something like $80 million in operating costs. We allocated $40 million to the hospital to do with what it wanted to do, and $40 million went back to the doctors for their programs and research. One of the reasons I told our board we should merge with the General was because they surely had a big Foundation.

In those days, the Foundation's financial statements were not public information. The Foundations were afraid that if the government found out what they had, the government would take the money. When we merged the two boards, I asked how much was in the Toronto Hospital Foundation at that point so that I could see how we could fund programs for Charles Tator, Tirone David, and others. There was really no money in the Foundation.

At my suggestion we met down at the Toronto Club. Fred Eaton and Fraser Fell were there as well as Fraser Elliott (lawyer and philanthropist), and Alf Powis, Vick Stoughton, and myself. Tom Bell, a previous chair of the hospital and Chair for the Eaton Wing Campaign at the Toronto General, had taken all the money out of the Foundation to finish the campaign.

There was only one endowed chair, and it was underfunded. It was the Eaton Chair of Medicine, and the university was taking a 15 percent fee out every year for administration. We changed that rule right away. I approached the Eaton family and in their usual generous way donated $2 million and re-endowed the Chair.

The Generation Fundraising Campaign

I didn't just go to lunch with anybody unless I thought I was going to get one $100,000 from them.

Clearly we needed to raise money to rebuild the Foundation with a campaign. At our Toronto Club meeting, I was told that Peter Godsoe, a rising executive at the Bank of Nova Scotia, agreed to organize a fund-raising campaign, and so far nothing had happened. I excused myself to phone him. Fortunately he was in his office and took the call.

"Peter, what about this campaign you're supposed to chair?" I asked.

He told me he was in line for a relatively big promotion and had no time for the campaign. Peter was also on our board, and I thanked him very much. I appreciated his honest answer. By the time I got back to the meeting, they told me they'd already decided I had to be chairman. Tom Bell had been chairman of the board, and the chairman had a lot of weight. I had to chair what we were going to call the Generation

Campaign to raise $25 million. Marie Dunseath was our new in-house Foundation manager and she was pretty good at it.

We got going and the University of Toronto called me asking for a meeting. Alf Powis and I met with St. Clair Balfour, Dr. Charles Holemberg, and others. Charles was the Vice Provost of Health Sciences at the University of Toronto, and known worldwide as a bright guy. He told us the university was going to have a campaign and there was no way they were going to allow us to have a campaign.

He went on to say, "If you're leading it, it's not going to be successful anyway."

"You can go blow smoke up your ass if you want, but I'm going to run the campaign, and it's going to be successful," I responded.

Campaign Success

We did run the campaign. I dropped pretty well everything I was doing as we went out all out for $25 million. I think we raised over $35 million. It was the largest campaign in Canadian history at the time. We had a lot of good people who gave money like the Reichmans, who postponed for a while for hard times and couldn't honor all pledges, but in time honored everything. The Reichmans gave a lot of money to a lot of people. The Jewish community were extremely generous people.

The board gave as well; Ralph Barford gave $500,000, the McConnell family gave $500,000, the Eatons refunded their chair with $2 million, and we got well on our way with the mining and oil companies. A great deal of time was involved in raising money because we would have to make two or three calls to everyone, and of course meetings were on their schedule.

Tirone David

I had an interesting experience during the campaign. About 3:00 p.m. one afternoon, I received a phone call from Tirone David asking if I needed a car ride up to Woodbridge—a large suburban Italian Community just north of Toronto. Tirone David was fast becoming the best-known cardiac valve surgeon in the world, and he and his beautiful wife Jackie were good friends of mine. I asked him what he was talking about. He told me I was the guest speaker as Chairman of then merged Toronto General and Toronto Western Hospital. I had no knowledge of the event, since it was not scheduled in my calendar. I agreed—I asked for the address, had to change some plans, and took Rosedale Limousine in case I had some wine and had no idea where the reception was.

Woodbridge is one of the most affluent areas in the Greater Toronto area. Tirone's father was Jewish and his mother Italian. He had been raised in Brazil and did post-graduate work at the Cleveland Clinic where he and Jackie met. I headed up to Woodbridge where the event was being held in a hall in a shopping mall. There were about 200 men and no women. Philip Orsino, CEO of our door company, was there.

I cautioned him not to give any money personally, "Don't you give any money. We have given enough already."

He said, "Okay."

I gave my talk on the research and teaching at the Toronto Hospital, and why we needed money over and above the government subsidies to attract great doctors like Tirone. He brought an artificial heart and proceeded to demonstrate how the heart worked.

At that point a burly chap about fifty years old stood up in the audience and said, "I have the heart of a twenty-five-year-old man that this doctor gave me, and I feel terrific."

Someone yelled out, "It's too bad they didn't give you his prick."

The hat was passed, and we raised over $250,000 that evening. I asked Phillip if he had donated. He said that he had no choice. He had to.

Tirone is still at the hospital operating, teaching, and doing research. When he is operating, the amphitheatre is filled with surgeons from around the world that have come to watch.

One time I had a call from the search committee Chairman for the Chief of Surgery, Cedars of Lebanon Hospital in Los Angeles. Apparently he knew me from a YPO event. He started to ask me about Tirone and how well he got along with his peers and so on. Then he told me why he was asking, and that they wanted him as Chief of Surgery. I asked what they would be paying him. It was without exaggeration about five times what we were paying him, and they were going to give him a large house rent-free. I figured Tirone was gone.

About two months later I ran into him at the hospital. I told him about the phone call and said I was surprised he was still in Toronto. Tirone told me he and his wife talked it over, and they wanted to raise their children in Canada. His wife Jackie had been born and raised in the United States. And when he came to the Toronto Western from the Cleveland Clinic, he was allowed to do the combination of work, teaching, and research that he wanted to do. Tirone is so dedicated that even on his vacation he would often go to Brazil and teach proper and new operating procedures.

Quadra Logic Technologies

I have never seen a company that was such a mess get turned around so quickly.

Quadra Logic Technologies (QLT Inc.) was a junior pharmaceutical company listed on NASDAQ and the Toronto Stock Exchange when I joined the board. Founded in 1981, QLT worked to create therapies and commercialize discoveries developed at the University of British Columbia in the fields of immunology and diagnostics for use with debilitating diseases. Duff Scott, a long time friend and well-known Toronto investment banker, invited me on the board. For several years, Duff had been Vice Chairman of Richardson Greenshields, a Winnipeg based investment banker. He then went on to be Vice Chairman of Merrill Lynch, and when they folded up, he became Vice Chairman for Canada of Prudential-Bache Securities, another US investment banking company.

They had just raised a great deal of money for QLT. The company thought they had developed a drug that would be absorbed by cancer cells, and when zapped with a laser, would have the possibility to eradicate the cancer. At the time I happened to be, among other things, Chairman of the Princess Margaret Hospital Board. My friend Duff felt that in order to protect the Prudential-Bache investors, the board needed some business people because it was composed mostly of scientists from the University of British Columbia. So Duff and I joined the board. He became the chairman of the board and I became audit committee chairman.

126

The cancer drug did not work as anticipated. However, they were working on other drugs, one of them being Visudyne—a drug that was developed in the hope it would stop the progression of age-related Macular Degeneration (AMD). In the USA alone, over 250,000 people were going blind with the disease. At the time it was a very important and profitable drug. Two other different manufacturers were manufacturing the drug.

Because of company growth, a few years later they decided to build a new stand-alone office building with a plant to manufacture Visudyne. Jack Wood, a retired CEO of a pharma company, fought the idea and he proposed we could buy it cheaper than we could make it. However, we lost the argument—it was built and there was a large cost overrun. No matter how you look at it, it was a dumb idea.

Issues, Solutions, Outcomes

In the meantime, the company was making a lot of money. The stock shot up to over one hundred dollars. They then started to spend a great deal of money on research and those kinds of people who like to re-search. We had a technical research committee of scientists who were not board members. The chairman was Dr. Julia Levy and she was to report on what research we should be doing, and more importantly, what we should not be doing. I do not think they ever told us to stop research-ing anything.

One of the problems was that not only was Julia Levy one of the founders of the company and a professor from the University of British Columbia, but also the CEO of the company and chairman of the scien-tific committee. This was a mistake from the point of view of corporate structure. Prior to Julia Levy being CEO of the company, we had had several CEOs while the company was very profitable. We had to deal with a major lawsuit over a patent agreement concerning Visudyne with the Massachusetts General. Our lawyers told us not to pay the approximately $20,000 that I believe we could have settled for. They said that we had a "slam dunk case." We lost and had to pay over $100 million.

We also spent about $800 million on the acquisition of a pharma company in Fort Collins, Colorado. This turned out to be a write-off.

We fired the CEO and made Bob Butchofsky, who was the marketing manager, the CEO, which was a move that proved to be brilliant. He went right to work cutting costs and waste, and re-focusing a quick turn-around with the company. Bob did an amazing job. He also appointed one of our new board members, who was the CEO of a US pharma company, as chairman of the scientific review committee. They started having meetings and cut out the inappropriate research.

Bob and his team did an incredible job and saved the company from going bankrupt. They now had a clean balance sheet with some very good potential products. Fortunately I was not standing for re-election at 2012 annual meeting after twenty-three years. Some hedge funds got together and threw out the board and fired senior management. As I understand it, they want to convert the assets to cash. I hear Bob has bought one of the products and is starting a new company in Austin, Texas. If it goes public, buy the stock.

The Toronto Hospital and Women's College Hospital Debacle

In our hospital, if you're getting a free doctor's office, or nursing assistants, or secretarial assistance, you give money back on an annual basis to pay part of the costs - or you teach, or do research, or all three.

At this time, a couple of years after the merger of the Western and General, I was still chairing the hospital and never missed a committee meeting, whether it was a building committee, audit, or scientific committee. In all my years as chairman of the board, I always attended and worked really hard at it to make sure it all worked.

The unified hospital was called The Toronto Hospital and was well under way when the Women's College Hospital approached us for what became a very interesting experience. Jim McCutcheon was on our board at the time, and his sister Susan McCutcheon was Chair of the Women's College Hospital with eighteen members on their board. I suggested we put the two boards together and build a new Women's College Hospital. It would have been the largest Women's College Hospital in the world. Not only did we have the space over by the General if we put it together, but we also had several women's programs that would've fit in nicely. Actually their merger committee basically agreed it too.

Some of the programs at the Women's College were our programs to the extent that they were manned and financed by Toronto Hospital staff and money. We had named the merged hospitals The Toronto Hospital, because the University was against us using the word "University" in our name at the time.

The Power of Boards and Doctors in the "No"

Through the negotiations, however, the Women's College board committee refused to take six of the eighteen board members onto the new Toronto Hospital board. The six members were the ones who started the campaign to say the Women's College should never merge with Toronto Hospital. In our hospital, if you're getting a free doctor's office, or nursing assistants, or secretarial assistance, you give money back on an annual basis to pay part of the costs—or you teach, or do research, or do all three. This was one of the issues for the doctors at Women's College.

The Women's College Hospital didn't have this arrangement and were getting free downtown offices and help. A couple of the doctors at Women's College immediately wrote to their patients telling them to find another doctor because they were going to lose their office and everything else. This was just absolutely wrong, but they did it. The six members of the board launched the campaign to save the hospital, stating it was too special to merge with the Toronto Hospital. That's why it never merged.

Of course it merged with Sunnybrook a few years later, and that was a disaster. It has now demerged, parted with Sunnybrook, and is a stand-alone downtown hospital. In my view, this makes no economical or medical sense. It's still a small hospital. When people get sick, often it's much more than one disease or illness, and they need treatment that the Women's College is not adequately prepared to treat. To this day, I believe it would have been much better if it had merged with the Toronto Hospital.

Cardiac Centre Campaign for the Munk Centre

One of the things about chairing a campaign is that you have to be quite generous yourself.

When I first returned from Vancouver after leaving Placer Dome, I chaired the Toronto Cardiac Centre campaign for the Munk Centre. I was able to get Peter Munk to give the first $5 million, which he very generously gave. The Cardiac Campaign was a success and I think we raised $45 million—a big number then.

I recall we were having lunch at the Toronto Club and Peter asked, "What are you going to do about my mother? You really screwed that up."

And I thought, My God, what have we done?

Peter went on to tell me that apparently when his mother got lonely, she would go over to emergency and sit there and chat with the folks. He said there was nothing really wrong with her. He told me she was wasting time and money. There were a lot of people doing this and getting second opinions when they were not required. I had tried before to get Premier David Peterson to charge ten dollars per visit when people went to the doctor, but there was no way politically that would ever fly.

When I had raised the money with Peter for the Cardiac Centre, he invited me to come onto his Board at Barrick if I was ever free to do so. He wanted on the Board of The Toronto Hospital, which I was able to do for him. Peter was an excellent hospital board member, flying back from Europe to attend meetings. He asked me to help get him into the Toronto Club, and as I was on the membership committee, that was easy to do. I had Fred Eaton write a very strong letter in support of Peter, and when I was kicked out of Placer Dome, Peter called to invite me onto the Barrick board. An hour later, Seymour Schulich invited me to join the Board of Euro Nevada, when just earlier I had accepted Peter's invitation.

The New Princess Margaret Hospital Building

It just made so much sense. And by reducing overheads, the attraction would be more money available for other things; the hospital was able to attract more money, world-class doctors, researchers and teachers.

I received a call from Premier Mike Harris to see if I would go in as Chairman of Princess Margaret Hospital, because they were having all kinds of issues and troubles. They weren't maximizing on services, or able to provide the services required by the people in Ontario at the time. I had spent several years on the Board of the Princess Margaret Hospital. As Chair of the Western and Toronto Hospital, you were automatically on the board. I told Mike that, Ed King, - the chairman then, had already confirmed he was going to stay for another term. I didn't know if I would take the chair and I mentioned to Mike I'd think about it. About a week went by when I received a letter—, an Order in Council saying that I was appointed. I phoned Mike and asked what the hell was going on.

I reminded him, "I'll think about it."

He said, "Well you didn't say no, and you didn't call us back, so we figured you'd do it."

"Has anybody told Ed King—the current chairman?" I asked.

And when the answer came back as no, I asked again, "Don't you think it would be a nice thing for somebody to call and tell him he's done a good job and that you're not re-appointing him? I like Ed; it's not right."

I was told, "Yes, but we want you. Ed is too nice, too busy, and we need a tough person."

"Don't announce my appointment for two months," I stated, "and if you're going to do anything other than that, then forget it."

They honoured my request and advised Ed. So I became the Chairman of Princess Margaret.

The Hospital Renovation Project Manager is a Woman: Board Approval

While I was Chairman of The Princess Margaret Hospital board, before we merged it with the Toronto Hospital (originally The Toronto General and Toronto Western), I had a call from Dr. Alan Hudson, the brilliant CEO of the Toronto Hospital. He told me there was going to be a board meeting of the Toronto Hospital. Their meetings are open to the general public and Alan wanted me to be there. He had a problem because he knew the board was not going to approve Susan Conner as project manager for the $100 million or so renovations. In response to my why, Alan said he suspected because she was a woman. Susan had been the Chief Financial Officer of the Princess Margaret Hospital. She's extremely bright without being arrogant, and she was in charge of building the new Princess Margaret Hospital on University Avenue when it moved from Wellesley Street.

I went to the Toronto Hospital board meeting and sat in the audience listening to the banter back and forth as to why Susan would not be the right person to be in charge. When I couldn't stand it any longer, I stood up and asked to speak.

"Can anyone tell me of someone they know who was in charge of constructing a $75 million building on one of Toronto's busiest streets on time and on budget?" was my question.

That was the end of the discussion. Susan was given the job, and once again she finished the Toronto Hospital project on budget and on schedule.

The Royal Visit

When the building was completed and as chairman of the board, I was advised by one of Princess Margaret's assistants that Princess Margaret would personally like visit Toronto to see our new facilities on University Avenue. This was the new hospital and moved from Wellesley Street, as mentioned above. I believe the lodge where people from out of town can stay during visits for treatments is still over at Jarvis and Wellesley. We used to have our board meetings in the basement where wigs were made from donated hair for people undergoing chemo treatment.

We were told we must supply three plane tickets: one for Princess Margaret, one for the lady-in-waiting, and one for her personal bodyguard. I approached the airlines to see if they would donate the plane tickets. They said no way—the cheap bastards. I believe I bought them.

We arranged a three-day visit, which was wonderful for our patients as Princess Margaret spent a lot of time with them. She was our guest for the three days. I must say I enjoyed every minute of it. Needless to say the Princess was a big hit at the hospital with the patients and staff. She took time to talk to everyone. She knew how to make them laugh. If they wanted her picture she would oblige. Along with her staff, Michael Baker, Hal Jackman—the Lieutenant Governor of Ontario—and I walked with her. The pictures were funny because Princess Margaret is about five foot tall, Dr. Michael Baker over six feet tall, Hal is six foot five, and I am six foot three.

Royal Entertaining in Caledon

I knew the Eatons were good friends of the Royal Family and generous to a fault. Fred had been High Commissioner to the Court of St. James and had entertained the Royal Family at dinners in the Canadian Embassy. Various members of the Eaton family had entertained the members of the Royal Family over the years at their Canadian homes.

I called Fred Eaton and asked him if we could put our guests up at his lovely country place in Caledon in the hills just north of Toronto. Always generous, Fred and his charming wife Nicky agreed. I was renting an abutting property to Fred's, and the Royal Canadian Mounted Police and the Ontario Provincial Police stayed in my house. I left a note inviting them to make themselves comfortable and help themselves to anything they wanted.

The lunches and dinners with Princess Margaret were up at Fred's and I usually wound up sitting beside Princess Margaret, which was a real bonus. We both liked our scotch. She loved her Famous Grouse Scotch and was an amazing dinner companion. Princess Margaret was quite funny, loved a good laugh, and is extremely well read. She could talk on any subject, and is up to date on world and Canadian events. She is maybe the finest dinner companion I have been with over the years.

When the Royal party left to return to England and I went back to my place in Caledon, I found a nice thank you note from the Mounties. They thanked me for my hospitality and, "Thought that it was interesting where I stored my guns," which they must have found in the master bedroom. I had totally forgotten I had about ten shotguns under my bed. I stored them there because it was dry and I thought safe. I was a bird hunter, and over the years I had bought and was given some guns.

Politics and Health

As Chairman of The Princess Margaret Hospital Board, I heard Premier Mike Harris was contemplating changing the Minister of Health Elizabeth Witmer, who had been appointed when the Conservatives had defeated Bob Rae's NDP party. She was a member of the Ontario Legislature, and I believe a member for Kitchener, Waterloo. Every time there was a change in the Ministers of Health, decisions with respect to approvals for the hospitals could be held up for at least six months while Ministers got up to speed with their complicated portfolio representing over 30 percent of the Provincial Budget. There was never enough money to fund all the needs. I had visited Health Minister Witmer's office, had met in her boardroom and was very impressed with her. I thought she was extremely bright. On the walls in Minister Witmer's boardroom hung pictures of previous Health Ministers, and over the years I had had several meetings with at least fifteen of them.

My source was quite reliable regarding the possible change, so I called the Premier's Office and was advised that he was on a tour of northern Ontario. I was told he would be speaking and staying that night at the Caswell Hotel in Sudbury. I asked for a private one-on-one meeting with him. It was agreed to. So I headed to the airport, flew to Sudbury, and went directly to the hotel. Just the two of us met.

I told him the problem was not with the Minister, but it was at the Deputy Minister level. He said they could not attract the kind of person required for the job, because of salary ranges. I responded by suggesting they could second someone from the hospitals because the CEOs of the major hospitals were paid more than Deputy Ministers. If you second him or her from the hospitals, you pay the hospital.

"Okay," he agreed, "however you have to call Tom Long and convince him of what you had just suggested."

Tom was the Chief Political Strategist for the Conservative Party. He had been a lawyer with Fasken and Calvin, the Toronto law office, and left there to run Mike Harris's first campaign, which had been lost. I received a call from Fraser Fell to see if I could help Tom out with an office. I provided a free office and secretarial help at no charge, which was something I had done for others. When I spoke to Tom, we knew each other well, and he was aware of my involvement in the Health Care System. He advised the Premier that my suggestion was a good idea.

The Premier had asked me who I thought could do the required job. I responded that either Dr. Alan Hudson (the extremely capable CEO of the then Toronto Hospital), or Jeff Lauzon (who had come in to The Saint Michael's Hospital), and who completely turned around the serious troubles financially and otherwise that the hospital had been in.

After talking to Tom Long, I notified Alan Hudson that he might get a call and job offer from the Premier to be Deputy Minister of Health. My advice was not to take the job because he had the best health care job in Canada, and was interacting with some of Canada's leading businesses. All that would stop. He was called by the Premier and did not take the job. Fortunately Jeff Lauzon did. Jeff did a fantastic job of streamlining the Ministry of Health bureaucracy, and he saw that the limited funds were not wasted and properly spent across the province of Ontario.

Practical Solutions and Problem Solving

At the time, one of the problems was that we didn't have the capacity for radiology machines that were required throughout the province. The other consideration is if you think about it, some people needed chemo-therapy, others radiation, some people needed surgery, and others still needed all three. The Princess Margaret didn't really have much money either, but they had a brand new building. Tony Fell had chaired the campaign and raised a lot of money.

We were sending people to Buffalo, Sault Ste. Marie and Thunder Bay for radiation and it seemed to me we were only using these radiation machines eight hours a day. In looking at the situation and after some discussion we decided to find a solution.

Dr. Tom McGowan, who decided he would be going into private enterprise, thought he could use the machines on afternoon and night shifts. He would find retired doctors, retired technicians, and retired physicists—all the people you need to run the machines and figure everything out and who wanted to work an afternoon shift or two a week. He said that way he could probably fill every day up. We just went ahead and did that.

Well by the time it got to the Ontario Legislature, the unions had found out about it, but we were already in business. I think the first year we saved the province of Ontario $18 million, but more than that, we saved people from travelling all over the province, or down to Buffalo to get health care.

At least here they could have their family with them. So in looking at that, it seemed to me to make sense, which is why we did it. Dr. Tom McGowan used spare capacity, retired people and people who were well trained, lived in the Toronto area, and who only wanted to work part-time, working afternoon shifts at the two cancer centres.

Positive Merger Outcomes

One thing I found out as Chairman of the PMH was that they had more people working in human relations and personnel management than at the Toronto Hospital. The Toronto Hospital was about nine times as big, so the PMH was a pretty fat organization. I decided we should start thinking about merging with the Toronto Hospital and started to push the merger very hard. We had a lot of people who really fought that: good people and smart people. David Brown, a very strong member of the PMH board and well respected by the other board members, was absolutely totally against it.

At about this time we were presented with the lottery. The board didn't want to do it; they thought we'd be taking advantage of people who were sick—or their family and friends who would feel guilty if they didn't buy the ticket. Anyway, I said we'd try it once, if it didn't work they had my word that would be the end of it. Anyway, we tried and it got going.

In the meantime the merger wasn't going anywhere. People were writing letters—an emotional campaign to try stopping that merger, which was crazy. The merger of the PMH with the Toronto Hospital did take place about fifteen years ago. Patients who were unable to get surgery at the Princess Margaret would be able to get it across the street at the Toronto General or at the Toronto Western.

There would be better communication between doctors, because they were members of the one institution; this meant more seamless attention for the patient. Their records could travel with them for visits at the General or the Western, getting various treatments that were required like surgery, chemo, or radiation. Patients could be moved along much more efficiently—one card, one medical file. It just made so much sense.

Previously patients had complained of being lost in the system when they were required to move from hospital to hospital. Prior to the merger they might have surgery that was not connected to a cancer hospital, and hope that in time someone would get them in to complete their treatment.

We got rid of an incredible amount of overhead. By reducing over-heads, the attraction would be more money available for other things: the hospital was able to attract more money, world-class doctors, researchers, and teachers. Now I understand the Princess Margaret has 1,100 full-time scientists on staff, which makes it one of the leading cancer centres in the world, compared to the University of Texas, MD Anderson Cancer Center, and Johns Hopkins Cancer Center of Baltimore, Maryland. You have to look pretty hard to find any other in that league.

I remember somebody with a cancer issue asking me if I could arrange to send them over to the Mayo Clinic. I agreed but asked why there. They said they felt they were better off if they went there. They went to the Mayo Clinic, and when there they were asked why they weren't at the Princess Margaret. Princess Margaret is an incredible institution, but the University Health Network and the combination of the Toronto Western, Toronto General, and the Princess Margaret Hospital, was much better and probably the finest tertiary care hospital in the world.

The University Health Network

You will learn there's more than one solution to a problem. Doctors are really always focused on the best and only solution; there's only one good one. Sometimes in business there's more than one, and it's important you broaden that.

One of the great things that happened when I was becoming Chairman of the University Health Network was that Vick Stoughton, who was the

CEO, decided to retire, resign, and go down and run the medical school and hospital at Duke University. So we did a search. I wasn't on the committee. Alf Powis was chair of the committee, and they got it down to three people to fill the position of CEO. They came up with Dr. Alan Hudson and a couple of Deputy Ministers who were working for the Ontario Government. Deputy Ministers were having a hard time because they didn't see eye to eye with the New Democratic Party. The selection committees were down to three, and I was told I had to make the choice because whomever it ended up being was going to work with me.

Dr. Alan Hudson: Expertise and Benefits

I chose Alan Hudson, and I said to him, "Alan, there's only one condition. You have to go to Harvard for ninety days and take a course at the Business School, because it will broaden your perspective."

He said to me, "Look, I'm a well-known surgeon."

He'd written some of the finest books on surgery worldwide, had several honorary doctorates—he was just a brilliant guy. He also knew the key problems in the Ontario Health System, and had some ideas as to how the now Toronto Hospital could help induce change and set a model for efficiency.

I questioned him, "Well then you don't want the job?"

"What the hell are you talking about?" is how he responded.

I told him, "Well, one of the conditions is you go down to Harvard for ninety days. You will learn how to read financial statements properly. You will learn a lot about human relations. You will learn there's more than one solution to a problem. Doctors are really always focused on the best and only solution; there's only one good one. Sometimes in business there's more than one, and it's important you broaden that."

Alan went on to become a great agent of change: he raised the standards of care, research, and teaching to the highest standards. Because he is so brilliant and respected for his integrity, Toronto Hospital became one of the best tertiary care hospitals in the world. When he arrived at the hospital, we had two endowed Chairs for teaching: The Eaton Chair of Medicine and The McCutcheon Chair of Surgery. When he left, there were over one hundred Chairs, and the total physical plant at the Toronto

General site was basically brand new. They are now endowed with an excess of $3 million each. I am proud to say that one of them is the Peter A. Crossgrove Chair of General Surgery.

The Hospital was able to attract some of the best teachers and researchers from around the world. Among Dr. Hudson's recognitions, he has been awarded honourary doctorates from Japan and the University of Toronto. He is a neurosurgeon and is considered a world expert on nerve injuries. He has co-authored the textbooks Nerve Injuries and Peripheral Nerve Injuries. He has many other achievements—they are too numerous to mention.

When Dr. Ken Schumack, the CEO of Cancer Care Ontario, died suddenly of cancer and Alan was ready for a change, I was happy to recruit him as the CEO of Cancer Care Ontario. He quickly made changes improving the quality of treatment and accessibility to our cancer centres across the province.

First he tied our centres directly into a hospital because previously they had been operating independently of the hospitals. This dramatically reduced administrative cost and these funds could be used for treatment. He had noticed that in the smaller hospitals across the province, doctors were doing cancer operations without the experience. There is a lot of data around to confirm that the more experience—the better results. Some doctors just dropped patients that might have needed radiation or chemotherapy. So Alan recruited Bernie Langer, the former Chief of Surgery at the University of Toronto, and the former Chair of The Canadian College of Physicians and Surgeons. Bernie dramatically changed the quality of the treatment in the smaller centres around the province. In order to deal with wait times at hospitals, the Government of Ontario recruited Alan Hudson away from Cancer Care Centre Ontario. Fortunately he had groomed a successor Dr. Terry Sullivan, who followed on and did a bang-up job until he retired.

Alan was doing a wonderful job of reducing wait times, through to collecting information and finding ways to clear up the bottlenecks. The other provinces envied his progress. Then one of his employees awarded a management information contract without putting it out for bids, and Alan did not notice it. Other consulting firms that didn't have an opportunity to bid complained. It became a major political issue and he took the fall for it. It was a huge loss to the health system across Canada. Now we have large backups for surgery and treatment hospitals that no one had a better chance of solving than Alan. His work has had an incredible impact on medical care in Canada.

One of the issues now is that over half the medical students are women, and only about half of those will graduate and practice because they generally go off to raise families after some years. People in the smaller communities do not have access to the quality and specialty of service they might need. There is a train coming down the track.

Bringing Dr. Bob Bell on Board

One never knows where good ideas pop up. For example, we had a Cancer Care Ontario Retreat up north of Toronto for a day and a half. At the retreat I ran into Tom Closson, who had taken over from Alan Hudson as CEO of the University Health Network in Toronto. I asked him what was new, and he shared with me that he had started to build a retirement home in Victoria, BC. A little later that evening I ran into Alan Hudson and told him Tom was going to retire.

He asked how I knew that and I repeated what Tom had said, "Alan and I discussed who we thought should be the next CEO of the UHN, and we both agreed that Dr. Bob Bell, who was the Chief Operating Officer at the Princess Margaret Hospital, would be an excellent candidate."

I asked Alan Hudson, who was the CEO of Cancer Care Ontario, if we could pay half the costs of Dr. Bell to go to Harvard for the ninety-day program. He thought that was a good idea and he would get Tom Closson, Dr. Bell's boss, to pay the other half. We did not tell Tom why we thought Bob should go to Harvard, other than it would improve his management skills. I must say that together Dr. Hudson and Dr. Bell, as well as Chief of Medicine—Dr. Michael Baker (who were managing huge operations) thought the Harvard experience was very worthwhile and improved their management skills dramatically.

About eight months later when Tom stepped down, Bob was a candidate for the job among others. He stood out because he had the business background and could understand statements. We are now at least five years down the road, and of course he is doing a fantastic job. The University Health Network is continuing to provide among the finest health services in the world. Bob has helped to raise a phenomenal amount of money for teaching and research, and this attracts great doctors who want to be where leading research is conducted and their peers are among the best in the world. Bob is one of the smartest people I have ever met.

Tony Fell and the UHN Chair

Between the time the Princess Margaret Hospital completed its merger with the Toronto General and Western, and I had gone on to be the Founding Chair of Cancer Care Ontario, Princess Margaret needed an interim chair who could eventually become chair of the combined hospitals. Fred Eaton called to see if I had any ideas and I said yes because I was thinking of Tony Fell. Tony was Chair of Dominion Securities, which was being bought by the Royal Bank, and he was becoming Vice Chairman of The Royal Bank. Fred called him and Tony said he had no interest. I suggested Fred set up a meeting with Tony; and if Fred would not, then I would.

Fred scheduled a meeting a few days later and we saw Tony at his office. Dominion Securities' policy was that at sixty years old you had to sell your shares and retire—no exceptions. I asked him what he was going to do when he retired. His only hobby was work. He was good at it and probably the top investment banker in Canada.

I said, "Well then you'd better get involved in the hospital because it will take all the time you can give it."

A funny thing happened when he turned sixty years old—they dropped the mandatory retirement age. In the meantime, he went on to be the Chairman of The University Health Network and he was a darn good one—just like his brother Fraser had been.

CHAPTER 11

Cancer Care Ontario

If there's something we can do to facilitate people—we do it.

The Premier of Ontario, Mike Harris, called me and told me, "I'd like you to be the Founding Chair of Cancer Care Ontario. We're creating this brand new Cancer Agency to control all cancer care in the province, because if they control the money, they'll control the quality of care."

This invitation from the Premier's Office came when I was the Chair of Princess Margaret Hospital but we had made the decision to merge with the Toronto General and the Western.

One time I was in Florida at the Ocean Reef Club in Key Largo playing golf, and when I returned home there was a call from Premier Mike Harris. Apparently someone from Cancer Care Ontario had said something that was perceived as negative and reported in the Toronto Star. He had appointed me as the initial Chair of Cancer Care Ontario, which I was for twelve years. He had left a few angry words on the message machine. So I called him back. He is a friend and a fellow northerner. I let him rant.

Then I calmly said, "Why do you give a shit? There is not a chance that anyone who reads the Toronto Star would vote for you anyway?"

"Yes. I owe you lunch," he replied. He still does!

The Whys and the Wherefores

What was happening was that general surgeons were being paid for surgery; they'd pick the towns they'd want to work in for smaller hospitals where they were paid for volume. They'd operate on cancer, and if the cancer patient needed follow up for chemo and other things, there was no quality control. The resources just weren't there. There were not enough radiation or cancer centres around the province. People had to travel long distances from home for traumatic treatment or to be diagnosed.

When I started, we had about two or three cancer centres and now there are about fifteen around the province. We started to build them when the province would be able to give us the money. I have chaired Cancer Care Ontario for twelve years. I think we've got some of the finest cancer care now throughout the province at several outstanding cancer centres. Obviously there's always room for improvement, but I think the smaller cities like Sudbury and Kingston and various cities across the province have benefitted.

Our first CEO at Cancer Care Ontario was Charles Holemberg, and the second was Ken Schumack—both were outstanding doctors and great administrators. Unfortunately both died of cancer while serving in the job. Then we had Dr. Alan Hudson who integrated the cancer centres with the nearby hospitals, which helped reduce costs and made things easier for the patients. When Alan was asked to do other things by the Government, Dr. Terry Sullivan took over, and he created a well-oiled efficient machine that serves the patients and taxpayers of Ontario very well. Since I left he has moved on.

There is now a medical school in Sudbury at Laurentian University and in Thunder Bay. Sudbury also has a very strong with some excellent researchers there having some help from the Peter Crossgrove Fellowships. The quality of cancer care is controlled by Cancer Care Ontario because they control the money. The cancer centres are managed by the local hospitals to save money. This system works.

A Philanthropic Aside

Regarding fundraising for the hospital and a philanthropic aside: a good friend Ellen Campbell called me and said she had a friend who needed help in the cancer treatment area. I made a call, and a couple of months later Ellen called to let me know the lady would like to buy me lunch as a gesture of thanks. About a year went by, however, because I had been unable to schedule the luncheon. Finally Ellen asked if we could meet for a coffee at a hotel in north Toronto. I agreed and went up one morning.

The first thing this lady did was to give me a beautiful leather bound bible with my name inscribed on it, which I still have and read from time to time. She told me she was so pleased for the help that she decided to give me $100,000 for what I had done.

I said, "No thanks."

She said, "Do you know that it has been over a year that Ellen has been trying to arrange this meeting?" When I said yes she continued, "About a year ago I gave the money to my husband to invest."

I thought to myself, Well I guess it's all gone.

"How much do you think is left now?" She asked me.

I thought nothing but said, "I have no idea."

She told me over a million dollars. She gave this to me and I added half to the Crossgrove Chair of Surgery at UHN and half went to CARE Canada. It was the largest donation that CARE Canada had ever received at that point. Julia Royer is the person who made this generation donation. She and her husband have donated several million more of their own money since. Every now and then amazing stories like this one crop up. You find very generous and sincere people who wish to make a difference in the lives of other people who may need the healthcare support, and they certainly do.

In the End—It's About How You Can Help

That's basically my background in the hospital field. I guess one way or another I'm still involved. I get called from time to time about various things, and certainly over many years had a lot of people thank me. One of the results of fundraising over many years is having nailed so many people for money, that there might be occasion for people to come back to me. This can occur in two ways: I have to give money for whatever they're raising, but also if they need help for family or friends, I have to pitch in and get that help. And I do that. Bob Bell, the current CEO of UHN, and all of the CEOs at hospital, have recognized that not only do I have this obligation, but the institution does too.

Any Way You Look At It: Healthcare Realities Today

It's important to look at healthcare realities today. The availability of good medical care in Canada is in a rapid decline. The further north you go in Canada's major provinces, the worse it gets. The causes are several: an aging population, people living much longer and requiring more medical care. In Ontario and most jurisdictions, there are not enough nursing homes, which cost a lot less to run than a hospital. Unfortunately the hospitals have many people taking up beds, which would be far more beneficial being filled by sicker people who could be treated and released quickly.

The current situation actually blocks beds and often the ability to take in very ill patients. Unfortunately some elderly patients need assistance, but there are no nursing homes to send them to. Some of the elderly patients have no family or their family will not help them. Nursing homes are much cheaper to build and operate than hospitals, and provide a nicer environment for elderly sick patients. With the aging population, this problem is compounding.

Another issue is that doctors are retiring from an age and time when few doctors were being trained. As I have mentioned previously, women count for over half of the medical students graduating today and statistics show that less than half of them practice medicine—if they do it's not a long-term commitment. This is just a fact of life.

Today people have access to the Internet and can see, for example, which hospitals have the best results for various procedures in the province of Ontario. It is very clear that the complicated procedures are mostly done in the teaching hospitals, and that is where one has the best chance of a successful procedure.

Clearly if you can get admitted to a teaching hospital when you have a serious problem, you have a better chance for a suitable outcome. Another problem is the lack of the newer, better, and expensive equipment that is constantly being developed.

With the thousands of new condominium complexes being built in Toronto, we wonder where these people will go when they are sick. The emergency rooms of all the Toronto hospitals are full to overflowing now. These problems are not unique to the province of Ontario.

We are told from time to time of doctors who are caught overbilling or double billing for hundreds of thousands of dollars. And we are never told what happens to them. How do the College of Physicians and Surgeons discipline them, and which is the doctor's union?

A Case in Point...

A case in point: I have recently had a call from a friend from northern Ontario, who is currently in Orlando with her husband who is in a hospital there. He has been diagnosed with three cancer tumours: two on the brain and one in his lungs. He is retired from a major Canadian Oil Company and is covered by their health insurance plan. He is seventy years old and, despite his current problem, he has always enjoyed good health.

He had been advised by the insurance company and was told that he was not sick enough to be covered by the insurance plan in the States, and had to drive home. The neurosurgeons say he will not make it and must have the brain operation immediately before the swelling is out of control. It becomes quite frustrating for the clients who have purchased their health coverage and yet feel quite powerless to get around resolving issues that might suddenly crop up. From the insurance company's perspective, they require third-party verification of the claim in order to avoid fraud—basically they had to speak to the client's doctor.

In order to get the insurance company, I had to call a friend who is in the group business. His office deals with several insurance companies, and he has a group of people in his office who hassle with the insurance companies on behalf of his clients. They were able to intervene as a catalyst between the two parties and the claim was approved. The insurance company has now agreed to fly him to Canada, but they are unable to get a bed for him.

My friend said when the wife called the insurance company; she was probably talking to a call centre in India. They are trained to deny, deny, and deny any liability. You would think they might also be trained in having some empathy when discerning difficult situations and how to resolve them quickly and efficiently. You wonder if they have been trained to consider individual cases with any sense of empathy and based on unusual circumstances.

One of the things I learned through this exercise was that you may have supplementary insurance, but if you are out of Canada, like Canadian snowbirds for example, who might be unaware of the thirty-day consecutive day's time restrictions, it is no longer valid. People are always encouraged to call their brokers so they clearly understand terms and conditions, and if they have health challenges the brokers can facilitate getting every claim paid efficiently. Check the fine print.

A Religious Slant on a Friend's Medical Story

We also need to look at the religious slant towards medicine and health. Let me tell you the story about my friend Eva Gougeon. Her late husband and their son Riki were my father's and then my general insurance agent, just as Riki's daughter Judy is for my two sons. Eva was a "pistol," who was always well dressed, wore a smile, and made us all laugh—just like her husband and three sons. They were a happy family. Her maiden name was Thornton. She was an Anglican and her husband Wilf was a Catholic, and he wanted his three sons raised Catholics. He insisted on this because he could get the insurance business and real estate business from the Catholic Church, as they were the pre-eminent church in northern Ontario.

The Gougeons had a summer cottage on Lake Penage, which is about twenty miles west of Sudbury. Their cottage was on the west end of the lake about twelve miles from the Summer Catholic Church and located on the east end of the lake. Every Sunday in the summer, Eva would drive their large and powerful launch up the lake to the church. However, before going to church, she would drop Wilf off at Gemmel's Store, where you could go into the icehouse and drink bootleg beer.

I worked at the Lands and Forest Station on the lake one summer when I was in high school, so when I saw the boat come by, I would go over and have a couple of beers with him in the ice house and whoever else happened to be there. After church, Eva would come by and pick him up and drive him back to their cottage. He always wore a three-piece suit and a fedora, even at the cottage. His liver gave up and he passed away. Eva continued to drive the fastest boats and cars in the Sudbury district. When Eva was about eighty-seven years old, her sons organized a taxi service for her.

A few years later this wonderful lady became ill and was admitted to one of the hospitals in Sudbury. She went into a coma. Her doctor happened to be of the Catholic faith, and after two years and many requests from the family, the doctor still refused to take her off life support systems. Her friends started a petition, acquired approximately 5,000 names, and sent it to the Premier of Ontario with no effect.

About a year and a half later, her doctor retired, and my late brother-in-law was appointed by the family to be her doctor, although he was an obstetrician and gynecologist. He had known her for years, and like anyone who knew her, he was very fond of her. Within a couple of days she passed away. When she died she weighed less than forty pounds. She spent all that time in a critical care bed. Just think of the cost to the system. Perhaps a father of three young children, who may have died waiting for a bed, could have better used her bed.

It is my opinion that everyone should be forced to have a living will so that if you are a vegetable, the instructions are clear: pull the plug.

Medical Relief Suggestions

What can we do to improve our medical system in Canada?

Rehire retiring doctors part-time: We can make it attractive for retiring doctors to work a day or two a week, or a couple of weeks a month. This arrangement actually worked very well to alleviate the situation that arose with the backlog of treating cancer patients who required radiation and chemotherapy treatment

These doctors who are retired could spend a few weeks of the year working in the northern parts of all the Canadian provinces. There are many doctors in the major cities in Canada who are unable to find jobs at this time. They should be encouraged to head to the underserviced areas of the country. Most of them born and raised in cities in the southern parts of the provinces are reluctant to leave. However, how can you beat the stress-free lifestyle of the north? There is no pollution, there many lakes for boating, sailing, skiing, and fishing, as well as golfing often within ten or fifteen minutes from the office. There's also no traffic stress going back and forth to the office. I have never yet met a doctor from the south whom after moving to Sudbury ever wanted to leave. Those provinces that are supporting medical schools had better take a hard look at these problems, particularly with our aging population.

Recovering costs for medical training: I would suggest that somehow the Canadian medical system has to recoup the substantial amount of money they have paid to train medical students who do not practice for several years after they graduate. This amount could be $100,000 per year for every year that they do not practice, or do not teach or do research up to five years. It must be possible to formulate some type of repayment system.

Recruit well-qualified doctors: Make it much easier for them to be certified to practice in Canada. For example, there are well-qualified doctors in South Africa, Ireland, Scotland, England, and the United States and so on, who may like to come to Canada. However, at the moment, you could be a graduate of a top medical school in the United States, such as a full professor at Harvard, but if you come to Canada you may have to take more courses and more exams. Some of the Maritime provinces have done an excellent job of recruiting and removing the roadblocks.

Hold doctors accountable for overbilling: Criminally charge every doctor who overbills and have surprise audits of their books and procedures. Take away their hospital privileges and have them pay for their medical training. I have never heard of one being put in jail yet.

Create patient awareness around non-threatening medical issues: Ensure that people do not show up at emergency when they do not have a serious problem. Some are not sick at all—they are just lonely or like to hang out at hospitals. For example, charge twenty-five dollars for a visit to emergency. As I mentioned before, I spoke to my good friend David Peterson about this when he was the Premier of Ontario. He said, "It's a good idea Peter, but if we do we will never be re-elected."

Having funds to maintain buildings and updating equipment: On the physical plant side, we clearly need more and to update many current hospitals.

We require the province, the municipality to pay a share, and community fundraisers to do a better job than they do now, and for wealthier people to step up to the plate and give more.

Clarabelle Lake on Clarabelle Road in Copper Cliff - Photograph Courtesy City of Greater Sudbury Museums, Copper Cliff Collection - CC0121. My father grew up in one of those houses, which were gone by the time I was about 5 years old.

Park and Clubhouse in Copper Cliff - Photograph Courtesy City of Greater Sudbury Museums, Copper Cliff Collection. CC0144

The high school was located at the end of the park. The football field and track were located in the park. The water tower up on the right supplied water to the town. This was the high school that I attended.

1937 - Inco's Creighton Mine – electric locomotive underground
Photo courtesy of Vale Archive.

1959 - Bombadier Work Horse to transport from Thicket Portage to
Thompson, Manitoba. Photo courtesy of Vale Archive.

1961 - Inco's Copper Cliff Smelter Converter Aisle West End
Photo courtesy of Vale Archive.

Creighton Mine
Photo courtesy of Vale Archive.

My father duck hunting with dog Rockey.

My mother Marguerite and father Alexander Davidson Crossgrove.

In my younger days prospecting for Canadian Nickel at Desperation Lake North Western Territories, south of Copper Mine in the Arctic - 1958.

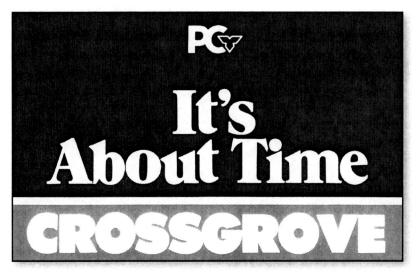

Campaign poster for the 1978 elections.

Skiing in Aspen with my sons Alex and Keith.

Salmon fishing at the Ristigouge Club in New Brunswick.

Princess Margaret HRH during her visit to the Princess Margaret Hospital. From far left stands Lieutenant Governor of Ontario, Hal Jackman, Alan Hudson, Princess Margaret, Fred Eaton and myself.

At the Toronto Hospital with Dr. Alan Hudson CEO (first left), Dr. Baker, Chief of Medicine (second left), and Dr. Paul Walker, Surgeon in Chief (second right).

With Dr. Alan Hudson.

Peter and Melanie Munk at the Toronto Hospital, Cardiac Campaign for the Munk Cardiac Centre.

Dr. Alan Hudson, CEO of the University Health Network.

Board meeting of QLT, with Dr. Julia Levy as CEO and E. Duff Scott as Chairman.

Attending a YPO Forum in Cape Canaveral, Florida with YPO members and an astronaut.

The Philex Gold Corp. Board of Directors Meeting in the Philippines, flanked by Gerald Brimo (CEO) left, and his father.

With Paias Wingti, Prime Minister of Papua New Guinea.

Meeting in Abidjan (Cote d'Ivoire); President Henri Bedie in the blue suit, Fred Eaton in white, and Joe Heinzer (first from the left), Chief Geologist.

Meeting in Indonesia with the Indonesian Provincial President on my way to the water project.

Shaking hands with Prime Minister Chretien at the CARE Canada meeting.

With Mike Harris, Premier of the Province of Ontario.

With Brian Mulroney, Canadian Prime Minister.

165

In conversation with President Clinton.

Fly-fishing with George Bush Senior in Labrador.

Portrait for the UHN.

CHAPTER 12

CARE Canada

It's really a wonderful organization because they work to make sure the money isn't going into administration and big salaries.

The other big charity involvement I had was with CARE Canada. I started out with CARE Canada when my old, long-time, and good friend John McDonald approached me. John, who is also from YPO, and his brother Bill who are still friends of mine, built Black and McDonald, a very successful coast-to-coast electrical contracting firm. John approached me about getting involved with CARE by taking over for him as chairman. And I did.

CARE does some incredible work around the world, and it's an extremely well-run organization. John Watson was the CEO when I took over. John was a very difficult person to work with, but he was very bright. In fact, he was so bright that it pissed off a lot of people internationally. I very quickly became the Treasurer for CARE International. I was treasurer for about twelve years and that entailed a lot of travelling. I guess the total budget would be about one and a half billion over all the members. It was a Federation with several members like CARE USA, CARE Britain, CARE Austria, CARE France, CARE Deutschland, CARE Japan, and so on.

To see that things were done properly and money was spent wisely was important. The head office for my tenure was in Brussels. I travelled to Brussels quarterly, but I often found the meetings would be held at various locations around the world. The work we were doing was incredible. There were some amazing stories and examples of CARE Canada's work and the results of that work. We worked very hard to make sure the money was spent in the field and not on overhead.

When I was involved with CARE in Indonesia we ran on five-year contracts with the government. We sort of told them what we were going to do and we were spending approximately $5 million a year. When our third five-year contract was up, somebody called me from CARE's office in Ottawa and told me we couldn't renew the contract unless we paid off some Indonesian government people under the table. I promptly got the phone number of the CEO of the World Bank—an Australian, a very good friend of my friend in Australia, as well as Malcolm Fraser, the former Prime Minister of Australia on the International Board of CARE. I called the World Bank to discuss our problem. Within twenty-four hours, they were signing the contract. However, some of these countries are extremely difficult to do business in.

I went to a project in Bangladesh where we had 40,000 women in the program. It was a four-year program with 10,000 women rotated out every year. They built roads by hand. They shoveled the gravel into baskets, carried it on their heads, and built these roads. When we paid them we kept half the pay, which wasn't much money, and then in the fourth year, we taught them how to manage money, and how to manage their affairs and basic business. We had around 40,000 applications every year but only room for 10,000 participants.

In order to get into the program, you had to be a single mother. You had to be abandoned. These were all single mothers who had one or more children. By the time I came onto the Board of CARE Canada, the program had been running for several years. By the time I came over to Bangladesh, I met some of the women who had worked in the program and were now successful politicians, and some developed big business. It was pretty interesting. They were quick to tell you that the men who dropped them all wanted to get back with them. They told the men to more or less go to hell.

Water Pipes and Womens' Empowerment

I was in Indonesia where CARE had been for several years. CARE Canada has CARE offices in various countries: Kenya was a big one, Eastern Africa, Bangladesh, and Indonesia. I arrived in Indonesia and almost immediately had to meet for lunch with the provincial people.

There was a big ceremony about 9:00 a.m. and then I was invited for a second lunch with the town people; this more or less happened as we were made our way up into the mountains. I got to the village and heard what had happened in this village regarding the women.

They had all been carrying the water two kilometers up the mountains and down into the villages. When they heard that CARE had put water in other villages, they approached CARE for assistance. We sent an engineer or water specialist in and he reported there would be no problem to install a water system. He said we'd have to have a two-kilometre line of buried plastic pipe up the hill to the well because we didn't know what the animals, the sun, and everything else would do to the pipe. The men would have to dig and put the pipe down. However, the men didn't believe in gravity. I went to the town hall meeting and listened to a gentleman who was the town elder. He explained that the women raised such a stink about the fact that the men refused to participate in digging a line for the pipe that I have to tell you this story.

There I was sitting in the hall—the dimensions were approximately eighty feet in each direction. All the women sat on one side to the right—about seventy of them and they were all Muslim. I only saw their eyes. They were all dressed in white with white scarves on their heads. The men sat straight ahead of me, and some government officials on my left. All dialogue was going through a translator. There were a bunch of laughing and giggling children hanging through the open windows. There was no glass of course. The old guy in the village was elected to tell the water story. I found out that he was younger than I was at that time.

He got up and spoke about the water project, telling us about the women hearing of CARE and requesting CARE to come, and about the men who wouldn't dig the two lengths to prove there was no gravity. Finally the women raised such a stink that the men dug the two lengths, and of course the water went down the two lengths. The men then refused to dig any more, saying it would never go two kilometres. Of course the women did all the work, and the men just sat around all day and came home at the end of the day. The women grew or raised the food, did the laundry, repaired the houses, and did everything else that had to be done.

The women got together and said they would cut off all sex; there would be no sex in the village. The men then quickly dug the required trench. All this was going through the translator, and by this time I was laughing so hard. It was so hot and humid. I was soaking wet with sweat and I already had two big meals—it was not even 2:00 p.m. yet, and I was about to have another meal. They prepared and placed the biggest banquet I had ever seen in front of me. In any event, the women waited to see if I laughed. And I did. I laughed—and they laughed.

Finally when the old guy finished, I turned to the women and asked, "I'd like to ask the women what changes the waters made in the village?"

Clearly they'd been waiting to see what might happen here.

One woman got up—she'd been waiting for me to ask—and she said, "Well, old guys like him are still alive. He'd be dead by now, and our babies aren't dying at childbirth. We can grow all the fruit and vegetables and everything we need in our own backyard. And we can have showers, so when the men come home, we're nice and clean, and we can have wonderful sex."

I was just dying because I was laughing so hard. Of course, I had to eat the lunch and inspect one hundred and ten houses. Everybody showed me his or her house.

The Heartbreak of War in Sarajevo

CARE Canada was working in Sarajevo, capital of Bosnia Herzegovina, right after the siege of the city: the longest siege of any city in modern warfare. Historically known for being the setting for the start of World War II with the assassination of Archduke Franz Ferdinand, Sarajevo has through the millennia been the nexus for Roman Catholics in the west, the Eastern Orthodox, and Ottomans in the south. A city of great religious diversity, Sarajevo came under siege from 1992 to 1996, with over 10,000 people killed—mostly civilians, and many were children. Life and living conditions were pitiful.

In the Prosecution's Opening Statement 2003 against Serb officials in their convictions in crimes against humanity, it was stated, "The siege of Sarajevo, as it came to be popularly known, was an episode of such notoriety in the conflict in the former Yugoslavia that one must go back to World War II to find a parallel in European history. Not since then had a professional army conducted a campaign of unrelenting violence against the inhabitants of a European city so as to reduce them to a state of medieval deprivation in which they were in constant fear of death. In the period covered in this indictment, there was nowhere safe for a Sarajevan, not a home, at school, in a hospital, from deliberate attack."

CARE Canada was operating in Sarajevo to help the elderly by feeding them and getting them to doctors for medical aid. It is hard to imagine that just a few years before the siege, the city had hosted the Winter Olympics. There was not one tree left standing in a city that endured heavy military assaults. They were all cut down for firewood and fuel to keep city residents warm. There was no wooden furniture in any apartments either; it had all been burned for heat. People hugged me and cried when they found out I was Chairman of CARE Canada. When I left some of the apartments, I hoped the people would die soon because they were so sick and lonely.

The huge parking lot at the Olympics a few years before was now a large graveyard. All the people who were still alive between ages eighteen and sixty had fled to other countries. Just after the war, the Canadian Consul General had worked out of the Care office for several months. He threw a small cocktail party in my honour and among the people invited were some of the CARE staff. I was talking to a young lady and asked her where she lived. She said in an apartment on the other side of the valley. In my estimation that would be about six miles away: three down and three up.

"How will you get home after dark?" I asked her. She said she could only afford to walk. I asked if she was being properly paid and she responded, "Yes." However, her sister and mother lived with her and she had to support them from her salary. I gave her the equivalent of about ten dollars. The next day in the office she wanted to give me the change.

I had the opportunity to visit a beautiful City Square. It was spooky because people walked back and forth in silence. No restaurants, no bars, and no place to go. I imagine for the multitudes silently walking and walking this might have helped them to make sense of their lives—their grievous minds and hearts filled with unspeakable horrors and sadness.

The next day I went out to visit some of the surrounding towns where the Canadian peacekeeping troops were driving around in trucks and tanks. Houses had been blown up depending upon what their religion was, and that was determined by their name, which could have been incorrect by intermarriage. I then took the train to Croatia through Slovenia the next country and found the new terrain of beautiful farms refreshing. Quite a stark contrast I have to admit. With its recovery from the damages of war, thankfully today Sarajevo is ranked as one of the safest tourist destinations in South Eastern Europe.

Skirting Political Issues

Several years ago I was on safari with YPO as I mentioned earlier. We had a wonderful trip on the Maasai Mara, which is a large national game reserve sharing a common border between Kenya and Serengeti National Park in Tanzania. After the trip some of us went on to Johannesburg, South Africa. A few of us were invited to meet with the City Council of Soweto because they knew I was involved with CARE International.

At the time, and this was between twenty-five to thirty years ago, they were very concerned about Canada's policy of encouraging the United Nations to have member countries not purchase anything from South Africa because of the efforts to stop apartheid. Media events were all staged they told us, and South African manufacturers had moved their operations offshore. The resulting situation was that people were desperate for jobs.

After the meeting I asked to see Archbishop and South African social activist Desmond Tutu's house. I pointed out that it looked like a humble dwelling. The mayor chuckled and told me Bishop Tutu lives in the "Bishop's palace" in Pretoria. I then asked to see Winnie Mandela's house. It was a big house with a swimming pool and tennis courts located on the only hill in Soweto. I was really curious to see how profiled people lived and whether they had been affected by the economic sanctions imposed to mitigate the political climate of apartheid. I wanted to understand as well how the man in the street was being affected by these same sanctions, suffering the consequences in their ability to earn a decent living. It was an interesting study of outcomes.

When I returned to Toronto I outlined some thoughts and sent them to the government. There was no response. George Currie who was then in YPO and publisher of The Globe and Mail, asked me to meet with the editorial board of the Globe. We did, but nothing came of it. The whole situation seemed to be a mute issue, and try as I did, was not going to illicit any action or reaction from anyone in government.

In an earlier chapter I mentioned Peter Munk's bone of contention about a year ago, and that I had spoken to The Globe and Mail about the perceived weakness at Barrick. I have never spoken to a Globe reporter in over twenty-five years despite the fact that I know the current Globe and Mail publisher, who was a volunteer on CARE Canada's board. I did at the time when I returned from Africa to report on my thoughts and suggestions on the issues they were going through there as a member of the CARE International board. It was a tough situation at the time.

Those were such moving experiences—some of the work we did and some of the work CARE does. It's really a wonderful organization; the people were decently paid, but not overpaid. Every dime is accounted for. I was very proud of the way CARE is managed. A lot of the money came from the Canadian Government who funneled money through there, and there was a lot of money that came from private citizens. I eventually left CARE. After so many years it was time to go. John Watson the CEO and I weren't seeing eye-to-eye. He felt I was being over critical and perhaps I was.

I was on the Board of CARE Canada for ten years as member of the board, and then chairman for six years of the ten. I was also Treasurer of the Board of CARE International for twelve years with the last two years as treasurer and vice chairman. I donated a few months a year out of my time to travel extensively abroad. There are so many stories I can tell about all my experiences with CARE—imagine that just part of their work is the daily feeding of 5 million children in India. I decided to step down because the travelling became too much for me, and because of the heavy commitment in time, which I just didn't have enough of across my work schedule. However, my time with CARE was very rewarding.

PART FIVE

CHAPTER 13

The Best Corporate Board I Sat On

It just goes to show: when relationships are in alignment and supportive,
then all kinds of doors open for many opportunities.

I was on the Board of United Dominion for about eight years until it was sold. It was originally called Dominion Bridge—a Canadian company based in Charlotte, North Carolina. The company originally built railway bridges and steel engineered structures. An example of their work was the retractable roof at the Rogers Centre that they built. However, they branched out into the steel door manufacturing business and made specialty doors for prisons. They had a huge pump division in Wisconsin that made pumps for the manufacture of drugs, food, and other products. They also had a heavy equipment manufacturing business in Germany called BOMAG. The company was listed on the Toronto and New York Stock Exchange.

The head office had been moved from Montreal to New Hampshire because that's where the CEO liked to live. The next CEO, Bill Holland, moved the head office to Charlotte, North Carolina. He liked to play golf and it was far easier to attract executives because of the convenient transportation hub; they also had plants and operations in many places. The major shareholder was the Canadian Pacific Railway and Bill Stinson was the CEO of the CPR at the time.

The company had gone through some tough times before my arrival, and Bill Stinson backed them through these tough periods. By the time I arrived, the company was working its way out of its financial problems. We held our meetings in various places in Charlotte, and from time to time in towns where we had factories—even in Germany. When I joined the board, it was close to being bankrupt, which I soon found out as a member of the audit committee. But for the grace of Bill Stinson, I think it would have been.

Experience, Experience, Experience

The board was composed of very experienced people. People who were or had run large companies like Bill Stinson, Alan Taylor (the CEO of the Royal Bank), or others like John McDonald, who I mentioned along with his brother Bill, built Black and McDonald, Canada's largest electrical contractors. Also on the board was Stuart Dixon, who together with his brother built a very successful grocery chain in the United States called Harris Teeter in addition to having created the largest thread company in the world. In fact, they had a plant in Quebec.

The meetings were always spread over a couple of days and included a board dinner, sometimes with management and sometimes without. Everyone was well prepared for the meetings and carefully went over corporate goals, objectives and compensation. I think the last director appointed to the board before the company was sold was George Taylor, the CEO of Labatt's at the time. Bill Holland wanted him because he was so tough on negotiating the costs of construction on the fully motorized retractable Skydome roof (the complex later renamed the Rogers Centre in 2005), which Labatt's owned when it was constructed. George was very bright and had been raised on a farm and continued operating a large farm as a hobby. He was a chartered accountant by training and always asked a lot of good penetrating questions.

When I joined the board, I went on the audit committee. I thought this company was going under and it had been around for a hundred years. More money was required. Bill Stinson backstopped a financing and the stock went from eight dollars to about forty-two dollars when the company was sold around eight years later after also paying some dividends in the meantime.

Connecting Connections

I feel connecting people is important, and I endeavour to do that when the occasion arises. One time, we were having a board dinner on the third floor at the Toronto Club. As I walked up, I noticed Loblaw was having a dinner for someone on the second floor, because I saw Galen Weston and Richard Currie. I recalled Stuart Dixon commented on what a terrific help President's Choice had been in the Harris Teeter Stores in the Southern States, which were owned by him and his brother.

When I arrived at the third floor, I asked Stuart if he had ever met Galen or Richard and he said no, but he surely would have liked to. I went down to the second floor and beckoned Galen to come out of the room, asking him if he'd like to meet the owner of Harris Teeter, and he was agreeable. I told him to wait there and brought Stuart down to meet him. Everybody was happy and so was I, because Stuart sent his jet to pick me up for a couple of golf games at Augusta.

Bill Stinson: Wise Business, Sage Advice

Bill Stinson, then CEO of CPR (Canadian Pacific Railway), is a bright, first class gentleman. We laughed because we could never have a meeting if he was unable to get a Wall Street Journal. One time I was fishing with him in Labrador as the guest of Harry Steele, founder of the Newfoundland Capital Corporation and Past Governor of the Atlantic Provinces Economic Council, and they had the Wall Street Journal flown in for Bill.

That was an interesting trip because there were some intriguing guests like Seymour Schulich (entrepreneur and philanthropist), Jean Charest (the Premier of Quebec), and George Bush Sr., who is a wonderful man. He had lost the election the previous fall and I took the opportunity to ask him some questions like what he missed the most. He said not the press. When they would call and ask for opinions, he'd tell them no comment, and it would drive them nuts. He told me he then had time for his kids. Two of them at the time were running for governor, one in Texas and one in Florida, and they had a good shot at being elected. He continued to say if that happened it would make him very happy. At one point President Bush was on Barrick's advisory committee and we had a meeting in Paris. He was going to talk to the investment community. Unfortunately the traffic was halted and he was not going to get there. He walked a half an hour in the cold pouring rain not to disappoint the folks.

Bill Stinson placed all the CPR businesses of petroleum, railways, real estate, and hotels into separate public companies to enhance shareholder value. And did it ever! The dividends of the new companies that were created went out to the CPR shareholders who now owned shares in several companies. This unlocked the value that was buried in the CPR, which the company had not been receiving credit for. When this separation was being completed, Bill retired as CEO. He was in his early sixties and certainly could have stayed as CEO for a few more years. I asked him why he didn't.

"Some people stay as CEO too long and lose perspective," he said. "I have had the job long enough and it's time to move on."

What a class act. And what sage, honest, and a truthful statement that was.

Board Strengths: Alignment, Dedication, and Integrity

One of the board's strengths was that some people at one stage or another had been through difficult times building their businesses. So collectively and experientially, the outcomes were effective and the whole board was strong. The board liked the management and each other. The question, of course, is how we should act upon the opportunities that present themselves when relationships are in alignment and supportive.

There was not a director on the United Dominion board who was not tough and experienced, but a gentleman. We were actually looking at an acquisition and when we decided not to go forward, some investment bankers had us in play, which means they went to some other companies and said, "We think you should buy United Dominion."

If there is a transaction, they make huge fees. A good offer was made and another company acquired United Dominion. It was a good run. I thought it was one of the strongest boards I ever sat on.

They were all experienced businessmen: smart, tough, fair, and did not need the board seat for income. They were used to putting management through their paces. They were men of great integrity who said exactly what they thought. The board dinners were interesting because there were lots of great stories and it was a wonderful learning experience for me.

Friends, Board Members, Thoughts, and Reflections

When you lose a good person,
you've lost all that training and institutional memory.

The make-up of people on the boards is interesting because you have people of varied backgrounds and experiences around the table coming together for a common purpose. Sometimes it works well and other times it doesn't. Still throughout all the years I have been on the boards, I have learnt much from all the members of the boards I have served on, I have made valuable friendships, keep them still to this day.

I remember when Brian Mulroney joined the Barrick board, I ran into Peter on Wellington Street and asked him what was new.

He said, "I've invited Brian Mulroney, and I've had thousands of shareholders write in saying they're going to sell their stock."

I asked him why he invited Brian on the board, and he said, "He's the former Prime Minister. He really doesn't have any money."

Well Brian has turned out to be a great director. He's so wired internationally—if you're going to be doing business in this country, he's been a great asset. It's not Brian's fault that the company may be in high-risk areas. He did what he was asked to do and he did a really good job of it.

When Brian left politics, he immediately joined Barrick's board and Peter sent him around the world to talk to Heads of State to convince them to stop selling gold. Given the costs of mining gold at these prices, it's a good buy, which is why the Chinese are looking to buy gold, oil, and strategic metals with their American dollars.

Prime Ministers and Presidents Among Friends

Brian's also a very good friend; he always tells a good story. One of the stories I love is how Brian really supported Nelson Mandela and Mandela's party, the ANC, when Mandela was in jail. When Mandela got out of jail and was on his way to becoming South Africa's first black President, one of the first countries he visited of course was Canada.

He came to see Mulroney in his office, and he said, "Mr. Prime Minister, I would really like to thank you for all the help you gave to our party while I was in jail, and to allow us to eventually succeed in our ambitions."

Brian thanked him very much and just before Mandela left, he said, "You know, I hate to ask you this, but we're a little short. We've got to clean up the finances," he continued, "and we need about $10 million. Do you think you can help us?"

Brian replied, "Well, you know, I guess we could. Sure we'll do that." I guess this was before he was President of South Africa.

Mandela was about half way out the door, he turned around, walked back, and confirmed, "And that'll be US dollars of course."

Brian tells the greatest stories; his memory never stops. He's just a fun guy to be with, and his intentions are always good.

And in honouring first South African President Nelson Mandela:

"There is nothing I fear more than waking up without a program that will help me bring a little happiness to those with no resources, those who are poor, illiterate, and ridden with terminal disease."
Nelson Mandela

The Players Around the Table

So who are the players around the table? Anthony Munk is a really good director; he is a big deep thinker who's involved in so many things elsewhere. He brings another perspective to board meetings. He is always well prepared and asks good questions. Barrick does not have any experienced miners or geological people on the board. Nat Rothschild is Peter

Munk's partner in the Porto Montenegro Yacht Basin. Bill Birchall has been the bookkeeper since day one. Howard Beck has been his lawyer for a very long time, and Howard is a solid citizen and gives him sound advice, but he really doesn't know the mining business. Don Carty is on so many boards—he flits in and out. He's a smart guy, but not really always present because he's so busy. Together with Rob Franklin, I guess you'd call them professional directors. Steve Shapiro from Houston is the chairman of the audit committee, and he's the best I have ever seen.

So you start to look around the table at all the players. Brett Harvey runs a coal mining operation. He tries to get mines he understands, but it's pretty hard to come up against Peter Munk as Aaron Regent found out. Aaron did a terrific job, starting to get them out of Africa and cleaning out a lot of the overhead.

One of the things I did when I took over Placer was to get rid of two floors of management who were blocking decisions. That's exactly what was happening at Barrick. Decisions weren't being made. George Potter was in charge of a project in Peru, Dominican Republic, and a $10,000 decision would have to be held off if he couldn't get in to either those mines for a couple weeks. That would hold up a billion-dollar project. It's crazy because nothing would get done. A lot of the good people left because of the frustration.

At Detour, all the senior people there are from Barrick—every one of them. They're wonderful people and they're building the largest Canadian gold mine, which is going to be ahead of schedule and on budget. But they're Barrick people, and they were trained at Barrick. They should be at Barrick.

They sent good people over to Tanzania, but with these people they lost all the training and institutional memory that they had. They bring them in from Australia and elsewhere and then forget about them. It's no wonder they quit. It's pretty tough going.

Barrick has got some adjustments to make. They have got to get their debt down. Thank goodness they didn't go with Donlin Creek, which was another one they were pushing. I was fighting that. I honestly don't think that Aaron Regent was for the Equinox Copper project in Africa at all. I think the finance committee and Peter and Nat Rothschild seemed to be the big promoters of the deal and that they overbid the Chinese by a substantial amount. I believe that Aaron would have preferred to do the Detour deal, which they had completed the due diligence on because they would be greeted with earnings right away, thereby reducing their gold country risk. They would have also been able to write off a huge amount for tax reasons with another asset in Canada. I was not party to all the discussions because being Co-Chair of Detour I had a conflict of interest. Time will tell. Gold probably still has a lot of luster.

Banks, Brokers, Bonds, and Boards

There are some times when bidding wars escalate prices beyond reason. That's when egos and the investment banks go to work. If a deal does not get done, then the investment banks that may provide fairness opinions and bridge financing do not make their humongous fees.

In the past the commodity prices have sometimes been able to get bad deals back on side. How do you plan for dramatic increases in materials, fuel, taxes, and royalties? That is why ETFs are so popular; they take the risk out. ETFs are Exchange Traded Funds, which are a variation of mutual funds. ETFs are created by financial institutions purchasing blocks of stocks, bonds, or commodities; in this case, gold, which is stored in vaults. When they are instructed to sell and the price is up from your original purchase price, you get the profit less a small fee. If the price is down and you sell, you take the loss plus a small fee. ETFs were not even invented ten years ago. The premise is that mining companies must take a very conservative approach.

Seymour Schulich

Seymour Schulich is one of the world's great people. He is not only successful and generous, but quite humorous as well. Before getting into the mining business, he was the third partner with Beutel Goodman Money Managers in Montreal, where he met a brilliant, extremely funny, and also generous mining engineer—Pierre Lassonde. They left Beutel Goodman to form Euro Nevada and Franco Nevada, a company that initially financed mining companies in Nevada by putting up cash and taking a royalty. These companies made them not only wealthy, but a lot of other people wealthy as well as creating several successful mining companies.

One day Seymour called and told me they were thinking about getting going in Australia and asked if I had any ideas. I gave him the name of Ronny Beaver at the Sydney Rothschild Bank, and told him to use my name, because the chap was a good friend. He knew everything about mining and everyone in mining in Australia. About a year later, I was invited to a company dinner and given one of their famous cowboy belt buckles.

A few years went by and I had to call Seymour. He told me my son Alex in Sudbury worked hard, further commenting that he had called Alex, and he was in his office on a Saturday morning. I asked how he knew that and Seymour said he was a client of Alex's. Alex had never told me this. Alex has a company in the financial planning business.

I did not know what to say to Seymour so I said, "I guess you have to work hard if you have seven children."

I was referring to my son and his family. Seymour cracked up.

Several years went by when I had not seen Seymour until recently when Ned Goodman was being installed into the Mining Hall of Fame, and I thanked Seymour for his thoughtfulness. I had done Seymour a favour, getting him into Australia and putting him in touch with Ronny Beaver in regard to royalties. I have a lot of time for Seymour; I think he's a straight up guy. He's so smart it blows me away. He's a basic guy—I've been fishing with him, and I just enjoy his company. And because I did him a favour, ever since, he's been a client of my son Alex. I didn't ask him to be my son's client, and didn't even know he was for several years. That's the kind of straight-up guy he is.

Ned Goodman

Ned Goodman was the Chairman of the Board of Dundee Realty. I had known Ned for a long time and was involved with him in my Placer days because he had a company called Eskay Creek, which he wanted to sell to Placer Dome. I tried to sell it to our board; my recollection was that we were going to pay about $200 million for it. Ned sent Peter Cole, a member of their board who was well known in the Toronto Banking community and a person I knew very well. Peter Steen was their CEO, who I also knew very well. We used to work out at the Cambridge Club where a lot of business is discussed. I became a member of the Cambridge Club within a few months of it starting and have been a member ever since. Peter Cole and I met and I reported back to the boardroom.

"No goddamn way," they said because they didn't trust Ned Goodman. On and on they went.

Ned sold Eskay Creek to Homestake Mine of South Dakota, which then merged with Barrick mid-2001. Barrick ended up buying Eskay Creek. I don't think Barrick ever made less than $400 million a year on that mine and I think they paid $200 million for it. Not a bad six-month payback. It was the most profitable mine they ever had. Turning that deal down was the dumbest thing in the world. I think if Ned Goodman had been from Vancouver we'd have probably done the deal.

It's interesting how the world goes around because I'm now involved with Ned in a couple of other things. He's invested in a silver, lead, and zinc mining company in Mexico—a company that I'm temporarily running—and we've finally got it turned around. We've had a lot of trouble with water and with management. We've made a lot of changes, and I think we have turned the corner. His advice and counsel are terrific and he's a very good friend.

He's done so much for this country. It's interesting that he doesn't have the Order of Canada. Somebody up in Ottawa must not like him. He has made incredible contributions to Canada in numerous areas. He started an investment school at Concordia University—look at what he's done as Chancellor of Brock University and what he's done in so many other ways. He won this huge award from the Fraser Institute and is in the Mining Hall of Fame. He has founded the Goodman School Of Mines at Laurentian University in Sudbury, where the mission is to be as good as The Colorado School Of Mines. He never stops helping. He does not only help with his intellectual capacity—he's brilliant—but he also helps financially. He writes cheques constantly. He's just a great Canadian. He's the son of immigrants. He is proud of his success, and he's a funny guy. Ned is a good and loyal friend. He's the kind of friend everybody should have. He's very smart, very tough, and he's very straightforward. If you don't want to hear the answer, don't ask the question; he's going to tell you what he thinks. You may not like what he thinks—probably because it's right.

Funny story: Ned had this oil and gas company, and he said to me, "I'm looking for a director. You got any ideas?"

He asked me who when I said yes.

"'Hard as Nails'—tough as bricks—Cam Berry '56," I responded.

He asked, "How the hell do you know him?"

"He graduated with you in 1956 from Westhill High School in Montreal and he was on the football team. When he had a few beers he would tell us how good a ball player he was, hence 'Hard as Nails,'" I continued, "and he went and took geology with you at McGill. He's a fraternity brother and a very good friend of mine."

Cam had been in the oil and gas business forever. He had a company called Camel Oil and Gas. His wife, Eloise, was the daughter of Moose Cryderman, a well-known Sudbury prospector. She trained as a nurse in Montreal, and I think I might have introduced them. Cam was the perfect fit because they had been friends even though all those years Ned hadn't seen him. Now they get together all the time for board meetings. Cam has all kinds of experience—in oil and gas—exactly in the areas that Ned is interested in. It's amazing how these things work.

Conrad Black

I first met Conrad Black at the home of Fred Eaton where we had dinner with Fred's lovely wife Nicky. Conrad was coming up from Sherbrooke, Quebec where he was working on his first newspaper probably to visit his parents and brother. I was in Toronto down from Sudbury on business for Pioneer. After dinner, we adjourned to the library with a lovely fire going and talked politics until the wee hours of the morning. Over the fireplace hung the painting that Fred had purchased from the artist Ken Danby: "The Goaltender." It is of course a favourite of many Canadian hockey fans. It's nice to see that Fred in his typical generous way has donated the painting to the Ontario Gallery of Art, so that many generations of Canadians may enjoy it.

A lot of people know how bright Conrad Black is, but what they don't know is that he has a great sense of humour. I was in Highland Beach Florida with Alan Manzer, one of our employees, visiting some properties we had foreclosed, when I was CEO of ITCO Properties. It was near Palm Beach. So I called Conrad to see if he was available for lunch. He was, and when we went to pick him up, he asked us to join him in an old Lincoln limousine. He told us to sit in the back and he drove with a chauffeur's hat on. He knew the history of every major home and the history of the city, which he explained to us in great detail.

He and I would have lunch at Winston's on Adelaide Street in Toronto about once a month. We paid turn-about and they were long lunches where we talked politics and world events. John Robarts, the seventeenth Premier of Ontario, ate there most days with some of his cabinet members and his friend Joe Barnicke. Doug Creighton, the publisher of the Toronto Sun, and many leading businessmen frequented the restaurant as well. It was the leading restaurant in Toronto at the time and was run by John Arena.

One day we were having lunch, and it was my turn to pay. We were both scotch drinkers and John came by and told Conrad, "I have this great scotch in a pewter bottle worth about $300 per bottle. Would you like to try it?" Conrad responded positively.

John did not offer me a drink. He came back about a half hour later to ask Conrad what he thought. Conrad said he liked it. John told Conrad he would send a case to his house.

"That bastard," I said, "I'm buying lunch and I drink scotch, and he didn't even offer me a taste?"

Conrad sent the case to my house. I was able to get even with John Arena.

It was difficult to get reservations at the restaurant. Sometimes I wanted to entertain people for lunch, so I would have my secretary call to get a table for four, and there would be nothing available! I gave the instruction to have another girl in the office phone over for Fred Eaton and reserve a table for four—no problem! I would arrive a few minutes early and let them know Fred couldn't make it, so I was entertaining his guests and they would ask for me. Of course I told Fred what I was doing.

Monty Black

Monty Black was a wonderful friend of mine. We used to play golf and have dinner together. Our cottages near Beaumaris in Muskoka weren't too far apart, and he and I used to go for an eighteen-hole round at about 7:45 a.m. We'd both take a golf cart each and hustle around the Beaumaris Golf Course so we could play with our wives or whoever later on. If the ball went off the fairway into the bush, you had an option of putting it down right there where you thought it went in and take a stroke, or if you were longer than that looking for your ball, you had to take two strokes. We moved around the golf course pretty quickly.

We had lots of laughs. He had great stories and could see humour in every situation. He was a wonderful chef and we had some great parties. We would have dinner and he'd cook. Of course we had some pretty select cuts of meat ordered from the Dominion store in Bracebridge. Monty was Chairman of Dominion's board, so he would pick the meats up on his way to the cottage.

Monty and Conrad called me to meet with them one day and asked if I'd go in and have a look at Dominion Stores. Their profits and share of market were dropping. Monty was both Chairman and CEO of Dominion Stores, which at the time was the largest supermarket chain in Canada. The company also had a president, who was John Toma. I really didn't want to do it but I liked Monty so much that I did. I knew I was a saw-off. Conrad wanted David Radler, an associate of Conrad's for thirty-six years, to go in, and Monty wasn't a big fan of David Radler and asked me if I would do it. They agreed on me as the guy down the middle. Well, turned out to be an experience I'll never forget. I went in as VP of development. In the ninety days I was there, the CEO never showed up. That was the first problem.

Nevertheless, during that time, a lot of interesting things happened. Very early on they were going to build another store in Timmins and I requested to see the marketing research for this new store in Timmins. They didn't have any. I insisted I'd like to see some, and for them to go out and do a bit of market research. The research showed that instead of having one more store, they should have one less store.

I had a previous run-in with the developer, who as it happened was to be the developer doing the Timmins project. He was also in the vegetable, fruit, and the freezer business. When vegetables came in they were usually put in a large cooler for three days before they go into the stores. Dominion Stores got a brand new cooler building in Ottawa. They never used it. They rented the developer's freezers.

I ran into him a few years previously. Ken McGowen (the Mac of Mac's Milk and Hasty Market) and I were doing a small shopping centre with a grocery store in it in Chelmsford, a town north of Sudbury. We had a deal agreed with Steinberg's, another grocery chain at the time. Jimmy Hinds, a lawyer in Sudbury called to warn me to watch out. Apparently I was going to get a call from this guy—that he was a bad man and he was going to go after that property. He was originally from Sudbury and became a huge developer along with his large fruit and development business. He wound in court in Newmarket on tax evasion and the trial went on for seven years. My recollection is that he was not convicted.

In any event, when this developer called me, he said he would like to take over that property in Chelmsford. He wanted the grocery lease and he would build a Dominion's grocery store. I told him about the agreement with this particular chain, and he commented on the fact that we hadn't registered our title. I asked him how he knew that; apparently he had a lawyer up there look at it. The lawyer was at the registry office looking at the title as we talked on the phone. I told him that was true, but I had given them my word.

Interconnecting Business Partnerships: Ken, George, and a Sense of Humour

Ken McGowen and I had given them our word. And speaking of Ken, one of the most wonderful people in the world, here's a story illustrating his sense of humour: Ken and George Cohon, who were good friends, were also great practical jokers. When Ken turned fifty years old, a Harley Davidson appeared outside his office located across the street from the Manulife Centre in Toronto. A package was delivered to his office with a helmet, big motorcycle leather boots, pants, gloves, and jacket. It just so happened that Ken was going to his first meeting as a new board member of Variety Village.

The meeting was being held at the head office of an insurance office at the top of the Don Valley Parkway. Ken decided to go to the meeting on the motorcycle. He put on all the paraphernalia and headed up there. It was raining buckets. He arrived at the meeting knowing only just one or two of the twenty at the meeting. He took off his gloves, jacket, and helmet and introduced himself, apologizing for being late. Apparently the water was everywhere. Talk about how to make an interesting first impression.

On another occasion, there was a joint board meeting of the Canadian and United States McDonald's board members being held at the McDonald's offices, which were at Yonge Street and St. Clair in Toronto at the time. Ken hired a model to show up half way through the board meeting. She walked in with a baby in her arms, went up to George Cohon, and raised a stink asking how was it that he was not supporting his illegitimate child and what was he going to do about it. Initially everyone was in shock; the Canadian board members were fooled because they all know that George had a lovely wife and family. In fact, George's son is the Commissioner of the Canadian Football League, which has dramatically improved since he has become Commissioner. The hoax was up when Ken started to laugh.

One of George's great lines when asked if he was worried about security around his house in Forest Hill he would respond, "Hell no, I posted a sign saying Fred Eaton lives two doors south."

On yet another occasion, Ken knew that George was having a black tie fundraiser at George's house because he was attending it, and the Shriners Circus was coming to Toronto to Maple Leaf Gardens. Ken had a transport truck loaded with camels, an elephant, and a giraffe start to unload in George's front yard.

George went to Russia after the Cold War and established McDonald's in Russia. I believe it was one of the first large North American companies to establish in Russia. Ken McGowen, who was with him on many of the early trips to Russia, started to import container loads of things like Swiss army knives and small hand tools—things the average Russian was starving for. He noticed that the Russians had gained an appetite for coffee, so he imported tea from India. This business has gone very well.

Ken and I were partners in a small shopping centre development in the Sudbury area, and one day we were having coffee in the coffee shop of the President Hotel, which I owned. He noticed the paper placemats and asked me, "I own a resort in Tahiti. If you advertise my place in Tahiti on your placemats, then I will advertise 'when in Sudbury stay at the President Hotel' on our placemats."

Now seriously, what are the chances of that happening? This is just an example of how Ken thought and his quirky sense of humour.

Ken and George are wonderful examples of very hard working, successful businessmen who took time to have some fun along the way.

Supermarket Capers

In Chelmsford, which is a town near Sudbury, I had given my word to these people and my word was that I meant what I said. This guy decided that was not going to do.

"How do you like your wife?" he asked me.

"Not particularly," I responded, since I was right in the middle of a divorce. I guess he didn't know that.

And then he moved onto the children, "Well how do you like your children?"

I was getting nervous at this time. The next day when I arrived at my office at about 7:00 a.m. the Ontario Provincial Police were standing there and wanted to talk to me about this phone call. I was blown away; they had been listening to the whole call.

When I went into Dominion Stores, I ran into this guy again, and he made me extremely nervous. The COO (Chief Operating Officer) called me down to my office and there he was standing right in front of me. I was told I was stopping this deal going ahead up in Timmins, and he accused me of just being in there as a spy for the Blacks, which I was of course.

I had run into a few other interesting facts regarding the COO's partner in the horse racing business, who was the guy supplying us garbage bags with a huge amount of shelf space in our stores. I also found out coffee making machines were piled up at the cash registers at various stores. The question was, why were they there? I found out they were being sold on behalf of the COO's son. Well, things got pretty tough there, and the police called and warned me I had better watch out. They were listening to phone calls and there were people extremely unhappy with what I was turning over. I wound up with police watching my house, checking under my car in the garage, and up at Dominion Stores' head office.

Lessons in Supermarket Experience

One of the lessons I learned in the supermarket business that was quite interesting: Dominion Stores contemplated going into the bottled water business. They had a big lab and looked at all kinds of bottled water, and they found out a lot of it was contaminated with bacteria. This is a fact that I never forgot. I think the water out of the tap was much better.

I reconnoitered to the Blacks by saying, you know you're not in love with this business, and in the grocery business there's a lot of opportunity for theft. People will slide people cash to get more facings on the shelves, and there were a lot of funny things that used to go on in the grocery business. Galen Weston found that out when he took over his father's business. I don't know what happens today, but there was certainly a lot of cash that used to change hands in those days. I understood that unless you're right on top of it, you're never going to win. The Blacks had an opportunity to sell Dominion Stores to A&P and I recommended they do that. That's exactly what they did.

It was an interesting experience, and one I wouldn't want to repeat. Occasionally I would walk into a restaurant in Toronto and see that real estate developer and I would just turn around and walk out. He made me extremely nervous. I never wanted to see him, and to this day I'm a bit nervous; but I guess he's got other things he'd rather worry about than me. It was very stressful at the time.

Jimmy Connacher

Jimmy Connacher is a great friend who changed the whole way capital was raised. He was from Winnipeg and founded Gordon Capital. They were the founders of the "The Bought Deal"—in other words, if you wanted to raise $500 million they took it all and laid it off. They took all the risk. Previously if you were looking for money, you had to convince several banks to take a piece to get to the number you needed. Jimmy was very successful as were his employees, and I know that when I was trying to raise money for a good cause, I could always count on him and his wife Mary.

Jimmy and I share the same birthday—same day, month, and year. So every year I find out where he is going to be on January 31. I have found him in Hawaii, Boston, New York, or at his farm in Vermont. This has been going on for many years. I would find out from his secretary, so the call was always a surprise.

One year I was in Vero Beach Florida at Windsor, Galen Weston's development, which I believe is the most beautiful development in Florida. At the time I had a house there. My next-door neighbour was Andre Demerais whose father and mother were from Sudbury, and is married to our former Prime Minister Jean Chretien's daughter. On January 30 I was having dinner at the Beach Club, and the Prime Minister and his wife and some friends were at the next table. I went over, excused and introduced myself, and I told him that it was Jimmy's birthday the next day. He asked me how I knew and I told him. I knew that when the Prime Minister was out of politics he worked for Gordon Capital. He asked me to send over Jim's phone number, which I did. I waited until late in the day on January 31 to phone Jim and wished him happy birthday.

"You will never guess who called me today to wish me happy birthday," he told me. I told him it was the Prime Minister.

Eric Sprott

I have mentioned Ned Goodman and Seymour Schulich and I would also like to mention Eric Sprott, who is another risk-taker and supporter of junior mining companies. Eric held the position of CEO of Sprott Group of Companies and stepped down to assume the position of Chairman of Sprott and CIO (Chief Investment Officer) of Sprott Asset Management, a large corporation in the investment industry, asset and wealth management and private equity and debt and physical bullion, and traded on the Toronto Stock Exchange. Eric is not afraid to invest risk capital and he does not walk away if things get off the track or take longer than expected. He is a straight-up guy and expects you to be as well. He is exceptionally bright and knowledgeable.

Eric has been extremely generous: as well as founding the Sprott School of Business at Carleton University in Ottawa, he makes very generous donations to the University Health Network in Toronto.

When I took over as temporary CEO of Excellon Resources, the mine was full of water to the surface; we had no money and we had debts. I told Eric we had the richest ore body in Mexico but we needed $12 million. I told him the board would invest, and that Ned Goodman was investing.

"Count me in," he said.

John Ing of Maison Placements put the deal together. Eric likes to be kept up to date and so far it has been a good investment. It is a pleasure to go to his office and see his art and coin collection and spend time with him because he is so bright and knowledgeable on so many subjects.

Peter Brown

The high-risk taker in the venture capital business who really able to get junior mining companies up and running, which created a lot of head-office jobs for mining companies in Vancouver, is Peter Brown. He was the Founder of the Canaccord Genuity Group Inc. in 1968, and today is the Honourary Chairman with the corporation operating as Canada's largest independent investment dealer both at home and worldwide with sixty offices. Peter served on a number of private sector and crown corporations and is currently Chairman of the Board for the Fraser Institute and Vice Chair of the Investment Industry Association.

He is blunt, flamboyant, and driven. Peter is a deal maker and lots of fun. He is a mover and shaker and his nickname is "Peter Rabbit." Peter has retired and now focuses on philanthropic activities.

CHAPTER 14

More about Corporate Directors and Board Governance

I do think that there should be more women on boards.

Some companies have age limits for directors, which range from sixty to seventy-five years of age. In the Dome Mines Group of Companies we had two—what one would call senior directors. One senior director was Dr. Bill James Sr., who had been involved in mining all his adult life, and who was respected in the entire mining community. I believe he was ninety when he decided to retire from the Board of Directors of Dome Mines. His son Bill Jr., a mining engineer, was CEO of Falconbridge Mines—20 percent of which Dome Mines owned at the time.

Another person on the board was Jim Redpath, who I believe retired from the board at eighty-eight years old. He had run many mining operations; you just couldn't buy that kind of wisdom or experience. I had gone to McGill with Jim's son before I switched out of geology. After leaving McGill, Jim Jr. founded Redpath Mining, which is one of the largest mining contractors in the world. The company is still building large mines for clients all over the world.

When talking of old directors, we had a board dinner for Alan Lambert who had retired several years before as CEO of the TD Bank at the Toronto Club. He was retiring from the Board of Dome Mines.

Towards the end of the dinner Bill James Jr., the CEO of Falconbridge, rose to speak and he said, "Alan, you had better join our board as you are just getting to the age we like our directors. Like my father who is over ninety, and like Marsh Cooper, Bill James Jr.'s predecessor at Falconbridge."

Falconbridge was running large mining operations in Sudbury and the Dominican Republic. Alan graciously accepted. After dinner, Bill and I were standing on Wellington Street waiting for taxis.

I commented to him, "Bill, you are one of the most generous people I know."

"Why do you say that?" he responded.

"Because you are worried about a hostile takeover by Noranda," I stated, "which was controlled by Brascan. Alan is Chairman of Brascan, and the reason he is probably retiring from Dome is because Dome Mines have a 20 percent interest in Falconbridge and he has a conflict of interest."

"Why did you not say something?" Bill asked.

I replied, "Because I didn't know you were going to invite him on the Board of Falconbridge."

Women and Active Participation

My view is the governance committee of a board should review every board member's participation on an annual basis. It would be a peer review done through a lawyer's office, so no one should know what a board member said about them. This system seems to work. If a board member needs to contribute more, or be better prepared for meetings, he or she should be told. And if they are not prepared to change, they should not be put up for re-election.

I do think that there should be more women on boards. I also believe it is starting to happen. For example, Dundee Industrial REIT has just appointed a female to the board: Chair Joanne Ferstman. I have served on a board with her for about ten years and she will be an excellent chair. The chair of the audit committee is also female and extremely well qualified. Earlier, I mentioned QLT, a Vancouver Company for about twenty-four years. I was on their board. They discovered Visudyne, a drug that was developed with the hope of supporting clearing issues of Age Macular Degeneration. For most of the time, Dr. Julia Levy was on the board, and for about eight years she was the CEO. The female money managers across North America followed the company and supported the stock.

Considering the Shareholders

On boards not acting in the interests of the shareholders: one of the great Canadian mining tragedies is that Inco (now Vale), Falconbridge, and now Xstrata Nickel, were never put together in Sudbury Ontario. When I was a kid, there was thirty years worth of reserves. Yet, now over seventy years later, there are still thirty years of reserves. The synergies that would have been achieved would have made it probably the most profitable mining venture in the world. The benefits should have then been dividends put out to the shareholders.

During World War II, they were actually afraid the Sudbury operations might be sabotaged, because when nickel is added to steel, it makes it much harder for armaments for tanks and field artillery.

Over the years, rumour had it that Scott Hand, a lawyer and CEO of Inco, liked his job, and so did the board—and they could never get together. Inco had originally put in an offer to acquire Falconbridge in 2006 for $61.04 in a combination of both cash and shares. Xstrata came in with a cash proposal for Falconbridge for C$52.50 per share, increasing the offer about a month later to $59.00 per share—total value of approximately C$22.5 billion. The Swiss company Xstrata became the new owners of Falconbridge, and Brazilian company Vale acquired Inco for $18.9 billion, paying shareholders $17.7 billion with Inco's debt of $1.2 billion being absorbed. The Inco purchase came to be known as the largest purchase by a Brazilian company. Those companies were of great help to Laurentian University, Cambrian College, and many other worth ventures that will over time be reduced and dry up. Major companies always make their major donations in the country where the head office is.

Corporate Compensation

By and large, senior corporate management compensation is far too high. This is a result of several years of bad governance by the boards and compensation committees. In many cases, senior management hire a compensation firm. First of all, if management hires them this is already a conflict of interest. Compensation firms know if they do not come up with good numbers from the employee's point of view, they will not likely be retained again. They tend from my experience to select from the highest comparable in the industry and ignore the others. I refer to these compensation firms as "rachet-and-rachet."

In my view, the corporate executives are overpaid by an incredible amount reaching into the billions of dollars. If a senior executive does a spectacular job, they can be paid a one-time bonus; after all, if the people down below these senior executives are not doing a good job, it is not likely the company is going to do well. There is no way the small time investor can change this process and get those executives who are way overpaid under control; however, the pension fund and other large fund managers can. They have a fiduciary responsibility to do so. Senior executives as a collective group are paid billions—maybe hundreds of billions more than they should at a time when many pension plans are being underfunded with the result that not enough money will be available for employees when they retire several years from now. The overpayment is the shareholders money that could affect the company earnings and stock price, or reduce dividends—or both. An activist group has recently noted that Barrick's non-executive chairman along with three non-executive chairmen plus the directors receive more than the shareholders do in dividends. I would say this situation is grossly out of balance; benefiting individual pockets over shareholder rights.

I was told of a CEO who put his company in play even though the board thought it was the wrong time. He did it anyway. He did it because he was about to retire and go on pension. By selling the company, it brought the change of control policy into play; therefore, he received the average of his last three years pay and bonus. Then he went on pension. This happens from time to time, which may be in the best interests of the CEO, but not the shareholders. If an executive is fired with cause they should not receive a golden parachute. That is a waste of shareholders' money.

It is my view that the pension and major mutual funds push for an independent agency to approve the compensation, just like they do for credit ratings—for example, Moody's (the bond credit rating service), or the Dow (stock market index). Furthermore, in my opinion, bad or incompetent corporate governance by companies is bringing this type of control upon themselves, and we are well past the time to do something about it.

Young Entrepreneurs

You can start a business at any age, and many people have started businesses while still in high school. Years ago I had invited Riki Gougeon and Ron Christie, manager of the Lands and Forests, for northern Ontario based in Sudbury (now called the Ministry of Natural Resources or MNR), to hunt pheasant on Griffith Island, an island off the Bruce Peninsula near Wiarton, Ontario. General Motors originally owned the island to entertain major clients, until Ralph Nader, a shareholder activist, heard and complained about it; General Motors then decided to sell the island.

Griffith Island was purchased to run as a business. You could either land a small plane on the island, or travel to the island in a large boat, manufactured by General Motors, and which was about a twenty-minute crossing. As a commercial operation it did not work. It was set up for pheasant, turkey, and Hungarian partridge shooting. It also had skeet and trap facilities with wonderful accommodation, a big fireplace, and a sauna. After about two years of commercial operation, John Robarts, then Premier of Ontario, decided along with Ernie Jackson (an insurance agent from London Ontario), to run it as a private club.

Ernie called a bunch of his friends: Bruce McLaughlin, a real estate developer from Mississauga; Dave Campbell who owned Disher Ferrand—a road builder; Fred Eaton; Cal Kerr, who sold Pioneer Rock Crushers; Charlie Armstrong from Brampton who owned Armbro Brothers, a road building contractor; George Seegmiller from Kitchener, who owned a road building and sewer construction firm; Bob Fasken, CEO of the mining company that became Barrick Gold; and a few others to each put in $20,000 and buy the club. I went up shooting with Fred Eaton, and he "put the arm on" for me to join about a year later.

In any event, I had decided to invite Ron Christie down from Sudbury to shoot. He had invited me to shoot at his duck club on Lake Erie. I asked him if my friend Riki Gougeon, whom he did not know, could drive from Sudbury with him to Griffith. He said no problem. We had a good shoot and at dinner Ron mentioned that Lands and Forests were forcing the lumber, paper, and mining timber companies to replace each tree they cut with two seedlings. When Riki returned home, he told his children, who were then in about grade ten, eleven, and twelve, (in those days high school went to grade thirteen), that they should form a company and bid on the contract, which was paid for by the company doing the cutting but managed by the Lands and Forests department. The work was all piecework, and they were to have crews around the northern part of the province.

They were successful with their bid, and needed stoves, tents, dishes, pots pans, and a couple of trucks. They went to the Toronto Dominion Bank and Hugh Fox the manager said, "Your dad will have to sign the loan."

Michael, Jill, and Angela remonstrated, "No way. He will take a piece of the business."

Hugh called Riki to guarantee the loan. Riki said, "Only if I get a piece of the business," and then went on questioning, "Do you think my children are going to have a bad credit rating over a $10 or $15 thousand dollar loan?"

The banker finally agreed and lent them the money. Riki and I had a partner in land and building deals—an ex-pro-hockey player, Leo Gasparini—and he personally leased them some old trucks with lifts on the back.

Their company was called A & M Tree Planting, and there are many people who put themselves through university working for that company. Since the work was piecework, they worked from dawn to dusk Saturdays, Sundays, nights, and holidays. Those Gougeon children were very ambitious. Both Riki and his daughter Angela were on the Canadian Ski team, and Jill met her future husband fundraising for the team. The children were all great skiers, having attended a ski academy in the States for most of their high school years. With three sisters, Michael was always very quiet. He decided he did not want to go to college, but wanted instead to get into the car business. With that they sold the business, and he bought a car dealership in Elliot Lake with his money and a loan from his sister Angela, whom he quickly repaid. Michael now has four car dealerships. Last summer, Michael's sixteen-year-old son Matt flew a plane solo across Canada.

The point of the story is that these kids were hardly graduated from high school, and at today's rates all had about $500,000 each in their pocket. This story just proves with a good idea and some drive, you can control your own future. They certainly worked hard and industriously. We all know many successful businessmen who never went to college. Instead, they had a passion or burning desire to apply themselves in their own unique way, creating and building businesses that would ultimately reward their entrepreneurial spirit, their personal talents, and their abilities. The Gougeon childrens' success came from the solid foundation of their family's encouragement and support to be fearless, excel wherever they wished to channel their passion and energy, and have a big-picture outlook—appreciating what you have and how you can give back. Obviously it worked, especially when so many benefitted from the opportunity to work in this company in order to facilitate their personal endeavours.

Speaking personally, my entrepreneurial drive started at a young age as I have documented earlier. With the dogged determination to succeed and make my way in the world—in part instilled and inspired by my father's values and hard-work-pays ethics, but also because back in the day, you had to create your own fortune or luck—or just plain support yourself if you wanted to get anywhere in life. It meant putting aside any fears or apprehensions and just getting out there and on with it. Then you needed to be resourceful, be on the lookout to pick-up opportunities as they came your way, and have the stamina to run with them—give it your all. Now of course there are so many government jobs, and many people are happy to get their indexed pensions and accumulated sick leave.

Personal values have not changed since that time for success to come your way. You still need to be resourceful, face your own fears, and be determined and passionate to make a difference not only in your life, but for the greater good of the community in which you live, or even farther afield. However, the instant gratification—the accepted norm today—has bred a "take-for-granted" attitude by our very young generations; perhaps a contributory factor for the lack of drive and direction in the younger populace—generally speaking. If entrepreneurial success seems elusive, it is only in the mind of the beholder. We all have the same opportunity to make something of our lives, and in addition desire and having the means to give back to our communities. In a way it's like feeding the circle: giving back to that which has pointed you in the direction and on the path to success and financial freedom. And on it goes.

Enjoying Good Business Savvy and Strategies

One thing I know about business is that if you have that edge, the savvy, or good business sense combined with a sensible strategy, you do not need to build or work a large company, or be a well paid professional to have a wonderful lifestyle. After all, it's the balance and enjoyment in life that a good lifestyle brings that we are really want and need at the end of the day.

Rick and Laura Scully happened to be Don Cherry of hockey fame's partner in Don Cherry's twenty-eight restaurants and sports bars across the county. The Scullys lived in Toronto at the time and went up to Muskoka for a vacation in 1993. They fell in love with the area and the lifestyle. Since they were both excellent golfers, they decided to move up to Muskoka full time in 1996 where they opened a REMAX real estate office. After a couple of years, Rick decided he no longer wanted to be a broker, preferring to be a REALTOR®. Being a broker was a pain in the ass, and he did not want the liability nor manage other people. He sold the brokerage and became a REALTOR®—and a good one at that. Out of 18,000 fellow REMAX reps across Canada, Rick was just beaten to being the top representative by a fellow in Vancouver selling condos to the Chinese.

Harvey Kalles was his next stop. It was Scully's intention to align himself with this high-end brokerage out of Toronto so he could focus on high-end clients. I have bought cottages through Rick and I asked him why he has done so well.

"Because I service my clients to death," he replied. "If you need a plumber or electrician at 11:00 p.m. I will find them. I take every call no matter when."

Shelly in the office answers the phone and Don Matthews goes ahead of time to turn the lights on to make sure everything is presentable before Rick gets there with the clients. He then turns the lights off after the showing. Having someone do this for Rick avoids wasting both his and the clients time. That way he can show them more cottages. The Scullys leave Canada every October to go on a cruise and then go to their home in Fort Myers. They return to Canada at the end of April.

About four or five years ago they sold their interest in Don Cherry's restaurant business as did Don. Every second year they build a cottage. Laura is the general contractor and I have to say an exquisite decorator. They live in the cottage for a year. That way they can make a tax-free profit on the sale of the property. I asked how he was doing this year and he told me on September 8 he had sold $95 million worth in cottages. He also plays golf about five times a week. What a lifestyle! With a well thought out strategy and hard work you can do very well.

Board of Director Dynamics

With respect to directors, there are many who are very experienced and who know a lot and work hard at being a director. They often make a significant contribution and go way above and beyond the call of duty for the shareholders.

Boards of directors are intriguing entities—of course, I've served on many of them. Some good, some not so good, some have stunk. When I originally started sitting on boards of directors they weren't paid very much, it was more of an honorarium. But, the workload on directors seemed to mount up.

Directors really have to scrutinize management, see that goals are set and achieved, capital expenditures are approved, and that the rationalization is correct. A lot of the people on the board, particularly in mining, don't have the faintest clue as to what the hell is going on. They don't bother going out to see the mines and the smelters, or even talk to the people and get a sense of the business the company is in. I have mentioned this issue a number of times, and you can tell I am passionate about driving this point home. A lot of directors are lawyers and accountants, which sometimes is useful. Certainly the accountants on the audit committee are quite useful. There are a lot of directors around who don't make a contribution.

Active Communication

The funny thing about directors is the person you tend to sit next to is always the same person you sit next to in the same position around the board table, and it becomes a bit of a club. You get to know everybody and look forward to the meetings and to seeing the people. Sometimes there are phone calls back and forth between meetings if there are matters concerning directors. Directors are playing a much more active role these days. They're being held much more responsible and accountable as they should be.

It's interesting to note that when a company gets off the track, you never see them publish the board of directors in the papers. I think they should. I don't know why the business papers don't do that. If a company's in trouble they may talk about the board, but they never say whom they are, which is public information in any event. I've never understood why. I think that would make directors pay a bit more attention to doing the right job. In my view, I don't see that happening to the extent that it should.

Owning Stock, Discipline, Accountability

I've mentioned earlier that directors should always own stock, and if they don't initially, they should take all their fees in the stock and DSU (Deferred Stock Units). You can set them aside and build them up. You pay no tax. You pay tax when they're sold. At least the money coming in is set aside over there, and you start to share the interest of the shareholders in the company.

In Canada of course, we have thousands of junior mining companies that are Canada based usually in Toronto or Vancouver. A lot of them aren't operating or exploring in Canada, and a great deal of the money has not been spent wisely—in many cases by overpaid management. It's time to have more discipline in all the financial aspects including the treasuries of these companies to make sure the money is being properly spent, and properly accounted for. I believe the Ontario Securities Commission is underfunded. I'm not sure they have enough of the right people to monitor the activities of some of all these companies.

Dedicated Directors

With respect to directors, there are many who are very experienced who know a lot and work hard at being a director. They often make a significant contribution and go way above and beyond the call of duty for the shareholders. Any shareholders who don't think that directors should be properly paid are absolutely wrong. Why should a shareholder benefit from the work of a director? Some of the books these directors are given for board meetings now are three inches thick, and they've got to spend a lot of time wading through them. Meetings are often quite inconvenient. Sometimes directors are called on short notice and meetings last a long time. Good directors push other commitments around to attend meetings to make sure they're there. Board dinners are often held the evening before board meetings. Sometimes senior management is invited and sometimes they are not.

I've worked hard over the years to attend most of the meetings in person, and if not, occasionally I've had to attend by phone. Some days we'd have phone meetings to verify and final approve a lot of the work already been done in a meeting session we'd all attended. In some instances it might have been a situation that needed a bit more information, and when we got that information we'd have a phone meeting to agree or to disagree about it. It has come to recognition that the chairmen of the various committees generally have a lot of extra work, particularly the chairman of audit committees. The result is that they receive additional compensation.

Good CEOs

As with everything in life, experience is the greatest teacher. We hopefully learn from our mistakes and failures, and even our successes.

What makes a good Chief Executive Officer of a company, or a not-for-profit organization, in my opinion? The best CEOs I have observed over the years have most of the following qualities:

1. Very bright with an overabundance of common sense.

2. Extremely hard working and focused.

3. A clear vision and strategy.

4. Not afraid to make tough decisions.

5. A bit of "prick" in them.

6. An overabundance of integrity.

7. A certain degree of insecurity that powers them up to exceed.

8. Generally well liked and respected by their peers and senior employees.

9. Anticipating potential problems rather than just reacting to them.

10. Ability to stay calm and focused while working through challenges.

11. Ability to delegate to others and to be a mentor to them.

12. Be able to fire others if they do not perform to the standards the CEO thinks and feels the job requires.

13. Ask the people who work with them a lot of questions and listen to the answers.

14. Have a good working relationship with the board of directors, use them as a resource, and seek their advice even between meetings if they can help clarify their thinking.

One thing is for sure: age is not a draw back. The examples are of Philip Orsino, starting to build Masonite International in his mid-twenties, and who is currently building Jeld-Wen into the largest, and I am sure most profitable, window and door company in the world. Michael Cooper built four very large companies starting in his early thirties: Dundee Realty, a large real estate development company; Dundee REIT, a large office REIT company; Dundee Industrial REIT, an industrial REIT company; and Dundee International REIT, a REIT operating in Europe. These are large profitable, extremely successful companies; three are public and one private, and the shareholders of the public vehicles have done and are doing quite well.

By the time this book is published, Brendan Cahill will be the CEO of Excellon Resource's silver, lead and zinc company in Mexico. Brendan has been the President of Excellon for the past eight months, and he is developing a corporate strategy to build a major company.

The one common thread with the three individuals above is that they all had mentors who they could run to and who they could go to for advice.

Good Corporate Governance

The makings of a good corporate director: There are directors' courses now taught by organizations and universities. Unless the people teaching the courses have a great deal of experience being a director, I am not sure they understand what the qualities of a good director are. On the corporate or not-for-profit boards that I have sat on, the best directors have most of the same characteristics as mentioned above.

Builders from small beginnings up: The best directors have started companies or started in small companies. They have built companies up, had to meet payrolls when cash was short because it was being used to finance growth, and they have experienced hard times as CEOs or senior officers in a company.

Ernest desire to be of service: Good directors have accepted a board appointment because they are interested in the company and perhaps the other board members, but not because they need the money or prestige.

Stating the truth where truth needs to be stated: Directors are not afraid to state an opinion, even if it might lead to not being re-elected to the board. They are unafraid of creating a situation where they would be too uncomfortable to stay.

Desire to fully understand all aspects of an industry: For CEOs, even from another industry, it can be a good learning experience to see how a company, even in a different business, operates and arrives at decisions.

Basic good values: A good director must have integrity and the courage to state what they really feel on an issue.

Understanding the power of working collaboratively: Directors should be open and willing to work with other company directors—considering team players all have their own perspectives on issues.

Resourceful: Directors often have contacts in other companies. They can be a good resource person when recruiting executives, and through their contacts in checking out a potential candidate for a job or position. They are often able, through their experience, to suggest business opportunities to the companies they are on the board of.

At ease in drawing upon and applying their skill sets: Good directors have a great deal of experience and wisdom and are able to question the company executives and point out potential problems.

Have a global vision and workable, practical strategies to steer through issues: Directors have vision, understanding, and foresight for future arising potential issues; they determine the best direction and course of action required in the highest interests of the company or corporation.

Holds command and consideration of proceedings at hand: A director should insist that before board meetings start and at the end of a board meeting that management and any conflicted directors are excused, so that sensitive items can be raised that might not be dealt with if management were in the room. After the meeting, an independent director should report back to the CEO any concerns or thoughts the independent directors had.

Hold due consideration to avoid conflicts of interest based on circumstance: The directors should insist that the CEO and chairman's job be separate. There are certain times when this may not be practical, for example, when the CEO is fired or quits, and the chairman may assume the CEO role for a short term.

Ability to create board structure based on what is relative and pragmatic: A director is responsible to see that the right boards and committees are set up with a knowledgeable chairman and committee members. It seems to me that these days the executive compensation is far too generous. The compensation committee should hire its own advisers who should not be hired by management. I refer to these consultants as "ratchet-and-ratchet" because they seem to pick comparative companies on the high end. That includes salaries, bonuses, and options.

Taking responsibility over approval and dispersal of donations: Companies should have a board committee approve donations. Most do not have one. You often see the CEO donate a large sum of money in the city where he or she is located and where the head office is. It clearly gets them invited to major social events. Sometimes it's important to give in areas where their plants are.

Integrity over shareholder responsibility: As Fred Eaton once said to me, "You know, Peter, it's the shareholder's money. It should be dividend out, and the shareholders can give it away." This is an interesting thought from a very generous man who has given to and raised money for many good causes.

Makes an effort to be present and prepared: If a director is missing meetings, arrives unprepared, not having read the material, or does not visit the operations, then he or she should not be reappointed to the board.

Committed to investing in the company: *Directors these days are generally* well paid unless it's a junior company, where they're given options, and if the company does well they make some money. Therefore they should be prepared to have some money invested in the company over time. It's known as having "skin in the game." If they do not have the money initially, they should take their board fees in DSUs (Deferred Stock Option Units) at least until a predetermined ownership level is reached. They receive these units instead of board fees and if they go up, they and the shareholders have done well. When you leave the board, the units are sold at that time and that's when you pay the income tax.

Enquiring, interested, and informed: It's interesting that over the years I am unable to recall fund managers and investors asking about the board. That is about to change, and it should. Of course, there is now a great deal of information about companies on their web pages.

Holds attention and is focused: A good board chairman is important. In this area, experience from having been on many boards helps from my observation. Board meetings should be focused on things that are important, or will become important. Some board members get off on topics that are not all that relevant, and some just like to hear themselves talk. A good chair has the respect of the board and will focus the board on the important issues, making sure that they are fully discussed. These days board members often have iPads in front of them, and if things are drifting, they may start reading emails, which is a huge distraction and disrespectful to the proceedings at hand.

Exercises discernment: The board governance committee has the responsibility to remove and replace someone on the board who is not making a contribution to the company and the interests of the shareholders'. The governance committee must check out the references of a potential director prior to them coming on board.

As with everything in life, experience is the greatest teacher. We learn from one another: we are each others' teachers. When experience is varied, well absorbed and integrated, our skill sets are that much more engrained and strengthened. These values, successes, failures, attributes, focused and agreed-upon goals, and open-ended, fair, and honest communication through relationships carry us forward in any and all situations.

Good Old Fashioned Values, Morals, and Ethics

"I am sure that in estimating every man's value either in private or public life, a pure integrity is the quality we take first into calculation, and that learning and talents are only the second."
Thomas Jefferson

In my view, many directors only want the status and the income. And sometimes if you want to stay on the board, you had better not rock the boat. With that, *truth* is fundamental—it is foundational for why one embarks on any course of action in business and life. No matter which side of the table the individuals sit or where they are coming from, it's important to consciously understand motivation and actions.

Examine your reasons why you wish to engage in something: purchase a business, become a board member. Ask yourself not once, twice, but numerous times delving deeper to uncover your core motivation. Analyze this motivation. Check the pros and cons relative to the strength of your passion. How deeply do they synchronize with your why? This process can help you in your decision-making process.

The core reason for doing anything is cemented in positive intentions, which hold strong and true in any situation.

Open transparent actions create teachable, demonstrable leadership skills to directors' peers. Action speaks louder than words. We set the example to up-and-coming generations of directors, board members, investors, and shareholders.

Accountability is ultimately a personal pre-requisite, also to employees, local communities, shareholders, and public at large.

Working cohesively for the highest and greater good of the company is paramount. Keeping alliances strong and active is also important. You never know from which corner your connections will stand you in good stead. Experience becomes the master of teachers.

Relationship development 101: In many of my experiences with numerous people, each has brought to the table their best and in some cases their worst. I guess in the great world of business and in life this is to be expected. What makes the boardroom an interesting experience is the collage of personalities. The question begs: how do personal and collective relationships and thus situations around the boardroom table get ironed out?

1. Take the time in hindsight to learn from your experience with relationships and situations. Acknowledging perspectives of past failures in both places you on the healthy road towards accumulating successful, cordial friendships, working relationships, and workable situations.

2. Purposefully continue to work step-by-step pushing toward your vision. Enjoy the process.

3. Conviction of your goals strengthens and encourages you to traverse chasms, realities of the highs and lows, and grow companies with confidence in a cohesive fashion.

Constantly reevaluate projected targets and goals, stay on task, and be focused; diligence is key. Around the board table unity as an expression of purpose is a powerful motivating force. It needs to be initially agreed and acted upon in all board experiences. In some cases, directors hold office in absentia. Full participation allows the load to be equally shared and is more impactful.

Courage and conviction gets to be called upon now and then. If something is not working, examine probable causes with reason, conscionable logic, perhaps gut instinct, and take courage to cut your losses and walk while you can.

The win-win principle applied across boardroom tables and everywhere else in life results in perfect scenarios to everyone's benefit. What benefits and profits one will be bound to benefit and profit the other. This dynamic ensures people walk away from the table happy in knowing they have achieved or acquired something great.

Learn to care: Care about the company, care about the employees, and care about the shareholders.

Social responsibility should be taught in business schools and directors' courses. Students going out into the working world should be prepared to serve on not-for-profit boards and donate to worthy causes. The Jewish community does this so well. They do not restrict their large donations to Jewish organizations, but to community needs as a whole.

Give of your time. Give of your energy, basic compassion, and humanity, and make a commitment to co-create a difference in this world.

"There is not a man of us who does not at times need a helping hand to be stretched out to him, and then shame upon him who will not stretch out the helping hand to his brother."
Theodore Roosevelt

"You have not lived today until you have done something for someone who can never repay you."
John Bunyan

"For attractive lips, speak words of kindness.
For lovely eyes, seek out the good in people.
For a slim figure, share your food with the hungry.
For beautiful hair, let a child run their fingers through it once a day.
For poise, walk with the knowledge that you never walk alone.
People, more than things, have to be restored, renewed, revived, reclaimed,
and redeemed.
Remember, if you ever need a helping hand, you will find one at the end of
each of your arms.
As you grow older, you will discover that you have two hands:
one for helping yourself and the other for helping others."
Sam Levenson

PART SIX

CHAPTER 15

Early Days and Family Members

People tended to help each other above and beyond the call of duty.

I have taken the liberty to share my life with you starting from when I left University and got my introduction and start to corporate working experience at Seagram's in Montreal. Growing up in northern Ontario afforded me many an opportunity to make of my life what I would or could. The fifty-three years or so that I have been involved in business and the corporate world are important. The stories I have highlighted and endeavoured to convey specific messages and guiding corporate wisdom straight from the boardroom table were essentially attributable to what I had learned from my upbringing. Be it my values, ethics, and morality, or just the will and determination to committed, self-responsible, and dedicated hard work.

Reading about my family background, the community backdrop of Sudbury, Copper Cliff, and generally developing life in northern Ontario from the 1930s onwards, will give you more of a perspective—a taste of how I came to be involved in the corporate world, particularly in mining, and the not-for-profit sector. Giving back as much as I was able to receive out of the dividends of working corporately, so to speak.

The expression "humble beginnings" is quite apt here. My parents instilled in me a wonderful attitude and appreciation for life, and I still to this day wish to stress the importance of giving back to the community without any expectation of receiving for your voluntary efforts. I am both happy and proud to share this part of my life story with you now, as well as to introduce to you those friends, associates, and individuals who made life what it was in that era, coming through the war years, and then dedicating and employing much business savvy in developing Canada to what it is today.

The backdrop to my birth on 31 January 1937 was a modest apartment up on Mackenzie Street in Sudbury, northern Ontario. My mother Marguerite, whose maiden name was Fortier from Pembroke Ontario, had trained in Sudbury as a nurse at Saint Joseph's—a French Catholic Hospital. Born on my father's birthday, a chicken pox or small pox outbreak at the hospital at the time was the reason for babies being born at home. They assumed that being born at home was a safer choice except for the fact Doctor Lively, who was in attendance and my father celebrated my mother's labour pangs downing liquor. You might appreciate how I made my entry into the world if you can picture this scenario. My mother was very small at little over five foot tall, weighing about ninety-eight pounds—in stark contrast to my father, Alexander Davidson, who was about six foot five, and a big, tall, thin chap. She had a hard time with my delivery considering I was also a big baby. By the time I was born, both my father and the doctor had too much to drink and were clean passed out. I ended up being delivered by Gertie Boiven, my mother's roommate in nursing at St. Joseph's Hospital in Sudbury. Gertie later became Gertie Edward, my future mother-in-law, and I have to thank her for my safe delivery.

I have two siblings: one sister who is eleven months younger and another sister ten years younger than myself. My older sister went away to school in Pembroke Ontario—the same convent my mother went to. I was not home much while my younger sister was growing up; so neither were a big part of my life.

My mother came from a family of nine. She and her twin sister were the eighth and ninth—they were born when my grandmother was fifty. The story goes that when she was picking out her wedding dress with one of her elder sisters, the clerk in the store wondered out loud what her "mother" thought of the dress, but of course, it was my mother's sister.

Large families, being the norm in those times, were a contributing factor to the growth of the smaller communities located further out from the bustling urban centers. Everyone in the family was expected to participate in supporting the family in one way or another, from carrying out chores to getting out into the world at tender ages to learn the value of the dollar and what it took to earn it. You could describe it as a cohesive pooling together of energy, making the best to suit each family's particular situation in trying to make ends meet.

My father, Alexander Davidson Crossgrove, was the youngest of a family of eight children. Three died of childhood diseases in Scotland, and one died in Canada. My father came with his family when he was about six or seven months old and was raised in Copper Cliff. His father had been brought out from Scotland as an engineer. Inco, which as mentioned stood for International Nickel Company, and is now Vale, required an engineer be on hand for power plants. That was the law in those days. So they recruited my grandfather, who at the time was a stationary engineer on the ocean liners going back and forth across the Atlantic.

My Crossgrove grandparents lived at Clarabelle Lake by the time I was a young lad. Clarabelle Lake was about three miles out of Copper Cliff where the mining company had built a few residences on a lake on top of a hill above the town. When my father was a child it was a beautiful area. He went to public school in Copper Cliff, and high school in Sudbury since there was not a high school in Copper Cliff. He travelled by streetcar to Sudbury. It was a three- or four-mile walk to the streetcar, and the family home was on top of a large hill on Clarabelle Lake. The terrain sported some large hills. People often forget that the Sudbury area is in the Laurentians. At that time, the lake was wooded and quite lovely. This all changed soon enough.

After high school, my father went to the University of Toronto where he studied for a Bachelor of Commerce. There he played for the basketball team and was intercollegiate high jump champion. When he returned to Copper Cliff, he played in the fastball league as a catcher. Their best pitcher was Bill Durnan, who played as the ambidextrous goaltender for the Montreal Canadiens in the winter and inducted to the Hockey Hall of Fame in 1964.

My father went to work in the industrial relations and personnel department at International Nickel Company, and became director of that department after a short period of time. Among other things he handled negotiations with the union: the International Union of Mine, Mill and Smelter Workers (Mine Mill) Local 598—it was the largest single local in Canada at the time. The union president was Mike Solski from the town of Coniston and had gone to the same high school as my father. The union conducted its first strike at Inco in September 1958. I recall my dad saying Inco had labour lawyers from Osler Harcourt, and the union had their team of lawyers and union stewards. Apparently they would tussle for days, then just my father and Mike would go for a walk and settle the new deal and return to tell everyone what the new deal was. That's the way they did it for years. My dad was then made assistant to the president of the Sudbury operations. He worked for Inco his entire life.

In the same way, generations of families—fathers and grandfathers in the community—were employed by the company through their lifetimes. A flourishing company and prospering and flourishing community—you can only imagine the pride, dedication, and commitment these generations had for the company. In fact Inco's Quarter Century Club was composed of employees who had completed twenty-five or more years of credited service with the company, and Quarter Century Club buttons were presented to employees, including my grandfather James Crossgrove in October 1937.

My dad was extremely well liked and respected. He saw the good in everyone and liked to laugh. He insisted that everyone call him Alec and not Mr. Crossgrove. I never heard him curse ever. He made the miners and smelter workers feel appreciated, and always affirmed the success of the company was based on how well they did their job. I guess I learned that from him. In my own personal work practices, I arrived at my company Pioneer Construction, which was involved in mining, pipeline, and road building in Sudbury at 5:30 a.m. as often as possible, seeing the work crews go out to work. I feel I learned the importance of showing people respect and kindness from my father. Good working relationships go a very long way.

The Crossgrove Brothers, Sister, and Family

My father had two surviving brothers, Bob and George, and one sister, Molly, who married Keith Acheson. Uncle Keith was raised in Gogama, then a lumbering town between Sudbury and Timmins that was reached through North Bay in those days. My uncle's father was the chief ranger in Gogama with the Lands and Forests, now the Ministry of Natural Resources. Keith studied forestry at the University of Toronto. He eventually became Deputy Minister of Lands and Forests.

The Achesons came to provide a home for Archie (Archibald) Belaney who was sent from England by his family to live with them in Gogama. Archie famously became known as Grey Owl, and was honoured by the King of England for his efforts to control the slaughter of beaver for their pelts. It was several years before the English realized Grey Owl was not a member of the First Nations, but a Brit. Movies and a documentary were made about Archie. My friend Fred Eaton was fascinated with the story of Grey Owl, so I arranged for my uncle to have lunch with Fred and myself at Winston's in Toronto. He brought several photostat copies of letters from the Belaney family to my uncle's family in Gogama. Needless to say, we had an interesting lunch.

My Uncle George Matthew Crossgrove, who was my grandparents' second oldest son, was quite amazing. He went overseas in World War I, enlisted in the Canadian Infantry—eighty-seventh Battalion—at the age of twenty-one in December of 1915, and came back to Copper Cliff as the highest-ranking officer of anybody who had left Copper Cliff. While in France as a Lieutenant, he ran into his father who was a private.

When George returned, and in honour of his success in the army during World War I, Inco paid his way through University of Toronto, where he went without ever even going to high school. He had taken a machinist apprenticeship at the smelter before the war. George graduated as a mechanical engineer from University of Toronto (UofT) with enough money left over in the scholarship fund to send my father to the University of Toronto as well. George went on to work for Bell Telephone and became the Executive Vice President of Eastern Canada.

Bob Crossgrove, my uncle, also attended the University of Toronto.

His oldest daughter Margo is married to Fraser Fell. Uncle Bob had a stock brokerage company called Crossgrove and Company, which went bankrupt in the stock crash of 1929. A front-page article in one of the Toronto papers, which I have seen, ran the headline "Crossgrove and Company Bankrupt." My uncle's business success meant my dad, who was at UofT, could live with him and was chauffeured back and forth to school. My dad was a fan of live theatre at the Royal Alexandra on King Street, and my uncle made sure he had tickets for every show.

Bob moved to Washington after his problems in Toronto. He worked for the United States Government. During World War II, he had to approve the purchase of all strategic materials by manufacturers that were mostly producing for the war effort. When the war was over he was made the U.S. Ambassador to the Virgin Islands. Not for long after, though, it was found out he hadn't bothered to become an American citizen. He came back and worked in Washington.

I can recall as a high school student going to Washington and touring Congress and the Senate. Bob had a special pass to go anywhere and everywhere and certainly everyone seemed to know him. When he passed away he had left cash and a note in his wallet saying it was for the mourners to have a party. He even recommended the venue and dance band. Bob requested his ashes be spread in the North Channel of Georgian Bay in Lake Huron. My Uncle Keith, a good friend of Cliff Fielding, had been allowed the use of a cottage on the east end of La Cloche Island, and Bob and his wife Molly would come up there in his later years. They just loved it.

The Grandparents' Generation

In those days, my grandparents on the Crossgrove side, who had by then retired from the Inco Company, alternated visits with family members. They did not have their own home because when they retired they had to give up their company house. They would stay with us for a few months and move on to visit with their other children and grandchildren every couple of months. They would move around the family because firstly I guess their pension at the time wasn't sufficient to look after them, and secondly they no longer had a company house. I really enjoyed their visits with us and hearing what they had to say.

As a war veteran, my grandfather would go to the Legion Hall to have beers with the old war vets. My Crossgrove grandparents were married well over sixty years. I remember their sixtieth wedding anniversary because they received a note from the Prime Minister and the Queen.

In fact, talking of the Queen and Royal family, King George VI and Queen Elizabeth I were the first of the Royal family to visit Sudbury in 1939. I witnessed this visit as a youngster, enjoying all the excitement elevated from the heights of my father's shoulders and saw the Royal party up close at the start of their tour. It's recorded the Queen was the first woman to travel underground in the Vale's, formerly Inco's, Frood mine. A second visit in 1959 saw Her Majesty Queen Elizabeth II and His Royal Highness Prince Philip visit the same mine.

The night just before my grandfather died, I walked down from my uncle's house to the Sudbury General Hospital, went up to his room, and asked him how he was doing. He was badly jaundiced; I don't know if he had his liver operated on, or what the hell it was—it was toxic, but one of his buddies had been in with some rye. He told me he had a pretty good life, and if he went that night it wouldn't bother him at all. Well, he did die that night.

I remember my Fortier grandparents. They were wonderful people. I loved to play cards with my grandfather and always did when I visited Pembroke. My grandfather always had stories to tell about business and rents and tenants. He owned a lot of the stores in downtown Pembroke at the time. Their house was heated with waste slabs from a local lumber mill. They had a huge wood shed, and it seemed every time I arrived to visit there were new slabs to be piled in the storage shed. Their kitchen stove was wood heated as well, and there was always coffee and tea on the stove. They eventually were convinced to move to a house across the street from the Catholic Church. When any of the family visited, the priest was right over and stayed around until the family members left. When my grandparents died, most of their substantial estate went to the church.

Grandparents Fortier were also recipients of the Sixtieth Diamond Wedding Anniversary congratulatory note from the Prime Minister and Queen. Both sets of grandparents lived into their nineties; their longevity a testament to their hardy, resilient, and winning personalities.

CHAPTER 16

Moving On and Growing Up In Copper Cliff

Growing up in that environment encouraged us to ask questions and to get a friend to help, and because we had no preconceived biases about race and religion, we could get along with anyone.

From the small two-bedroom apartment on Mackenzie Street, we moved to a house on Howie Drive next door to the Burtons. The Burtons built an ice rink in our yard, which was quite large, and the three Burton brothers, Marty, Archie, and Cumming all became professional hockey players. In fact "Cummy," as we called him, played right wing in the NHL for several years for the Detroit Red Wings; later becoming a sports broadcaster for the local Sudbury station when he retired from hockey.

Their father, Archie Burton Sr., had been a catcher for the Philadelphia Phillies. He was also a prospector, and if you went over to their home there was drill core piled all over the place in the house: living room and kitchen. It was just everywhere. He was a typical prospector. Prospectors never threw core away—and they still don't. He had a shed out back where he split the drill core in half himself, so that it could be examined and sent to a lab for further analysis if the core looked interesting. I don't know how much was sent away as I was quite young at the time.

When I was six years old, we moved on to Copper Cliff. While Copper Cliff was only four miles from Sudbury, it could have been forty miles away from Sudbury because it was completely an Inco company town—self-contained and sustaining. International Nickel was located just west of Sudbury and is now part of the city of Sudbury.

Founded in 1902, Inco evolved out the amalgamation of two nickel companies and involved itself in the mining, processing, and refining of nickel, as well as copper, gold, and platinum metals—valuable especially through World War I, World War II, and thereafter—nickel filling the needs of the automobile industry, and much later stainless steel for household appliances and other applications. Metal production of the various ores including gold was so enriched and profitable, that the costs of mining nickel could be said to have been virtually free. The company name Inco was trademarked in 1919. Inco Limited became the new company name in 1976, and when shareholders approved a takeover of Inco by Vale in 2007, the corporate name Vale was adopted in 2009.

The company took care of everything. You lived in a company house and the rent was heavily subsidized, and depending on your job, they determined which street you lived on. The company painted your house. If you had plumbing problems, they sent plumbers. If you had electrical problems, they sent their electricians. They cut the grass and cleaned the driveway. As you moved up, you had a better house on a better street. You need to understand in that time people went to work with a sense of real purpose—really a combination of survival primarily, but also to thrive and move up in the world.

Inco employed and looked after approximately 20,000 employees in the Sudbury area at that time. In fact, you couldn't be a boss or rise above a certain level of Inco if you were Catholic. Things were pretty much controlled by Masons in those days. If you wanted the senior positions in the company, Catholics did not get them. This situation was never talked about. It was as though it didn't exist.

Living With the Winds of Industry

The land between Sudbury and Copper Cliff was extremely barren back then because prior to that time, nickel copper ore had been roasted on big open log fires and sulfur was burned off. Because of a prevailing wind from the west, the sulphur gas from the smelter killed the vegetation. And with the vegetation gone, there was erosion and much barren rock, very few trees, and not a lot of soil. In 1954 the company then built the largest smoke stack in the world at the time—637 feet tall—and most days the sulphur gas was carried away and dispersed at a much higher altitude by the prevailing winds, probably circulating through the Arctic and Nordic countries. If there was no wind you would still walk around Copper Cliff coughing. By the time I was old enough, we used to walk the four or five miles out of town to Clarabelle Lake to swim; the trees were all gone and most of the soil, and so were the houses. In later years, they drained the lake, and now it's a big open pit and underground mine. In 1972 a 1,250-foot gas-cleaning systems chimney was commissioned at the smelter in Copper Cliff in a bid to improve air quality and emissions. This system siphons off the sulphur given off from the burning ore and is collected and actually sold as a commodity. The aggregate stone used for the cement to build the base was actually supplied by my construction company Pioneer.

Growing up, the tailings would blow a fine grey filament around town. You could say we were living with the winds of industry. It would even filter into the house. They eventually started to use massive amounts of fertilizer, and were able to grow grain and grass in the many tailings areas that were each thousands of acres. In the last thirty years they have grown trees that are now quite large. They clearly were the leading environmental control mining company in the world prior to governments developing standards with respect to the environment.

Interestingly enough, several years later, prior to anyone landing on the moon, astronauts went up there to the Sudbury area to practice moon-walking. Another note of interest: nickel alloys from Vale were used in Neil Armstrong's historic journey to the moon in 1969.

Copper Cliff, Sudbury Culture, and Ethnically One Community

There were about 5,000 people living in Copper Cliff and about 60,000 in Sudbury. Sudbury is an interesting city; the north is a diverse area where people don't discriminate ethnic groups. Ethnically, Sudbury was one community. Aside from Inco disallowing Catholics, in Sudbury there were Finns, Croatians, Serbs, Ukrainian, Italians, Wasps, French—everything you'd want in an integrated community. It was a mixture with everybody basically equal. There was no tension between religious or ethnic groups. It was a great sporting community, and we all played sports together: football, baseball, and hockey. We chummed around together and got along very well. Those were carefree days.

In the north, people don't see social strata, and there's a great deal of intermarriage. Not the sort of social classes or ethnic groups you would see in other places. We could all count in different languages like Italian or Finn, and of course we knew all the curse words. And that's the way we grew up. I wasn't aware of discrimination until I went to McGill, where some people had a different view of Jews. Sudbury was a real melting pot. It was a wonderful place.

About half the people in the Sudbury area were French speaking. There were French schools, radio stations, French TV stations; a lot of people were bilingual. We had a very good Jesuit Catholic school there called Sacred Heart, Sacre-Coeur, and we had St. Charles College run by the Jesuits. The interesting thing was my mother spoke French all her life. After she married my father, she didn't speak French because he didn't speak it, which was unfortunate because I would have loved to speak French.

Copper Cliff was a great town of course, because they had a community hall where you could play basketball, tennis and badminton. They had their own hospital, and the Copper Cliff Club with a swimming pool, bowling alley, and a large beautifully well-maintained park with ball fields. There was also a curling rink, and when the first one became too small, they built a newer and larger one. I was always involved in sport. I really enjoyed it. We had the only artificial ice rink north of Toronto in Copper Cliff called Stanley Stadium after Lord Stanley. It was a well-utilized facility; we all skated and played hockey a lot.

It's interesting that the Copper Cliff Club at that time didn't allow Italians to belong to, or enter into the club. The Italians had their own club, the "Italian Club." In fact, every Friday night all the teenagers including myself would walk up to Little Italy to the Italian Club and watch a movie. The whole deal cost twenty-five cents: ten cents for the movie, ten cents for a Pepsi, and five cents for a bag of potato chips. Everyone who worked at the club was a volunteer. We always had a serial show first, usually including the Lone Ranger and Tonto, his First Nation's sidekick—whose real name was Jay Silver Heels, a Canadian from Alberta. The main feature would be screened after. It was an enjoyable outing for us.

The Copper Cliff Notes quotes, "Up The Hill: Italians in Copper Cliff," recording that children could not attend the theatre on school days. They were referring to the shows at the Rex Theatre built in 1911 in Copper Cliff. The Copper Cliff Public School principal, Mr. McPhail (from 1911 to 1945), always kept check at the door.

"We were all excited for Saturday to roll around to see the serials—The Masked Man and The Cowboys. Wintertime was bad, as there was only a large stove to heat the place. Most of the time the wood wouldn't burn and there was so much smoke that visibility was poor. We were very cold. It was bedlam with the loud piano playing and all coughing—but we stayed.'"

In those years in Copper Cliff the sidewalks were made of wood and in the winter were cleared by a horse pulling a plough. The chap driving the horse was Aino Jakala, a Finnish bachelor. He was about five foot two and weighed about 300 lbs. He always wore the same coveralls and the joke among the kids in town was who smelled worse—Aino or the horse. He changed his clothes once a week after having a public sauna run by the Salo family on Finland Street. Where could one get a sauna for twenty-five cents that included a Pepsi? Men were on one side and the women on the other side of the wall. We had a small hole and thought we could see the naked women, but I think it was all in our imagination.

Home Grown

We grew nearly all our vegetables in the backyard in a fenced-in garden. One of the things I recall very well was that we didn't have a fridge until I was about sixteen. My parents grew vegetables out in a garden behind the house: tomatoes, potatoes, carrots, radishes, beans, cauliflower, and many others. Some vegetables were put away for the winter. They would be wrapped up in layers of newspaper, placed in cardboard boxes, and stored away in a cold storage cellar down in the basement. That's where a lot of our vegetables would come from during the winter.

Groceries and milk were delivered daily. We had a milkman, Marcel, a French Canadian. He delivered milk six days a week with a horse and wagon. My mother put out milk bottles and tickets for the type of milk she wanted. Most people did not have a fridge, so they had milk delivered five or six days a week. The cream would come to the top and be scooped off for coffee. I remember my mother telling the story about Marcel. She asked him what he was doing on a Sunday and he replied he was, "Going partridge hunting." On the Monday she asked him how he had done. She repeated, "He had seen four partridge and shot them both." It's amazing what sticks with you over the years.

The year my parents bought their first car was in 1952. All purchases had to be for cash. My father did not believe in paying interest. As well as working in the mines, a lot of people worked in the mine service business, not only for Inco and Falconbridge who were based in Sudbury, but also for mines based throughout northern Ontario and northern Quebec. They were suppliers of equipment, parts, and hardware amongst other businesses. The region prospered.

Always Obliging

People were always obliging and tended to help each other above and beyond the call of duty. One day I was called out of my high school class when I was about fifteen and told to go up to Dr. Ferguson's office at the hospital, which was about a ten-minute walk from the school. I arrived there to find Dr. Ferguson with Wilf Gougeon, who was among other things, a Life Insurance agent. Apparently Mr. Gougeon and his wife Eva would get a free trip to an insurance convention in Mexico if he filled a sales quota, and my dad decided to help him by buying enough insurance to bury me if I died.

Dr. Ferguson and Mr. Gougeon had cottages on Lake Penage, or Panache as it was originally named, as far back as the mid-1800s—a lake located near Sudbury. They just kept talking on and on about Penage as Dr. Ferguson checked my heart reflexes and took a blood sample. He then handed me a bottle to pee in. I asked him where I needed to go to pee. He pointed me over to the corner. I tried as hard as I could but couldn't pee. Mr. Gougeon asked me what was wrong.

I admitted, "I'm too nervous to pee."

"For goodness sakes, give me the bottle," he said as he took the bottle out my hand, went to the corner and peed in it. And that was that. The whole thing was crazy. I didn't need insurance at that age, however, the trip was based on the number of policies sold, and this was the cheapest one he had. I trust he enjoyed himself in Mexico!

Education and Childhood Influences

My schooling in grade one started at Copper Cliff Public School. I went to both public school and the high school in Copper Cliff, which was built in 1937 and had 150 students and five teachers on staff. One of the great things that Inco made sure and did was to hire the finest and best teachers available. They were paid about 20 percent more than the average teachers in the Sudbury district. I was not an outstanding student, but I wasn't at the bottom of the class either. I loved history particularly, Canadian and American, but hated Latin.

If you were not doing well or living up to the teacher's expectations, they would haul you in and give you a lecture. They would threaten to report you to the principal who might use the ultimatum of cutting you off from sports as an incentive until you straightened up. Playing sports was important. If you misbehaved, you got hauled into the cloakroom. They had a big rubber strap and they knew how to use it. I remember my first time getting the strap. If you were really bad they took you down to the principal, and he might tell you to bend over the desk and give it to you over the rear end or on the arms.

Most of the students who were not interested in academics went up to the smelter or to the copper refinery, and took up a trade like a machinist, electrician, welder, and other such trades. People working at the smelter and refinery were well paid at every level of skill.

One interesting thing about Copper Cliff was that everyone had a nickname. Even the teachers called people by their nicknames, and no one thought anything about it. Some examples were "Cheesehead" Matte, "Oxy" Ogston, "Boggie" Signoretti, "Rocky" Canapini, and "Stinky" La Pointe.

Gordon Grey tells a great story. Someone had come to see him at his office. Gordon Grey's father was manager of the Toronto Dominion Bank in Copper Cliff. Gordon, or "Moose Grey," had gone to Queens University, studied Commerce, and later became a chartered accountant. Along with Brian McGee, Gordon founded AE LePage, which was for many years Canada's largest real estate company. In any event, this chap showed up at LePage's head office in Toronto asking if "Moose" is in. When they finally figured out that he was looking for Gordon Grey, they told him that Gordon was out and asked if they could leave him a message.

"Sure. Just tell him 'Spider' Kavanaugh dropped by," he quipped.

If we wanted to move around town in the winter at night, we'd wait for a car to come by and hop on the back bumper. Vehicle bumpers were the kind you could grab onto and slide on top of the snow. You could go four or five miles around town on the back of a car if you wanted. We had fun. I also had a dog that pulled a sleigh in the winter. He had a harness and would take me up town to get the mail. Of course, we knew everybody in town and everybody in town knew each other. If a kid got into trouble, the whole town knew, their parents knew, and the police knew as well. We had a pretty good life and we were all relatively well behaved.

War Effects

The communities were small enough that both wars affected the communities on many levels, what with the young men going off to war being posted overseas. The Rex Theatre in Copper Cliff provided entertainment during World War I, deeming its importance in "boosting community pride and the war effort."

The *Sudbury Star* reported the armistice on 13 November 1918 as follows: "Copper Cliff was up early—Star telephoned the first news—Citizens Celebrated in Style. News of the signing of the armistice was received at 3:06 a.m. Monday morning when the Star telephoned the Bell Telephone Central. Miss Crystal Biggs, night operator, was first to receive the joyful news, which was also sent through to Creighton Mine at the same time. The message was immediately given to the boiler rooms at both towns and the whistles set in action.

"Many citizens report first hearing the din in Sudbury and the Creighton whistles. Nearly everyone got up and dressed and by 4 o'clock the main street was black with people. An impromptu procession was formed, men, women and children, old and young, taking part, nearly all with some means of making a noise, tin pans, whistles and horns. The local

Orangemen's fife and drum band was also out. The parade wound up at Nickel Park, where the Maple Leaf, 'O Canada,' the National Anthem and other patriotic singing took place.

"During the morning Mayor Corkill called a meeting of his council and executive heads of the company to arrange for a formal celebration. An invitation was received to join with Sudbury in a monster community thanksgiving service at Sudbury. This was accepted and Copper Cliff's procession arranged for one o'clock. Enthusiasm was at fever heat. The parade did full justice to the occasion. It formed at the band hall at one o'clock and included: returned soldiers, united bands of Copper Cliff and Creighton, Royal Cadets, Mayor Corkill and Town Councillors, Fire Department, decorated autos, decorated trucks with effigies of Kaiser and Crown Prince, and citizens. The parade disbanded at Nickel Park, the bulk of the crowd leaving for Sudbury."

During World War II, we had to practice for air raids at school and at home. When the sirens went off, we headed to the basement of our house or school depending on where we were. We came up when the all clear was sounded. We all ate our food because we were told, "If we did not, we were feeding Hitler or Mussolini."

I remember the day war ended because there were so many families affected. My father had been turned down for the armed forces because he had heart arrhythmia. The night the war was over there was a huge bonfire lit on a hill. Everyone was crying with joy and relief. A day later the tension was gone and everyone was so happy. It was an occasion and experience one would never forget. We didn't have a car when we moved from Sudbury; I remember going out on the streetcar and watching my mother throw rifle shells out of the window on some abandoned vacant land on the way out to Copper Cliff. The shells I imagine had been souvenirs from World War I or II, and had been sitting on the fireplace mantle in our Sudbury house.

A Young Working Life

My father, being of Scottish ancestry, always believed that one should work. So I was quite young when I started working in my spare time. I believe this is a value passed to me that influenced in part how I have lived my life. One thing that was drilled into me was that the easiest money to make is the money that you do not spend. I also learned that you are not spending one dollar—it's really two dollars because you have to pay tax.

We would never dare to fib to our parents in those days because if we were found out, the penalties could be quite severe. It would not be tolerated. If caught fibbing, we were sent to our bedroom where we were made to wait for a while for my father to appear—that was part of the suffering. When he arrived, we pulled our pants down and had a red bum in short order. It certainly encouraged us to respond truthfully.

Of course, living in a close-knit community was advantageous because of the connections, friendships, and relationships that came out of all the interactions and life in those days—all of which gave rise to many interesting stories. Much of the varied work that I and many others engaged in was part of how these small communities built themselves up outside of the urban areas.

Growing up in that environment encouraged us to ask questions and to get a friend to help, and because we had no preconceived biases about race and religion, we could get along with anyone. The only status symbols I guess were the streets one lived on in Copper Cliff; however, over the years as businessmen became wealthy in Sudbury, the class distinction disappeared. I think one of the reasons that people left Sudbury and Winnipeg and did so well was because they were from diverse and ethnic communities. It mattered not when and where we grew up; the fact of the matter is we all got along and were not cliquish or prejudiced. The entrepreneurial spirit came early to me. I sold papers door-to-door and then up at the gate of the smelter when the shift came off. I probably sold a couple hundred papers at that gate per day and made a fair bit of money. Even while at public school, I had another job working at the Stanley Stadium cleaning the ice in-between periods. They didn't have Zambonis back then. Cleaning was done with scrapers. To flood the rink and make ice between periods and before and after games, they tied a blanket over the pipe out of which the hot water flowed.

As a kid, I remember seeing Jack Kent Cooke, who went on to own the Washington Redskins (NFL), the Los Angeles Lakers (NBA), and

Los Angeles Kings (NHL), and Lord Roy Thomson, a successful media entrepreneur in partnership with Jack Kent Cooke, with another man by the name of Mason talking business between periods in the hockey game. They owned the radio stations and newspapers in northern Ontario at the time, and I remember them standing under the seating stands in between periods right where I was coming off after cleaning and flooding the ice. These businessmen were obviously hockey fans and I'd listen to them, having no idea at the time who they were, or what they were discussing. They were talking about their businesses. And I was quite fascinated. Unconsciously, their conversations could have sparked in me a passion for success, and desiring an understanding of the workings of big business right from a young impressionable age.

Quite early on, I also worked in the restaurant in the rink at the Stanley Stadium. I was helping as well as selling french fries, hot dogs, pop, and other snacks out in the stands. I was paid commission and sometimes enjoyed the tips.

The Budding Entrepreneur

At the age of ten or twelve I went to work for the Canapini brothers. This was a side job on the weekends after school and in the summer, when I would bag coal. Coal was bagged in canvas bags, then delivered by truck to someone's house and put down a coal shoot. I was contracted two cents a bag to bag the coal. I recall coming home very black and dirty. My mother finally thought it was costing more for clothes than I was making, so I ended that job.

A few years later, I worked with the Canapini's clearing off the sawdust from the ice that they had cut in Ramsey Lake and stored in the winter. We would saw large ice blocks into smaller ones with big lumber crosscut saws. The smaller ice blocks would be sent to the smelter. The ice was used to cool the drinking water and the men's lunch pails. The smelter was very hot in many areas because the converters heated the metal up to 1,800 degrees Fahrenheit. Salt pills were always available for the men at the drinking fountains as well because they sweated so much. A much more efficient artificial ice plant was then built, which produced ice blocks, replacing the ice taken from the lake which had to be cut and stored under sawdust.

One of the chaps I worked with was Jerry Toppazzini, who of course went on to become a great Boston Bruin hockey player. Professional hockey players, even the good ones, did not make all that much money in those days. So they took on summer jobs; some sold cars. Eddy Shack worked as a butcher. Often people like the Canapini brothers who owned the ice, wood, and coal business all had nicknames, and were known as "Jiggs," "Rocky," and "Beef." I knew them for many years and never learned their Christian names.

I worked in the summers so I could make money to buy whatever I wanted in hockey equipment. If I wanted to hitchhike to Sudbury for a movie I could do that. Everything I ever did in terms of work was a learning experience. I liked the idea of being independent. I thoroughly enjoyed it. Travel gave me a great sense of freedom and felt good. One year before high school started, I took a train ride on the Canadian from Sudbury to the west coast and back. This adventure was a big deal in those days. I realize now that with all my worldly travels over the decades, I got an early start for the taste of travel.

At the age of about fourteen or fifteen, my grade seven teacher Elwood Sloss, who also happened to be a neighbour in Copper Cliff, suggested he would get me a job up in Manitoulin Island. I accepted the job and worked that summer cleaning fish. That's when I first fell in love with Manitoulin Island.

CHAPTER 17

Life on Manitoulin Island and an Early Start in Mining

Today people often do not care what they say. If it's not in writing and there is an opportunity to make a buck, there's no deal.

Manitoulin Island is the largest fresh water island in the world, located in the North Channel of Georgian Bay. It is approximately 140 miles long and forty miles at its widest point. The island can be reached by heading southwest from Sudbury over a swing bridge, which in the summer allows the large Canadian and US yachts through. It can also be approached from Tobermory at the top of the Bruce Peninsula—a three-hour car ferry ride to the port of South Bay Mouth on the southeast corner of Manitoulin. On a sunny day it's a spectacular trip.

There are many beautiful and large lakes on Manitoulin, and the water in these lakes is absolutely pristine and clear. When you look into the waters, you think it could be five feet deep and yet it could easily be twenty feet. Lake Manitou is one of the many lakes. It's where they gather up the female lake trout and milk them and raise fingerlings to stock lakes all over Ontario. It's the lake on which my parents had a cottage and where I now have a cottage. The lake is approximately twenty-five miles long and about six miles wide at its widest point and full of bass, pickerel, pike, splake, and lake trout, which are a combination of lake trout and speckled trout. There are two rivers that run out of Lake Manitou—the Blue Jay and the Manitou, where you can catch rainbow, speckles, and salmon in the spring. Manitou comes from the Native name meaning "Great God."

There are a couple of other large lakes, one being Kagawong and the other Mindemoya. There are many other lakes on the island as well. Manitoulin is sparsely populated with the main industry being cattle farming and tourism. The paper and lumbering businesses have disappeared.

There are still a lot of cedar trees cut for posts and rails and shipped south.

Many people think the most beautiful cruising scenery in the world is from Killarney, south of Manitoulin, through the North Channel on the north side of Manitoulin, to just east of Sault Ste. Marie. Some families like the Evinrudes' and Wirtzs' from Chicago have been bringing their huge family yachts up for three or four generations.

As I mentioned earlier, my first visit to Manitoulin to hunt partridge was with my grade seven teacher Elwood Sloss. His father owned the International Harvester Equipment Dealership in Spring Bay. We were hunting with the Beatty brothers and I recall we shot forty-two partridge that weekend. Other game and animals on Manitoulin include wild turkey, pheasant, ducks, and geese.

In mid-November every year they also have a one-week deer hunt on Manitoulin Island when about 3,000 deer are shot. They are counted at the bridge because the ferry is no longer running. All the land on Manitoulin is privately owned, so you need the permission of the landowner to hunt. This is to make sure that cattle, sheep, and cows are not shot as well.

I recall as a young person going to the farm next door to my dad's cottage and counting seven deer hanging in the barn a few days before the season opened. It would seem the neighbours were ahead of themselves. Their rationale was that the deer had been eating their grain and corn all summer, and it was not only too dangerous to hunt during hunting season, but they also had to keep their eye on their cattle in hunting season.

During the summer between grades seven and eight, I obtained a job at a tourist lodge near Spring Bay on Lake Kagawong. My job included picking up garbage and delivering ice for the ice boxes in the cabins and delivering firewood. At night I would have at least two wheelbarrows of bass to clean and pack in ice for the Americans who were taking them back to the States. I don't know whether they froze them when they got back there. I think some of them owned restaurants and sold the fish. In those days there were so many fish it was incredible. I hear the fishing is still good today, but you are only allowed to keep a few fish.

The Manitoulin Property Investment

About a year later, I spoke to my father about looking for some property on Manitoulin Island. He found a property with 900 feet of shorefront, a beautiful sandy beach, and ten acres at Green Bay at the north end of Lake Manitou. The price was $900. The farmer selling it was Mr. Wood. We went to the Manitoulin registry office located at Gore Bay, and the location of Mr. Wood's lawyer, Cliff Boyd. The idea was to close the deal and transfer the property. Mr. Boyd told Mr. Wood in front of my dad and I that he was selling the property too cheaply.

Mr. Wood, who really did not know my dad, said, "I gave this man my word and shook his hand to close the deal."

My dad and Mr. Wood subsequently became very good friends. Today people often do not care what they say. If it's not in writing there's no deal.

My father's cottage was all built by volunteer labour: his friends and me. I would go up on my days off from my summer job when I was working in the smelter and work on the construction of the cottage. The three-bedroom cottage was lovely and the total cost all in was $2,400.

Both my mother and father loved to garden. We had fresh flowers in the cottage every day. He raised the flowers to bloom at different times. We also had about an acre of vegetable and berry gardens. My mother baked delicious pies with the raspberries, strawberries, and rhubarb. The vegetables they grew were potatoes, cabbage, peas, beans, sweet corn, cauliflower, and carrots, and many more that were picked an hour before dinner. It was so wonderful. These days there is a growing trend towards kitchen gardens. Back then, vegetable gardens were the norm. They had to be, because each family had to be self-sufficient in that way.

Another interesting thing about the cottage is that even though it had indoor plumbing, there was an outdoor toilet without a door and binoculars hanging on the wall for bird watching. There were several bird feeders in the area, and there were probably 90 percent of the small birds to be seen in northern Ontario in the area of the outhouse. We had to put up with a little odour, but some sort of spray and lime usually worked. It was a great place to go if the cottage was too busy and you just wanted to read and watch birds.

Trucking and Manitoulin Transport

I ran into Cliff Boyd several years later at a transport hearing at the Sudbury Court House. Cliff was acting for Roy Cooper of Cooper's Transport who was primarily hauling bulk milk but wanted to expand his trucking license. Boyd was there as Roy's lawyer trying to help Roy, using Edwards Sudbury Limited as a potential client which would be using the trucking capacity and trucking license and would require Roy's services. Before we went into court we were rehearsing what I was going to say. One question Mr. Boyd asked me was how long I had worked for Edwards Sudbury Limited; this was just after graduating with a Bachelor of Commerce.

When I replied two months, he said to me, "I will not ask that question."

The first question he asked when the proceedings started was, "How long have you worked for Edwards Sudbury Limited?"

Not missing a beat I responded, "Ever since I left university." Mr. Boyd went on to become a judge.

Talking about Manitoulin truckers, I have to mention Manitoulin Transport. The company was started and is still owned by Doug Smith with the head office in Gore Bay on Manitoulin Island. Doug started with one truck hauling famous "Manitoulin Turkeys" to Sudbury and points south, as well as some cattle. Then for a back-haul he started hauling groceries. He has built the company to the point where he has over 480 depots in the United States and Canada. I rented him his first depot in Sudbury—an old railway roundhouse for $500 per month.

Doug had another talent; he played a saxophone in a band of four people from Gore Bay. They played in the town hall at Mindemoya on Friday nights and on Saturday nights at a barn in the village of Sandfield. Mr. Boyd was one of the other three players. He played the drums and delivered bread during the day. Mrs. Boyd, who was a big lady, pounded out on the piano and their son played the fiddle. Later in the night when the square dancers and the band were drunk, the building shook.

Doug Smith is a wonderful person—hardworking, smart, funny, and a real gentleman. He told me the story of the Ontario Provincial Police calling him once about his grandfather who was ninety-five years old and had surrendered himself at the Gore Bay police station. He had been driving himself from his house in his half-ton truck down the street to the coffee shop for years without a license. Of course, the police knew this and there was nothing wrong with his driving. Doug said he would handle it and tell his grandfather that he was on probation. He dealt with this by having someone from his office drive his father for his morning coffee.

Manitoulin Paradise

About fifteen years later, I bought a 360-acre farm with 200 acres of pasture and 150 acres of bush on the North Channel, about fifteen miles west of Little Current. The shoreline was about three and a half miles long and looked out to Clapperton Island, which had been owned by the Ford family. My farm manager's name was Billy White and he had a few chickens, pigs, cattle, and a couple of horses for my children. The cottage was on the water about two miles from the farm and was built from logs and lumber all cut on the property.

The fireplace was twenty-eight feet high and made from stone collected on the farm. We had a wonderful vegetable garden and a wood fired sauna on the shore. In the spring we made maple syrup. We picked it up with a barrel on a horse drawn sleigh and then boiled it twenty-four hours a day. It takes forty gallons of sap to make one gallon of syrup. When the sap was boiling, we threw in raw eggs, which started to cook and turn black as they absorbed the sand that had come up the tree with the sap from the tree roots. We also had a boat harbor with a forty-eight-foot Pacemaker, and would cruise through all those beautiful Islands from Parry Sound to Sault Ste. Marie. I married a girl from Toronto who wanted to be in Muskoka, so I broke up the property and sold it off in pieces.

Approximately three years ago, I bought one hundred acres of bush and 3,500 feet of lakeshore on Lake Manitou. I have built a cottage but I am not allowed to build a dock or boathouse. The Ministry of Natural Resources says it is fish spawning ground. I hired the two most prominent fish biologists in Canada who say it isn't, and the Federal Department of Fisheries under whose jurisdiction the land is also say that it is not a spawning ground. However, they will not overrule the Ministry of Natural Resources—but if I were to take the MNR to court, they say they will tell the truth. In the meantime, I am told I do not need a building permit to build an airplane hangar. Therefore, there is currently one under construction. I have to build a much larger facility than I wanted to build. An airplane hangar would have been less than half the size as the entrance to the boathouse. In addition, I had to cut down a lot more trees on the shoreline to accommodate the airplane wings. Not only that—I do not have to pay taxes on the hanger. How dumb is all that? The government is out of control. On the waterfront I bought, the previous owner was going to build seventeen cottages. You would think they would be happy to have one.

It is my view that in twenty years, the wealthy people will be going to Manitoulin because of big properties, beautiful water, scenery, and the best cruising in the world. It is only one hour and fifteen minutes from Toronto Island in a prop plane. We are most fortunate in Canada to enjoy the incredible nature that we have, and residents and visitors alike do appreciate this.

Working Summer Holidays

It was a good time learning how to start meeting people from all walks of life and to see that we were all raised with quite different perspectives on life.

I was never a good student; I was an average student, at least in public school and high school. Schooling was boring quite frankly. I guess I was more interested in athletics. I played hockey. We practiced five days a week and played on Saturdays. Some of the schools had outdoor rinks in those days. Of course we always had Stanley Stadium with the artificial rink. I also played football, and was football player of the year in the Nickel Belt area one year. I was very proud of that. When I was about seventeen, I went down to try out for the Toronto Argonauts. I don't know where I got that crazy idea from but I went down. They farmed me out to Balmy Beach. However, my father told me to get back home, which I did. It was an interesting experience. I was a somewhat disappointed, however, but somewhere deep inside I knew it was the right decision.

It was about that time too that I worked with the Junior Rangers, and I had some interesting jobs. My Uncle Keith was the Deputy Minister of Lands and Forest, which is now Natural Resources. I was hitchhiking one night from Copper Cliff to Sudbury and somebody stopped to pick me up.

The man asked who I was and I replied, "My name is Peter Crossgrove."

"Are you Alex's son?" he asked and to which I replied in the affirmative. He told me, "My name is Welland Gemmell." I knew who he was. He was a member of the Ontario Progressive Conservative Party who represented Sudbury, appointed as Minister of Mines and after the Minister of Lands and Forests—as it was known then until 1954. He asked what I was doing for the summer and I told him I had tried but wasn't able to get a job at the Junior Rangers.

He asked me, "Would you mind sending me a telegram on Monday and I'll look into it?"

By Tuesday I had a job and was hired for the summer up at Thessalon, primarily cutting pulp, building roads, and working at a place called McCreight's Dam just outside of Thessalon. Every weekend we were in Blind River or Thessalon where they held big country-dances that we used to go to. We had fun because they held canoe races and canoe tilting, and all kinds of things during the day as well. Of course there were prizes, and being young and strong we'd enter everything. We were all between sixteen and eighteen; although we were far too young to drink, that didn't stop us. We would go to the pub to drink and nobody worried too much about it in those days. Sometimes if we missed the truck home, we'd have to walk the twelve miles home—and that didn't seem to bother us very much either.

Peshu Lake

In the second summer, I worked at Peshu Lake in an area that had been burned over by a huge forest fire, and the government and lumber companies worked up there. We lived in tents, and by the end of the summer the water was so cold that we would have to break the ice to wash our faces and shave. My work that summer was to drive a bulldozer pushing gravel up a ramp onto the back of a truck. We didn't have a loader—that's how we did it. We built a large base with a huge deck so that bush planes that might be servicing forest fire fighters might pick up supplies and people to fly them into lakes closer to where a fire might occur in the future. Peshu Lake is on the road between Thessalon and Chapleau, and at that time was the only way one could get up to Chapleau, which is a township in the Sudbury district and home to the Chapleau Crown Game Preserve—the largest animal preserve in the world.

Those were wonderful summers. I met people from all over the province. I can't recollect any of them staying friends all my life, but some of them were friends certainly through high school and when we'd play a hockey tournament in Toronto. I would seem to wind up staying at a friend's house that I'd met through those summers.

Life in the Interlude

Living and working in community teaches you a lot about yourself and others and how to make do with what you have—the value and power of resourcefulness. It was an invaluable learning experience for me. The next phase of my life spanned through the last couple years of high school. In my first year after high school, I took a couple years off before I went to university. I wasn't quite sure what I wanted to do, and I needed to make money for university. My father felt that if I wanted to go to school then I should pay for it.

So the first summer I worked up in Chibougamau, which was originally a mining town in central Quebec with difficult access to this remote area at that time. I am not so sure the public really has any idea of the conditions up there and what we endured in order to stake claims in those days. It was rough; however, we just had to put up with it. We were cutting line and staking claims. It was so wet up there. It never really dried out. I think there were only three or four days where we didn't have rain. Our sleeping bags were wet. Our tents were wet. Legs were raw because everything was so wet. The food we ate was out of a tin can, and we had no refrigeration. Food was Klik or Spam. We tended to eat a lot of heavily fried food and there wasn't a lot in the way of fruit or anything else. Food was flown in without any refrigeration. We had propane for lights and we slept in canvas tents. It was a pretty busy time. Occasionally we'd get into Chibougamau, which was a rough town and it was full of tough miners and hookers. We'd go for a weekend or so and have a good shower, go into the hotels, drink beer, and look at the girls.

I recall an interesting story about the local United Church. The trailers where the hookers stayed were located just on the edge outside of town and that's where you went if you wanted to have some fun with a lady. The United Church took exception to these trailers being there, and one Sunday the minister raised heck at a service. The church told the town they should get rid of the trailers. The next weekend the priest got up and said we shouldn't get rid of the trailers, because the next thing we know the miners would be after all of their young daughters in and around town. The trailers did stay after all that, which was probably a wise decision on behalf of the Church elders.

From Chibougamau, Quebec to Moak Lake, Manitoba

My mining experience then went further afield when Canadian Nickel (the exploration division of Inco - now Vale), then sent me from Chibougamau to Thompson, Manitoba. Actually it was Moak Lake, and we were doing the original prospecting there. They thought the mine would be at Moak Lake; however, the mining operations were built at Thompson several miles away and which has become a very large town. In those days it was just a couple of tents in the bush.

Coming on the train from Winnipeg we arrived in a place called Thicket Portage. From there we had to travel about twenty-five miles in the old bombardier skidoo with the skis on the front and tracks on the back. It carried about six people. However, the first night we spent in the hotel at Thicket Portage, I recall beer was about twenty-four bucks a case, which everybody thought was absolutely outrageous. There was no room in the hotel, so people paid to sleep on the floor. There were people snoring, farting, and dreaming. It was quite an experience. We got up and they brought us out to camp on the skidoo.

It was in the winter and quite interesting, since it was geophysical work cutting lines. In those days we slept in tents that had wooden walls and floors and oil stove. We would get up in the morning in the winter and if we had been working the day before, we would find that our socks were frozen to the floor.

At our camp at Moak Lake, we had First Nations people build a sauna out of logs and we lined it with heavy construction paper. One Sunday the construction paper caught on fire from the propane lantern, and of course everybody ran out of the sauna with the First Nations running for their cameras to take pictures of these white men running around nude. It was funny as hell. Anyway, we eventually got that thing fixed.

I can recall the line cutting was really tough work. The snow was very deep. We had to wear heavy clothes, and have four or five sets of snowshoes, because they had to dry out and then we would have to shellac them. We started out with a very dry, newly shellacked pair every day, and would go out into the snow that would be up to your waist. One time, I was out cutting line with a First Nations man, and I gave him the compass and said it was his turn to go first. He said he guessed we'd have time for another circle before lunch. I don't think he thought much of the way I was cutting line or the direction. They were Cree (Aski), who lived in the area.

We had a supply plane that would fly in and land on the ice in the winter, and on the water in the summer. One of the First Nations wanted to buy a radio and it had to be brought in from Winnipeg. He didn't read or write so he had one of the more literate First Nations men order it for him. As a joke they ordered one that required an electric cord—not a battery radio. He sat waiting for the plane to come in with his radio and, when it got there, they all had a great laugh. It had come up from Winnipeg and was electric and would never work in the bush. They thought that was the biggest joke in the world. If the First Nations men decided they wanted to head home, they would sit in the camp until the plane arrived, even if it was not going to be coming in for a few days. They were fine to work with and still are of course. There was no booze allowed in the camp. They are hard workers and can be quite funny.

I recall the spring breakup, when of course the plane was unable to land on skis and pontoons, and they were bringing out a side of beef for us. They flew over and they dropped it from the plane. They wanted to drop it as close to the camp as they could. But, they dropped it too close, and it hit the dining tent and broke the table. Stuff flew in every direction. The First Nations thought this was the funniest thing they had ever seen.

Northwest Territories

The following summer I worked up on the smelter for Inco, and the summer and winter after I went to work up near Copper Mine in the Northwest Territories to work for Canadian Nickel. We flew in from Yellowknife and worked up there. In fact Max Ward (who owned Ward Air, then a smaller bush airline), was the pilot who flew us in. They had Bristol Bombers and Otters—huge planes that would land on the ice and unload barrels and gas. We were doing geophysical work there. I was running the radio shack.

Sometimes I would be on the radio looking to get some information and the Russians who were on the ice floes in the Arctic Ocean would answer in very good English. They were monitoring everything that was going on up there. Those were in the days of the Distant Early Warning Line (DEW LINE).

One day we had a plane crash. It was snowing quite hard and visibility was poor. The plane couldn't see where it was landing, the landing strip was on the ice, and the plane actually landed flying into a hill on the side of the lake not only because they could not see the horizon, but also they were out of gas. Fortunately no one was killed or badly hurt. The plane was an Anson made out of plywood that dragged a bomb underneath it, with an instrument that sent an electric current down to the ground. Instruments in the plane would analyze the results to see if there might be mineralization that acts as a conductor.

It was my job to send a message back to Copper Cliff in code notifying them of the crash. To do this you took whatever letter in the code book you wanted, counted ahead ten letters and wrote down the encoded word. When they received the message, they had the same codebook and subtracted ten letters to create each word and arrive at the original message.

We were instructed to burn the plane before the federal aviation people arrived, which we did. Before we did that, we took both engines off which happened to be the same engines they use in Beaver Aircraft. Max Ward had use for the engines, so we sold them to him. With that money, we bought a big heater that would heat and supply us with hot water. We could have showers and we even hooked up a steam bath. We also bought a washer and dryer, which was unheard of at that time in the Arctic. We gave ourselves a few other amenities because it was cold there and everything was frozen up tight. When using the outhouse, your feet would be level with your rear end because the fine dry snow had drifted in. A ring of ice would form around the hole from people sweating and then freezing. It wasn't very pleasant.

I remember thousands of caribou crossing right in front of the camp on the lake ice and the wolves would be following the caribou picking the odd one whenever they wanted to. This went on for a couple of weeks and was quite an amazing sight. In the winter, we would get several days of snow when we couldn't work, so we would play bridge sometimes twenty-four hours at a shot. When the snow stopped, we would be too tired to work and went to bed to sleep it off.

In the summer, the fishing was phenomenal. You could fill your boat with lake trout no matter what you threw over. Sometimes you could find a three or four pounder inside a large lake trout because as you know they eat other fish. You could catch all the fish you wanted in about twenty minutes. We had a tent down right on Copper Mine River with a couple of geologists living in it in the summer. One day they radioed us that a grizzly bear had destroyed their camp, and in fact it was so strong it pulled a rope through a three quarter inch piece of plywood. We sent a helicopter down to pick them up. It was a mess, and the grizzly was shot from the helicopter.

Another experience in the Arctic was going up to Kugluktuk (formerly Coppermine—the village), which was at the mouth of the Coppermine River on the Arctic Ocean. I once had to go into the hospital to see the doctor and found the Eskimos or Inuit having sex in bed right in front of me, but no one seemed too concerned.

Something else we did was to name some of the lakes up there; we sent the names in to Ottawa. We gave them crazy names like Desolation and Desperation, which they still have to this day.

Discovering Anomalies and Finds

At the time, International Nickel used to do a lot of geophysical work, initially from the air. They had an airbase at the Frood Stobie Mine in

Sudbury. They had a big hangar and electronic operation there to prepare their geophysical equipment. They also had an Anson aircraft made of plywood—the type used in World War II. The plane was loaded with electrical equipment and towed something that looked like a bomb about fifteen metres below the plane. They would fly the plane winter and summer in grids over what appeared to be areas of interest. The electrical equipment could detect conductive material that was below the surface and was used in any season. An electrical signal was sent down and depending on the strength of the conductor if they found something interesting, they might follow up by doing a ground electro magnetic survey over the same target. They would also look for outcrops—rock formation or mineral veins appearing at the surface of the earth, and they might diamond drill to see what was causing the strong electrical signal. It could very well be mineralization. This was how the Thompson Manitoba Mine was found.

They would bring the plane and the instruments in for recalibration from time to time. When they were finished and before they sent the plane to Chibougamau, Thompson, Coppermine, or anywhere else, they would send it up to Timmins to check the equipment out on a well-defined anomaly just off the end of the airport. They never checked out the anomaly. It turned out to be a huge copper ore body, which became Texas Gulf.

CHAPTER 18

University Choices, Practical Mining, and Business Experience

I always found ways to try to make a buck on the side—that's how I got by.

We've arrived full circle in my story. The time had come to think about going to university. I decided to go to McGill. Everybody around Copper Cliff pretty well went to Queens because the mayor of Copper Cliff was a man by the name of Collins, and the football stadium at Queens had been named after his father. Inco had created many scholarships and fellowships at Queens in mining and geology, so most people headed in that direction.

I chose to go to McGill because I could live in the field house if I played football. That would give me free room and board; however, it was awfully noisy being right in the stadium behind the scoreboard. Before the college season started, we could watch all the Canadian Football League games in McGill stadium for free.

Not long after, I joined the Phi Delta Theta Fraternity, which was known as the athletic fraternity on campus. Shortly thereafter I became the Phi Delta Theta House Manager, which came with free room and board.

I started in geology but very quickly switched to commerce. My father of course didn't know that I didn't take geology. I knew I didn't want to take geology but rather be in commerce. One of the reasons for the switch was because up in the Arctic, I remember Keith Diebell telling me he had an undergraduate degree in geology from Queens and a graduate degree from UBC, and he was always away in those days. Geologists would be out in the bush four or five months at a time. You couldn't get away with that today, but that's how it worked then. They'd come home and their wives and children didn't know them. Sometimes their wives would find a boyfriend. He advised me not to do that; it was not a career he would choose.

I loved accounting, I loved commerce, and I loved those business courses. At the end of the second going into my third year, my father was pushing me hard to return home, and in doing so to work in the purchasing department at Inco. I had worked a couple summers in the warehouse and Mac Forsythe, the purchasing agent who quite liked me, thought I should work under him and perhaps inherit his job that was a big job at Inco in those days.

My father was convinced that I would work for Inco, so I switched to Sir George Williams Concordia University for a year with the permission of Eric Kierens, Dean at McGill, to take a purchasing course that McGill did not offer. I quite liked Concordia and thought I'd like to stay, but I knew I wanted to go to Western and take an MBA. I contacted Western to ask if it mattered where I graduated from—either McGill or Concorde. I would have to get permission to go back to McGill for my fourth year and graduate from there. I was told no and that it didn't matter at all. I continued at Concordia for my fourth year and graduated from there at the top of the class and then left Montreal. By that time I was married and went to work at my father-in-law's company Edwards Sudbury Limited.

While at McGill and Concordia, as Phi Delta Theta House Manager, with free room and board, I always found ways to try to make some money on the side. Others also used their imagination and ingenuity to get by. This reminds me of the story of Bob Gougeon who went to Upper Canada College and then on to the University of Western Ontario. Being a relatively small person, he knew he would never make the football team. So he decided to try out for the University of Western Ontario band. When he showed up, he was told all the positions were full. He asked the bandmaster if there were any instruments he didn't have that he would like to have. The bandmaster said he needed a snare drum. Bob went to a used instrument store and bought one. The store manager arranged for a couple of lessons for him and he painted the drum purple and white—the university colours. Bob became a member of the band and was then able to travel on the train together with the football team and cheerleaders to McGill, Queens, and the University of Toronto—all expenses were paid and it was a bundle of fun.

During my time there I also took a year off and worked underground up at Creighton Mine—about ten miles west of Sudbury. I became a fully qualified miner and gained valuable mining experience, working on bonus at a mine stope, which is the excavation in the form of steps to remove ore from vertically or steeply inclined veins in the rock. I ran a slushing machine as well as a jackleg drill and worked on timbering the mine stopes. I was away prospecting another year trying to make money, since my father believed it was a total waste of time going to graduate school. He didn't understand why I couldn't come back to Inco and become an assistant purchasing agent, because "they'd look after you for the rest of your life."

Inco had a hospital in Copper Cliff. One summer while I was home from university and working during the summer vacation for Inco, I had to have a hernia operation, which I had at the Copper Cliff Hospital. The company kept on paying me as if I was still at work. In those days it took about two weeks to recover from that type of operation, which was before Dr. Bob Jackson developed laparoscopic surgery at the Toronto Western Hospital. Inco were wonderful to their employees and their families.

Laurentian University

In the summers if I was home from university, I attended classes in the evening in courses at Laurentian University that I was interested in. The classrooms were situated over a movie theatre downtown while they were just building the university. The courses were quite different from what I was taking elsewhere. For example, I took a course in industrial relations from Roy Pella, head of Industrial Relations at Falconbridge. He was a well-known athlete because he had represented Canada in the Olympics as a javelin thrower. He was an all-around athlete and had been a football star at Queens.

Laurentian University is a federation of Huntington College—the United Church and Thorneloe College—of the Anglican Church and the University of Sudbury—French Catholic. When I returned to Sudbury many years later in 1971, I was a Huntington College representative on the Board of the Laurentian University. And then I represented the Laurentian University on the Board of the Senate. After a couple of years I resigned from the board because they spoke French at the Senate meetings. I could not keep up, and they would not speak English or provide translation. The Senate had a lot of professors who felt an English speaking person should not be on the Senate.

However, I worked hard with every Premier of the Province and the Ministers of Health to get a medical school in Sudbury because, in my view, it was the only way to get enough doctors in northern Ontario. Once you get them there, they stay because of the lifestyle. I was extremely pleased and gratified to be invited to the first graduating class of the medical school.

Laurentian University has a very dynamic President and Vice-Chancellor—Dominic Giroux. They have approached me to help them raise funds. However, with all my other commitments and running a mine in Mexico I don't have the time. I did arrange to have lunch with Dominic Giroux and introduce him to Ned Goodman. Ned has now funded the Goodman School of Mines at Laurentian University, and is determined to make it as well known as the Colorado School of Mines. I am sure he will. Ned commented the day the Goodman Family Foundation announced the historic gift to the Laurentian University, "Greater Sudbury has the best orebody and largest concentration of expertise in mining supply, products and services in the world. We want to be associated with the Laurentian University because it's undoubtedly the go-to for university for mineral exploration and mining in Canada."

Executive Director Dick DeStefano is quoted as saying, "I was exceptionally pleased to watch the northern Ontario mining cluster emerge with a clear focus on being a world centre of mining excellence and building on its historical expertise and assets as its foundation. The Goodman School of Mines is another step forward and adds value to the importance of northern Ontario mining activity at all levels."

I would like to help Laurentian if and when I get the time. Clearly this region of Ontario is an important asset to the province and to Canada as a whole with respect to the mining industry amongst other considerations.

More on the Mining Industry, Life, and Personalities

As I mentioned, during my stint at university I took a year off school to make some money at Creighton Mine. At the time the mine was about 6,400 feet deep, and I was assigned to work in a bonus stope at the 6,200-foot level. First of all, underground mines are designed with a shaft that goes straight down from surface to the bottom of the mine. They have a container in them called a cage. The cage is pulled up and let down by massive drums located on the surface, and wind up or release these massive cables.

For our first week underground, we were sent to a school stope run by an old miner. The focus was on safety: how to operate the machinery and install mining timbers and wedges. Independent contractors, who are specialists in this type of work, often do the job of installing the shaft. Once this is complete, the next job is to drive drifts to the areas where the mineral is located. In my time, this was about every 200 feet. Some drifts following the ore could be a couple of miles long. Between the drifts were raises every so far. A raise is a vertical or inclined excavation, leading from one level to another and may also extend to the surface. The raises served several purposes: first, in the event of an accident it could be an escape route. Secondly, it could also be used to drive forced air into the mine, because mines could be quite hot, and lack oxygen, which is required by the men and the machines.

When you arrived underground, you had to place your brass nameplate in the lunchroom. Miners are paid from portal to portal, which refers to the time you get on the cage until you get back to surface, because it could take forty-five minutes just to get to the work face. This regulation was as a result of the great union battle by John L. Lewis and The United Coal Workers in the United States. The union's lawyer was Edward Lamb who spent his summers at Kagawong on Manitoulin Island. Known as the "portal-to portal-case" and won in the Supreme Court in 1946, it held that workers were entitled to receive pay for required necessary duties when arriving at the workplace. If workers were made to wait by the employer either before or after shifts, then they were required to be paid as well for time spent traveling as they were from time clocked to their workplace.

Edward was a very interesting man; he wound up owning the Seiberling Rubber Company (one of his largest businesses), a TV Station in Erie Pennsylvania, and a TV station in Toledo Ohio, among fifty-five other manufacturing and financial concerns. Joseph McCarthy took on Edward in the hearings that Senator McCarthy was running with his lawyer Cohn. The premise was that Mr. Lamb was a communist, because he had visited Russia a couple of times to try and encourage trade, believing that was the way to beat communism. He subsequently wrote a book No Lamb for Slaughter. It's a great read. I invited him to come to London and speak to the University of Western Ontario Graduate Business School. Needless to say, he was a big hit.

Back to mining: you dressed and worked in long underwear, pants, safety boots, wire goggles, and gloves. It was very hot, especially working at the 6,200-foot level. There were four men in a team and one was the stope boss. We were basically mining above the drifts, and the ore was pulled to a spot to drop into ore cars in the drift. The process was to drill the face with a jackleg drill powered by compressed air and load the holes with dynamite sticks. They were set to go off from the centre out, so the blast would not freeze. You could get a severe headache from the chemicals in the dynamite sticks. Blasting was done at the end of the shift or at lunchtime.

Next you would go in and scale. That meant seeing if there was any ore or rock that had not fallen down. The scaling bars were about ten feet long, made of steel, and were heavy. The basic idea was to scale down loose ore. You could actually tell by the sound of the ping if it was loose, and then you would pry it down. The next operation was using the slushing machine to haul the muck over to the hole above the ore car. Mining timbers would then be placed over the area we had just mined. Then the cycle started again. It was hard and dangerous work, but paid well.

The day and afternoon shifts were the production shifts, and night shift was for repairs and to haul materials down. In the middle of the winter you would go underground when it was dark, and when you came up it was dark. You enjoyed your days off. One time we came up and it was dark and foggy, and as we were pulling out of the parking lot our driver decided to be smart, so he allowed someone to pass him and we followed behind them, except they went right into a ditch and we followed them.

What bothered me the most was getting into my long underwear, because after work I hung it up on a chain about twenty feet in the air where it dried. The next day it felt like pulling on sandpaper. I was not comfortable until I started to sweat.

Many things have changed in mining today. They now use fertilizer and diesel oil for blasting, unless it's very wet. They use big jumbo computerized drills. If the mine is not too deep, they truck the ore up with trucks and scoop trams.

There are a lot of accidents in mining, primarily because people do not follow safety procedures. One thing that I didn't mention is when I arrived home at about 1:00 a.m. from the afternoon shift, I could hear my mother close her door and go to bed. When I worked underground she always worried about whether I would arrive home safely. Around the world there are many mine accidents and deaths. We do not hear of them as they may be in Australia, China, northern Ontario, Africa, or Peru. We only hear when there are several fatalities or miners are trapped in a mine. The miners not following the safety rules and taking shortcuts causes most mine accidents. Now they have random drug and alcohol tests. I can recall getting on the cage to go underground when some people smelled like a brewery. Today that would mean immediate dismissal.

Building Communities Commercially: Rick Major's Story

Rick Major was an interesting character who belonged to the same Fraternity as I did: Phi Delta Theta at McGill University. He had a mind like a computer. He was without a doubt one of the most brilliant people I have met so far in my life.

He was not a live-in at the fraternity like I was because he was a native of Montreal. In those days you went to university if you had completed grade eleven in the province of Quebec, whereas in the province of Ontario, you had to finish grade thirteen. So, the locals were quite young when they graduated. Rick graduated with a Bachelor of Commerce Degree.

He took a job with the Imperial Bank of Canada, which had earned the nickname the "Mining Bank." That was before the 1961 merger with The Bank of Commerce and which became the Canadian Imperial Bank of Commerce as it is today. Noranda, a mining and metallurgy company originally based in Quebec, was starting a new mine up in northern Quebec, and would be building a town. Canada was experiencing a frontier push at the turn of the century, and between that time and World War I, the mining industry was exploding. The bank was trying to get the business. So they erected two tents with wooden floors, walls, and oil heat. Rick was to be the bank manager and only employee. The bank would be in one tent, and he would live in the other until they had something more permanent.

We had a departure party at the Queens Hotel in Montreal at the time, which was just across the street in those days from Windsor Station. Rick's train was departing about 10:00 p.m. My recollection is that we started the departure party at about 4:00 p.m. He had his clothes packed and he had a cash ox with several thousand dollars in it, which we all counted from time to time as we drank more beer, just to make sure it was all there. Rick also had a pistol. He had the shells, but fortunately they were not in the gun, because from time to time we also fiddled with the pistol as the evening went on.

When the time came, we poured him onto the train and he was off. About three days later he was back because Noranda Mines didn't want the Imperial Bank on the property. They wanted the Bank of Commerce.

The head of the Imperial Bank in Montreal was Russ Harrison, who later became the CEO of the Canadian Imperial Bank of Commerce after they merged. Russ then gave Rick the assignment of reviewing the compensation packages of all the management and bank managers in the province of Quebec.

When he completed the assignment he handed it in and said, "Unfortunately I have to resign from the bank." When Russ asked why Rick went on to say, "After completing this project, obviously I cannot afford to work for the bank."

Rick went on to work managing money for Starlaw, which was the name derived from the Montreal Star and the St. Lawrence Sugar Company. The McConnell family owned both companies and they were the largest money managers in Canada at that time. They owned Montreal Investment Management, Toronto Investment Management, and Vancouver Investment Management. Their family foundation at the time was the largest in Canada over $700 million.

Rick was eccentric to say the least. He would work to about 1:30 p.m., then go over to the old Hy's Steakhouse on Adelaide and have lunch and plenty of wine. Peter Cole, a brilliant guy from the CIBC, would be there, as well as Pat Sheridan, one of the smartest mining people in Canada, and Murray Sinclair, another brilliant Canadian investor. Occasionally I was invited and really enjoyed the lunch and the discussions. Fortunately I did not have the capacity for wine that they did, so I would leave and go back to work. Most days Rick did not bother to go back to work. Every four years he took a sabbatical and went to Cognac in France for a year. Unfortunately his liver ran out of capacity. In spite of a liver transplant, Rick died at about fifty.

Edwards Sudbury Limited

In the mining industry today, petroleum theft is still a big concern. You have to stay right on top of it. Every business, aspects of and dealings in, is an opportunity for holding to your honesty, and it protects the interests of those you work for and with.

Edwards Sudbury Limited was in various businesses and I was running the tire retread division. They retread tires for the mining companies, which was a big business. Thousands of tires were retreaded for Canadian Tire and it was a relatively large operation. We also sold new tires.

Working for Edwards Sudbury Limited was interesting; not only did they have the tire and retread division, but in addition they had about seventy-nine gas stations. They sold wholesale petroleum products to the Elliot Lake Mines. The oil and gas arrived at a storage depot at Algoma Mills on the CPR rail line between Sudbury and Algoma Mills, and from there it was trucked north to Elliot Lake about thirty miles away. In fact, they were hauling gas on the rail line up to Algoma Mills, which was on the CPR line between Sudbury and Saulte Ste. Marie. They stored the oil and gas in storage tanks at Algoma Mills, and then hauled it by tanker truck to Saulte Ste. Marie. Oil was delivered to both the mines and to the employees' houses, and whatever they dropped off at the houses could be charged to the company. The company would then deduct it off the employee's pay. This was a pretty good deal. But, Edwards found out that some of their drivers were stealing or dumping the load before they even got to the mines. The meter would show so much and they would get paid for that amount, but half of that petroleum would actually be delivered; half would be stolen and sold somewhere else. The trucks would then arrive at the mine half full. No one checked the metres coming in—just going out. Ultimately, the mines would pay for a full load while receiving a lot less.

Edwards also had both a chain of electronic stores and automotive stores. They supplied their gas stations with everything; they even had furniture and hardware stores up in northern Ontario. One of the reasons Mr. Edward got into all of these businesses was because during the war when everything was rationed, he was able to get whatever he wanted in terms of gasoline and tires—things like that. Another big consideration was that he had six children. He used that thought and motivation to develop these very successful businesses.

He also had a large grain and feed business, which was run by his son Peter Edward, who was a graduate of McGill's Agricultural College. The grain elevator was located on the main line of the CPR, and the passenger trains went by it every day on their way to Western Canada. Thomas D. Edward (or T.D. the father) had a real sense of humour. He had a rooster painted on the side of the grain storage elevator and a huge sign that read, "Cock of the North." Only if you looked to the bottom of this huge elevator would you read "Feeds." He thought this was quite funny.

Here is a refreshing story speaking to the power of honesty and good customer relations: Herb and Dorothy Bisset were the owners of the Sudbury Steam Cleaners back in the day; this was a business that was opened up in downtown Sudbury in 1901. Their promise of service to their clients reads, "Over 100 years of unwavering commitment to dry cleaning excellence and community service." In fact, their motto stands true from the earliest days. At that time, my mother-in-law Gertie Edward had pinned her jewelry into the curtains of the Edward home. Perhaps insurance might have been costly, and she thought this was a secure hiding place. One time she sent the curtains in to Sudbury Steam Cleaners to be cleaned and she forgot to remove her jewelry.

Dorothy returned the curtains and politely asked Gertie, "We cleaned your curtains. Would you like us to clean your jewelry as well?"

Sudbury Steam Cleaners acknowledges today, "there is no doubt that the people who have stood behind Sudbury Steam Cleaners have been the key to the steady growth of the company since its beginning in 1901." This is a wonderful testament to the fact that honesty really does pay.

Selling Tires and Other Salesmen

When I was on the road selling tires, I would run into other salesmen also on the road. We often stayed at the same hotels throughout northern Ontario. One of those in the group was Billy Duncan, who was a salesman for Heinz Foods. Billy had grown up across the street from me in Copper Cliff. We called him "Screwy," a great left-handed baseball pitcher who could throw a screwball, which is why I imagine the reason why we called him "Screwy." He was a funny man—always laughing. We were selling different things for the paper mills and the mining companies, but he sold food.

Billy decided to quit Heinz Foods, because he was tired of being on the road. He was working out of Barrie, and decided to sell sandpaper and abrasives in the Barrie area. One night at a hotel while we were having dinner together he warned us of what he was up to. He had told us that he hated his boss and he hated one of his customers who ran a big grocery store Highway 17—west near Algoma Mills just before you turn north up to Elliot Lake and east of Blind River. He suggested that we should be in the store at a specific time because he was making the last trip with his boss, to the guy he also hated in the store at Algoma Mills.

Screwy told the owner of the store that his boss was coming with him on his next trip, "My boss is deaf, and you really have to yell at the guy. You'd be doing me a really big favour if you did that."

Then he told his boss that the owner of the Red and White store in Algoma Mills was a good customer, but deaf. He would have to yell at him. Neither knew it was Screwy's last trip. It was a large grocery store, and we arranged to be there. These two guys were yelling off the top of their heads at each other—Screwy was yelling too. It was the funniest damn thing in the world, and of course we started laughing. The boss figured out what was going on, and we ended up having to give Screwy a ride back to Sudbury because his boss took the company car away from him then and there. And that was the end of his job right on the spot.

That was part of the life of being a travelling salesman. I learned about selling because when Mr. Edward travelled on the road with me about once or twice a year. He'd ask me a lot of questions about the customers before we arrived to see them. We talked and he took notes. When he'd come back a year later, he'd ask customers, "How's your son so-and-so, and how'd your wife's operation work out?" These people would be blown away. I'd walk out of there with orders I'd never seen from them before. He was just a super salesman.

Something funny I recall was from when I used to drive. I was always in a hurry, being young, and I knew I was driving too fast.

He'd ask me, "Well—what's the speedometre reading on your side?"

I worked for Edwards Sudbury for a couple of years to save some money. I didn't have quite enough because by then I also had a young son, and I was heading off to the University of Western Ontario to the MBA program. We had enough money to buy a house next door to Kingsmill's Farm, which ended up as part of the University of Western Ontario's campus in the 1920s). I recall the address was 48 Edgar Drive. Our house backed right up on Kingsmill's Farm and I could walk to school in fifteen minutes. From the back of the house there was a wonderful view, and the cattle fed right up at the fence in the backyard. We paid $12,000 for that house and I think I sold it for $16,000 when I left two years later. With that I was able to pay off all my school expenses and my debts, so that worked out pretty well.

Other Families of Mention

The Sudbury community raised many fine and successful entrepreneurs in numerous businesses from the earliest days. The other tire dealer in town was a man by the name of Art Duncan. He sold Goodyear tires but did not have a retread plant, whereas Edwards Sudbury Limited sold Firestone tires. In later years there was a connection between Art Duncan, T. D. Edward, and Paul Desmarais—the founder and still chairman and

CEO of Power Corporation, a substantial Canadian mogul company out of Montreal with investments in Canada, United States, and Europe and sizeable holdings based in Europe. The financial sector had interests in life, health insurance, and retirement and asset management services, and direct and various investment platforms in Canada, United States, Europe and Asia. These platforms range from steel manufacturing, iron ore mining, property development, and biotechnology and clean energy fields, as well as subsidiaries in media—the press, online, and independent television production.

When Paul took over his father's bus line and the Sudbury-Copper Cliff Street Car Railway Company, they were in receivership. This company ran some buses in the city, but most of the business was transporting workers to Copper Cliff in streetcars. Paul's grandfather had established Sudbury Bus Lines. Paul's father was a lawyer in Sudbury. I knew him quite well because he parked a car in a lot that Leo Gasparini and I owned. I would often chat with him. He was basically retired then but kept an office at his son Bob's practice. He was a real gentleman—always well turned out and a big Conservative. I knew some of the rest of the Desmarais family. Bob, Paul's brother, was my CFO when I subsequently ran for Sudbury MPP of the Conservative Party of Ontario in 1978.

Paul was married to Jackie Maranger, and both the Desmarais' and the Maranger's lived up near where the Edward family lived in Sudbury. Jackie's mother Tonoss and father Ernie were friends of my parents. My mother, Marguerite Fortier, and my mother-in-law Gertie Boiven, nursed with Mrs. Maranger at St. Joseph's hospital. Everybody seemed to know everybody.

While Paul was attending law school in Toronto, the business was basically going bankrupt. Paul quit law school and came to run the bus lines that were sold to him for a symbolic one Canadian dollar. To run the business, he got the money from putting the tires down on credit from Art Duncan, oil and gas from T. D. Edward, and secured a loan from Lawrie Martin at the Royal Bank who helped him expand the business. Paul was on his way. Art Duncan and T. D. Edward decided to take a chance on him because he left school to help his father and they liked his plan.

Paul did eventually have a run in with Peter Edward, T. D. Edwards' son. Peter was trying to collect on some money and raised so much hell about how fast it was being paid that Paul had the whole thing delivered in a truck load of coppers—what we called pennies back then. This whole deal became the basis and foundation of Power Corporation, one of Canada's largest corporations, as Paul started to buy city and intercity bus lines and went from there.

The substantial and successful investments and story of Power Corporation is introduced as, "one of remarkable leadership, extraordinary people, and steady, sometimes spectacular growth. It is also a story intricately bound with the economic, political and social history of Canada, through good times and bad." From humble Sudbury beginnings and great intentions, "Power Corporation evolved from a Canadian utility company into the diverse, multibillion dollar management and holding company that today spans the world." A Quebec and international resident, financier Paul Desmarais, is described in 2007 as being the fourth wealthiest person in Canada, and well up there in the top 200 richest people around the world. A couple of years back he was estimated to have a net worth of US $4.5 billion.

Sudbury was a pretty small town and everybody pretty well knew everybody else. I knew Paul quite well, and I used to love talking politics to his brother Louie who was a chartered accountant and a city councillor. I served on the Senate and Board of Laurentian University with another brother Jean, who was a surgeon up in Sudbury, and worked with Paul's youngest brother Bob, who was my CFO when I ran for the Conservatives. Bob was a lawyer and was eventually appointed as a judge. Paul Desmarais of Power Corporation turned around at the ceremony when I received The Order of Canada and made this comment to me, "We didn't do too badly for a couple of Sudbury boys, Peter."

Success is to be measured not so much by the position that one has reached in life as the obstacles, which he has overcome.
Booker T. Washington

Take up one idea. Make that one idea your life—think of it, dream of it, live on that idea. Let the brain, muscles, nerves, every part of your body, be full of that idea, and just leave every other idea alone. This is the way to success.
Swami Vivekananda

The price of success is hard work, dedication to the job at hand, and the determination that whether we win or lose, we have applied the best of ourselves to the task at hand.
Vince Lombardi

A successful man is one who can lay a firm foundation with the bricks others have thrown at him.
David Brinkley

AFTERWORD

"I have always felt compelled to give back to society and to make it as good for my children and grandchildren as it was for me."

At my age, it's nice to be asked to be involved and I enjoy being involved. I never understood when I was young that as you get older, you do get wiser. I think I've learned a lot—all the good lessons cost you money. I've always told my children, and I think they don't listen very well, but the easiest money you make is the money you don't spend. I remember my son saying to me something only costs one hundred dollars.

"The hell it does. It costs $200," I came back.

He asked, "What are you talking about?"

"One hundred dollars plus tax," I responded glibly.

Well now he's got seven kids so he understands how it all works. He had three or four of them in university at the same time, as well as kids in private school. Now he understands the value of a buck.

Looking back, I feel very lucky and privileged to have grown up in the Sudbury area where ethnic backgrounds and education were not barriers. The people of Sudbury are very proud of those who have done well. For example, Cliff Fielding, who became a billionaire without going to high school. Emil Pidutti, as I mentioned earlier, who built substantial commercial and residential buildings in Ontario and Saskatchewan. We can talk about Robert Campeau, a carpenter who went on to own Brooks Brothers and several large retail chains in the United States. Then there is Alex Trebec who grew up in Sudbury, and whose father was a chef in a Sudbury hotel. There's Paul Desmarais whom I have mentioned above and Leo Gerard, the head of the United States Steel Workers in Pittsburgh. And I mention as well Dean Muncaster, who recently passed away, and is given most of the credit by the Canadian Tire Dealers for the success that Canadian Tire is today. Our current Governor General lived over the Cochrane Dunlop Hardware Store in Copper Cliff, where his father was the manager until he was transferred to Saulte Ste. Marie. The Governor General mentioned that when he was presenting me with the Diamond Jubilee Medal.

From time to time, I am invited to speak in Sudbury. I always feel good because the Sudbury people give me more credit than for what I have achieved. It's a very warm community and a wonderful place to live. That's why Laurentian University, Cambridge College, the Health Science Centre, and the Cancer Centre are able to attract the type of people they do—simply because they love the lifestyle with numerous lakes in the city, several golf courses, and a low crime rate. For example, my oldest son does about 90 percent of his business outside of Sudbury, but Sudbury is where he wants to raise his family. Where else in a city can you live on a lake with great fishing, be in your office, at the golf course, at the hospital with a medical school, a good restaurant all within ten minutes from your house?

The urban core of Sudbury is where the population resides with numerous smaller communities scattered around 300 lakes in the amalgamated region. The hills have been blackened by the historical mining activity, having once been a major lumber centre and world leader in nickel mining. Mining and related industries dominated the economy for much of the twentieth century. Sudbury has seen much growth over the years from the earliest of days when the community began to grow through mining and expand through all the attendant services that opened up to accommodate the community's needs.

Over the years, I think that I have been involved in many businesses because I like the variety of knowledge and challenges in the diversity of economic endeavours. I have also found that I like and enjoy most people and learn from them. What I do not like are people who lack integrity. I do everything in my power to avoid them. I do enjoy mentoring young people who are willing to listen to what has worked for me and what has not.

The three greatest honours I have received are two paintings of me— one placed in the lobby of the Princess Margaret Hospital. I constantly hear from families particularly from northern Ontario, about how much better they feel when they come to the Princess Margaret and see my portrait there. It helps reduce the fear they feel in a strange place. There is another portrait in the boardroom of the University Health Network, and a third one in the boardroom of Cancer Care Ontario.

I have always felt compelled to give back to society and to make it as good for my children and grandchildren as it was for me. I think we have all been failures at this. In the past, people were much better at volunteering, for example as town councillors, or on school boards—we were happy to run for the position and do the work free and gratis without a secretary and without an office. I am unable to recall a year in my working life when I have not made a financial donation to worthy causes and I think we all have a duty if we are able to donate to a good cause.

I trust the stories I have told you, the reader, from the earliest days of my life, through my varied corporate and not-for-profit experiences to the present and where I am still involved and sitting on boards, will give you an understanding illustrating the complexities of life as it spills into the boardroom, around the boardroom table, and fills the seats of each board member to make life challenging, opportunistic, fulfilling, and hopefully not to be taken too seriously at the same time. Such are the boardroom games of life!

In Memoriam: I would like to pay tribute to my good friend Riki Gougeon who passed away 4 July 2013—tragically taken in a plane crash with his son-in-law and nephew, Georgian Bay Ontario. Riki was a life-long friend of mine. We partnered together in all kinds of businesses for fifty-three years with only a trusting handshake and never a harsh word between us. Riki had a great sense of humour, and was a wonderfully talented man. He will be missed.

> *"There comes a special moment in everyone's life; a moment for which that person was born. That special opportunity, when he seizes it, will fulfill his mission—a mission for which he is uniquely qualified. In that moment, he finds greatness. It is his finest hour."*
> **Winston Churchill, British Prime Minister**

Appendix

Peter A Crossgrove
30 Adelaide St. East
Toronto, ON Canada
Born and Raised in Sudbury Ontario

Academic Background
BCom, Concordia University
M.B.A., University of Western Ontario
Sloan Fellow Dr. Program, Harvard Business School

Honours
Order of Ontario
Order of Canada
The Upper Canada Medal
Queens Golden Jubilee Medal
Queens Diamond Jubilee Medal
Chairman Emeritus, Cancer Care Ontario
Honorary Board Member, University Health Network

Mr. Crossgrove joined Seagram's in Montreal, and at the age of twenty-eight was appointed to the VP of Marketing.

Mr. Crossgrove left Montreal in 1968 and returned to Sudbury where over time purchased Pioneer Construction, Bidwell Investments, and Edwards Sudbury Limited.

Mr. Crossgrove sold his Sudbury companies in 1978 and then moved to Toronto where he worked for Coopers and Lybrand. At that time he was also one of the two original investors in Interior Door, a private company that later became Masonite, a public company, which was sold to KKR for $3.2 billion in 2004.

In 1990 Mr. Crossgrove served as Vice Chairman and C.E.O. of Placer Dome Inc. in Vancouver.

Mr. Crossgrove is currently a director of the following companies:

Blue Goose Cattle Company
Detour Gold Corporation (Co Chairman and Lead Director)
Dundee Industrial REIT
Dundee REIT (Lead Director)
Excellon Resources (Executive Chairman)
International Advisory Board for The Goodman School of Mines
Lake Shore Gold
Nordex Explosives
Pelangio Mines
Radon Environmental Management Corporation

Past Corporate Boards:

Acadia Mineral Ventures Ltd.
A.M.T International (CEO)
Alcan Tire and Rubber Company
Astro Dairy Products
Band-Ore Resources Ltd. (CEO)
Barrick Gold
Bidwell Investments (CEO)
Brush Creek Corporation (CEO)
CIBC Mellon
Campbell Red Lake
Camreal Realty (Chairman)
Detour Gold Corporation
Dona Lake Mines
Eaton of Canada
Eden Roc Minerals (CE)
First Silver
Gentra Inc.
Glenayre Electronics
ITCO Properties (CEO)
Kiena Mines
Mellon Bank Canada

Ontario Road Builders Association
Ontario Store Fixtures Ltd.
Orbite Aluminae Inc.
Philex Gold Corp. (Philippines)
Pioneer Construction (CEO)
Placer Dome Inc. (Vice Chairman, CEO)
QLT
RM Trust
Sigma Mines
South African Minerals (CEO)
SUNY Petroleum
T. Eaton Company
United Dominion Industries
Waters and McDonald Associates Ltd.
West Timmins
York-Hanover (CEO)

Past Volunteer Positions:

Canadian Association, Provincial Cancer Agencies (Vice Chair)
Cancer Care Ontario (Chair)
Canadian Partnership Against Cancer (CPAC) (Founding Member)
Cancer Teaching and Research (Foundation Chair)
CARE Canada (Chair)
CARE International (Treasurer)
CARE International (Vice Chair)
Chair of Canadian Association of Provincial Cancer Agencies
Commercialization of Medical Research (Chair)
Generation Fund (Chair—raised $50 million for UHN)
Grace Hospital Vancouver (Board Member)
Laurentian University (Board Member)
Montreal Board of Trade (Board Member)
Munk Cardiac Centre (Campaign Chair—raised $35 million)
Ontario Government Committee for Capital Available for Princess
    Margaret Hospital (Chair)
Senate of Laurentian University (Board of Governors)

The Princess Margaret Foundation
The Toronto Hospital Foundation
The Toronto Western Foundation
Toronto Hospital (Chair)
Toronto Western Hospital (Chair)
Young Presidents Organization (Chair)

Index

A

B

C

H

I

J

Orsino, Philip, 53, 56, 60, 73, 125, 209

P

Palmer, Arnold, 9
Panneton, Gerald, 111, 112
Paprazian, Rick, 105
Parsons, Steve, 116
Pattison, Jimmy, 28, 29
Paul, Carl Otto, 69
Pella, Roy, 253
Peterson, Ontario Premier David, 121, 130, 150
Peterson, Shelly, 121
Peterson, Tim, 121
Pidutti, Emil, 31, 51, 267
Plaunt, Donald, 38
Player, Gary, 9
Potter, George, 183
Powers, Stefanie, 62, 63
Powis, Alf, 119, 120, 121, 123, 124, 138
Prince Philip, HRH, 223
Princess Margaret, HRH, 132, 133, 159
Purchase, Greg, 72

Q

Queen Elizabeth I, HM, 223
Queen Elizabeth II, HM, 223

R

Radler, David, 189
Rae, Ontario Premier Bob, 134
Ranger, Lone, 228
Redford, Robert, 64
Redpath, Jim, 197

Wood, Jack, 127
Wood, Mr., 239
Wozniak, Graham, 112

X

Y

Z

About the Author

Peter A. Crossgrove is a Canadian citizen born and raised in Sudbury Ontario. He received his BCom at Concordia University and MBA from the University of Western Ontario. He participated in the Sloan Fellow Doctorate Program of Harvard Business School. Appointed VP of Marketing for Seagram's in Montreal at the age of twenty-eight, Peter then went on to purchase Pioneer Construction, Bidwell Investments and Edwards Sudbury Limited. In 1978 he sold his Sudbury companies and moved to Toronto where he worked for Coopers and Lybrand on corporate turn-arounds.

Peter was one of the two original investors in Interior Door, a private company that became Masonite, a public company sold to KKR for $3.2 billion in 2004. He served as Vice Chairman and CEO of Placer Dome Inc. in Vancouver, and has sat on forty-six corporate business and mining boards, twenty-three past volunteer board positions in the not-for-profit sector, as well as university and government boards. He currently sits on ten mining, real estate investment trusts and other business boards.

Peter Crossgrove is the recipient of the Order of Ontario, Order of Canada, The Upper Canada Medal, Queens Golden Jubilee Medal, Queens Diamond Jubilee Medal, Chairman Emeritus, Cancer Care Ontario, and is an Honourary Board Member of the University Health Network. Peter travels extensively while still actively participating on corporate boards. He currently lives in Toronto.

Based on his experience of fifty-three years both in the mining fields, business arenas, and close to seventy corporate and not-for-profit boards, Peter Crossgrove shares thought-provoking, informative, and insightful presentations at business and mining schools, to the health profession, corporate settings, and other group settings for both public and professional audiences.

Described as the all-accomplished Renaissance man, Peter was raised in northern Ontario at a time when commerce and industry was developing and expanding. Life offered its challenges and Peter speaks candidly of his upbringing and successes in his entrepreneurial endeavours: the values instilled by his parents, the importance of giving back to the community without expectation of receiving anything in return, and as far as boards are concerned—good board governance and how imperative it remains for all directors to carry out their designations in a responsible, authentic, and transparent manner, especially considering shareholders interests.

On the not-for-profit side, Peter talks about the necessity for boards to be cognizant and open to the forward movement and change of those scenarios that are for the highest good of the organizations they represent. Peter also speaks to the need for directors to forgo the personal glory of privilege in the boardroom. Peter has travelled the world on behalf of CARE Canada and CARE International. He has witnessed much and has many wonderful and amazing stories to share with North American audiences.

Peter can be reached at pacrossgrove@gmail.com
Excellon Resources 1-416-364-1130
Executive Assistant—Rocio Zavala

If you want to get on the path to be a published author by
Influence Publishing please go to
www.InspireABook.com

Inspiring books that influence change

More information on our other titles and how to submit
your own proposal can be found at
www.InfluencePublishing.com

CPSIA information can be obtained at www.ICGtesting.com
Printed in the USA
LVOW12s0612081213

364355LV00021B/2341/P

9 781771 410199